THE ECONOMICS OF
COLLECTIVE BARGAINING

This material was prepared pursuant to Contract #99-8-1383-42-20 from the U.S. Department of Labor by the author who was commissioned by the George Meany Center for Labor Studies, AFL-CIO, in partial fulfillment of its Tripartite Program for Apprenticeship and Associate Degree in Labor Studies. The opinions contained in this material do not necessarily reflect those of the George Meany Center for Labor Studies, the American Federation of Labor-Congress of Industrial Organizations, or the U.S. Department of Labor.

THE ECONOMICS OF COLLECTIVE BARGAINING
Case Studies in the Private Sector

Charles Craypo

The Bureau of National Affairs, Inc., Washington, D.C. 20037

Library of Congress Cataloging-in-Publication Data

Craypo, Charles, 1936–
   The economics of collective bargaining.

   Bibliography: p.
   Includes index.
   1. Collective bargaining—United States—Case studies.
I. Title.
HD6508.C74   1985   331.89'0973   85-28373
ISBN 0-87179-490-X
ISBN 0-87179-491-8 (pbk.)

Printed in the United States of America
International Standard Book Number: 0-87179-490-X (hardcover)
0-87179-491-8 (softcover)

31

To Mary

Contents

List of Tables

List of Diagrams

List of Charts

Preface

The purpose of this book is to explain the economics of collective bargaining in privately owned and managed industries. The book reflects my combined training and experiences as academic labor economist and university labor educator. Neither theoretical concepts nor practical events alone explain fully the collective bargaining phenomenon; both are essential. To assess the impact of economic bargaining we must know the subject matter in great detail, and also we must have an abstract method of organizing and analyzing the facts. Formal academic work and practical field experience are not alternatives, therefore, but instead complements. So I have used the analytical tools of the institutional labor economist and the empirical knowledge of the classroom labor educator. From this perspective I have tried to describe the parties and processes in the bargaining relationship, the traditional and changing economic environments within which bargaining occurs, and the impact of bargaining outcomes on workers, industry and community.

The book consists largely of case studies of economic bargaining that are analyzed in an "ability-to-pay" model of relative bargaining power between labor and management. Unlike other interpretations, which might emphasize organizational communications or procedural strategies or interpersonal relationships, this approach focuses on economic power. Collective bargaining in the American private sector invariably reduces to the use or threatened use of economic power; dominant trends and directions in bargaining are best identified and understood in the context of such relative power.

The analytical framework I have used is derived mainly from the power bargaining model constructed by Harold Levinson in the 1960s. The framework is inspired conceptually by the work of the early institutional labor economists, notably George Barnett and Robert Hoxie, who posed important questions regarding industrial structure and technology that were not addressed adequately by John R. Commons and the other Wisconsin School scholars. I have asked their questions and applied a modified version of Levinson's model to recent events in economic bargaining in order to try to answer them.

The cases chosen for detailed study and structural analysis here were often the result of chance and circumstance. For example, the importance of industrial organization in the Litton-Royal Typewriter case was brought to my attention by Gordon Brehm, who was then with the Allied Industrial

Workers union; the issue of bargaining structure in the intercity bus industry by John Lantz, former bus driver and local union business agent; technology in the printing industry by my colleague Greg Giebel; crisis in the
steel industry as a result of my years of labor education with local steelworkers; deregulation in airlines by papers and discussions in my graduate labor
economics class. But the particular cases selected for study are less important than the analytical method that was used to interpret them. If these
cases are microcosmic analogies of the most important trends now occurring
in the larger arena of economic bargaining, as I believe they are, then their
almost random origins are inconsequential because much the same findings
would result from another set of cases.

Such an eclectic method of study makes the writer dependent on others:
for their theoretical concepts and research methods, for their shared experiences and discoveries, for their information and documentation, and for
their insights and observations. But the complete list of scholars, students,
labor educators, trade unionists, labor and management negotiators, and
public officials who have enhanced my own understanding of economic bargaining is now too lengthy to enumerate here. This does not lessen, however,
my appreciation for their help and encouragement.

I am indebted to several persons at the George Meany Center for Labor
Studies for their encouragement, assistance, and patience during the
preparation of the manuscript. Among them, Richard Z. Hindle conceived
the idea for such a book; he and David Alexander administered the larger
project to which this volume is related. Russell Allen—who first made me
aware of the major themes presented here, and then let me claim them as my
own—and Woodrow Ginsberg both made critical corrections and insightful
suggestions for improvement. Jacqueline Brophy provided valuable editorial and organizational assistance. I also want to acknowledge Andrew Cuvo
and Robert Glaser, two full-time union representatives whose cooperation
enabled me to include case studies of local bargaining in construction and
metal manufacturing.

Colleagues who looked at portions of the draft and offered useful comments and recommendations include Lawrence Mishel, Michael Podgur-
sky, Leonard Rapping, Ronald Seeber, Gregory Giebel, Keith Knauss, and
Donald Kennedy. Whatever mistakes and misinterpretations that remain
are my doing.

My early and final drafts of the manuscript, all of them equally illegible,
were typed by Irene Kirk, Raefa Miller, Melissa Harrington, Debra Wool-
ston, and Toni Maefield. My thanks to them.

Charles Craypo
January 1986

1

Economics of Collective Bargaining

The Nature of Industrial Conflict

Every society must reconcile the opposing interests of workers and managers. Regardless of prevailing economic, political, social, and religious institutions, a potential for conflict exists as long as some people work while others supervise. Eric Hoffer, a West Coast longshoreman turned social commentator, identified the source of industrial conflict:

> To the eternal workingman management is substantially the same whether it is made up of profit-seekers, idealists, technicians, or bureaucrats. The allegiance of the manager is to the task and its results. However noble his motives he cannot help viewing the workers as a means to an end. He will always try to get the utmost out of them; and it matters not whether he does it for the sake of profit, for a holy cause, or for the sheer principle of efficiency.
>
> One need not view management as an enemy or feel self-righteous about doing an honest day's work to realize that things are likely to get tough when management can take the worker for granted; when it can plan and operate without having to worry about what the worker will say or do.[1]

Workers and managers never see things in quite the same way. A worker for someone else is more interested in the job than in the final product. The manager has the opposite interest. At every turn their priorities differ. A slower work pace is lost production for the employer. Higher wages are cost increases for the firm. Job security for labor means less control over the workplace for capital. Man-

---

[1]Eric Hoffer, "The Workingman Looks at The Boss," *Harper's* (March 1954).

agers often persuade workers that together they are a team and that their interests ultimately coincide, but labor history shows that sooner or later events convince the workers otherwise.

Unions and collective bargaining are labor responses to the organization of production in a market economy. Through these responses, workers try to gain some control over the conditions under which they make goods and provide services. Collective bargaining functions entirely within the established order of industrial ownership and management. Nevertheless, it reduces considerably the employer's natural bargaining power by giving workers a collective voice in how labor is used in the production process. Bargaining does not threaten the wage system but seeks a more balanced distribution of income; it does not expel supervision from the workplace but restrains the exercise of managerial prerogative.

Industrial Labor in America. Only recently in the United States' industrial history have labor disputes been settled through collective bargaining. Before that, unions and collective bargaining were tolerated reluctantly. Except for some union-dominated trades and certain industries where managers found it in their interest to have unions, differences between workers and owners were resolved arbitrarily in the workplace by management, in the courts under common law precedent, or in the streets through violence.

No statutes or social conventions restricted employers in the use of human labor as a production factor. Workers were hired and fired at will, depending on the job skills they possessed and the extent to which the employer currently needed those skills. Labor disputes that went into the courts typically were decided in favor of employers on the basis of property rights. Unions and workers also usually lost when disputes moved into the streets, as employers called in the police or militia to break up demonstrations and to physically punish the leaders. Large companies sometimes outfitted their own army of guards to enforce labor peace.

Labor Market Theory. Underlying this anti-union public policy was the economic philosophy of free markets. Called either free enterprise, neoclassical, or market theory, this approach argues that individuals and society fare best when economic outcomes are determined competitively by the unrestricted forces of supply and demand. Wages and working conditions should be determined this way, the theory holds, because free market outcomes are fair and efficient. Like any other price, compensation for labor should depend on availability relative to demand. An excess of labor depresses wages, a shortage drives them up. Neither workers nor employers can be exploited, because no individual must work for a wage below the ongoing rate and no firm must keep an employee who fails to meet its standard quota.

The free market also assures efficient production and maximum total output, according to the theory. If left to follow their own self-interest, each buyer and seller will find and pursue that economic activity which rewards them most. Competition will ensure that labor's reward and contributions are the same. The result of every individual's full commitment to self-interest, therefore, is the greatest possible production and supply of goods and services.

Free market theory in its pure form objects to unions and economic bargaining because they prevent or penalize the freedom and mobility of workers and employers that is necessary to make the market system work as expected. The employer who has signed a union contract specifying a $5 per hour pay rate for an "Assembler I," for example, cannot then hire a worker for the job at $4.50 an hour. Collective bargaining therefore precludes the benefits that the theory predicts.

If neoclassical labor market theory rejects unions on the grounds that they foster inefficiency, unions reject neoclassical theory as being irrelevant and inconsistent with the day-to-day job experiences of their members. All general economic theories make assumptions about human organization and behavior in order to explain and predict economic events and outcomes. Neoclassical labor market theory must assume, among other things, large numbers of independent buyers and sellers of labor, and employers and employees with an easy mobility relative to labor markets and a complete knowledge of market conditions. The result is a deductive theory of wage and employment levels which infers, generally and over time, that individual workers and employers have an equal footing in labor market transactions. "A worker is protected from his employer by the existence of other employers for whom he can go to work," say Milton and Rose Friedman, two of the ablest advocates of market theory. "An employer is protected from exploitation by the employees by the existence of other workers whom he can hire."[2]

Hourly and salaried workers do not believe this conclusion. Their job experiences indicate that most of the time there are too many workers looking for employment and too few competing em-

---

[2]Milton and Rose Friedman, *Free to Choose* (New York: Harcourt Brace Jovanovich, 1980), p. 246.

ployers, that available jobs are offered on a take-it-or-leave-it basis with no room for individual bargaining over terms, and that employment and earnings are as much matters of chance as of informed search. In addition, workers do not believe they have bargaining power just because they can quit and go elsewhere.

Relative bargaining power in free labor markets was depicted more accurately in the insightful writings of Adam Smith, the intellectual father of market economics, than in the abstract theory that followed. He described an imbalance of bargaining power between workers and their employers, who in his day were referred to as "masters." Employers tended to conspire rather than compete. "Masters are always and everywhere in a sort of tacit, but constant and uniform combination, not to raise wages of labor above their actual rates," he wrote.

Smith also noticed that even when workers combined to form unions they were at a disadvantage because they did not have enough savings or assets to outlast employers in lengthy disputes. Labor strikes "generally end in nothing but the punishment or ruin of the ring leaders," he concluded.[3]

Adam Smith's characterization of labor disputes certainly described most of American basic industry prior to passage of regulatory labor laws. Government at all levels was motivated chiefly by a desire to maintain industrial stability. While such a policy might appear neutral, in practice it favored employers. It was labor, not management, that wanted to alter the terms and conditions of employment from those which had been imposed upon workers. Since no orderly means of doing so was available, bringing about industrial change required direct action. But when the inevitable disturbance occurred, government would intervene in the interest of industrial order.

Although workers never overcame the combined efforts of industry and government, they might have done so had they been more solidified. Most of the time they were hopelessly divided. Native workers tried to keep out immigrants, craftsmen had little sympathy for less-skilled workers, white males resisted the employment of minorities and women, trade unionists and socialists could not cooperate—even the skilled trades fought among themselves.

Employers skillfully exploited the underlying fears and rivalries. They replaced striking workers and machine-displaced crafts-

---

[3]Adam Smith, *An Inquiry Into the Nature and Causes of the Wealth of Nations* (1776) (New York: Random House, 1937), pp. 66-7.

men with immigrants, minorities, and women; they worked different ethnic groups side-by-side, knowing that their inability to communicate would make them distrustful; they made deals with one craft to undermine the others and with crafts as a whole to abandon laborers at critical junctures. Labor's occasional successes usually disappeared with the next economic downturn.

Not until the severe depression of the 1930s did enough workers discover simultaneously that the industrial system was not in their interest and that change was overdue. Enough of them had also come to understand that collective rather than individual action was necessary. Industrial disputes erupted with increasing frequency, as working men and women all over the country began taking matters into their own hands. Rising labor militancy culminated in several urban general strikes, and fierce battles broke out between police and striking workers and their supporters. Thoughtful liberals and conservatives alike feared that the nation was on the verge of industrial revolution. Something had to be done to relieve the situation.

Labor's uprising had a decisive effect on public policy. It demonstrated that America no longer could have both industrial stability and nonunion workplaces. Given this choice, the federal government abandoned its commitment to unregulated labor markets and in 1935 enacted the nation's first comprehensive labor law. The National Labor Relations Act (NLRA) protected worker rights to organize unions, obligated employers to recognize unions chosen by workers in elections supervised by the National Labor Relations Board (NLRB), and required employers to bargain with recognized unions in good faith over the terms and conditions of employment.

The Extent of Collective Bargaining

Union membership as a percentage of the eligible work force rose sharply after enactment of the NLRA but in recent years has been declining. The level of nonagricultural workers belonging to unions (which excludes employee association membership) peaked in the post-World War II period at 35 percent of the work force in 1954, the year preceding merger of the AFL and the CIO. At that time the Congress of Industrial Organizations (CIO) had roughly 6 million members in 32 affiliated unions, and the American Federation of Labor (AFL) had 11 million members in 109 craft and craft-industrial affiliates. The level of trade union members in the U.S. labor force slipped to 31 percent in 1960 and to 28 percent in 1970. By 1978 the figure had dropped to 24 percent.

A more accurate measurement of union membership includes both union and employee association members. When this formula is used the 1978 figure for the United States rises to 27 percent, with a total membership of 22 million. The statistical reason for the declining ratio is that, although absolute union membership increased during this time, the number of persons in the work force rose at a faster pace. Between 1978 and 1980, however, the ratio of labor organization members to the total labor force fell by 1.7 percent, a loss of 391,000 members.

The losses were not uniform. The heaviest losers were six unions in the auto, steel, clothing, textile, tire, and oil refining industries which together lost 314,000 members. Some unions even gained, mostly in the nonmanufacturing sectors—public employment, retail trade, education, communications, and services. Five unions in this group increased their total membership by 259,000.[4]

Of the 87.5 million U.S. wage and salary employees in May 1980, 22.5 million, or 25.7 percent, worked under negotiated contracts in the private and public sectors. More than half this number (52 percent) were blue-collar workers, another one-third white-collar (37.7 percent), and the remaining 10 percent service workers. Blue-collar workers under union contracts belonged to unions more often than did white-collar employees.

U.S. unions suffered a disastrous drop in membership in the private sector of the economy between 1980 and 1984. During the 1981–82 recession total membership fell below 20 million workers for the first time since 1968. By 1984, despite the economic recovery then underway, union membership had declined to 17.3 million out of a total employed work force of 92.2 million. Membership as a proportion of employment fell from 23 percent in 1980 to 18.8 percent in 1984. Table 1 shows the ratios of union membership and representation by major occupation for 1984.

Table 2 lists the ratios of represented workers in selected industries. After railway and postal employees, workers in manufacturing and communications services show the highest ratios of union representation, followed by miners and construction workers. Still, the largest number of organized employees is in education. Repre-

---

[4]Union membership ratios do not fully reveal the extent of union influence in the economy. Because workers do not necessarily have to be union members to be covered by union contracts, a larger number of workers are in unionized workplaces than belong to unions. The law requires a union to represent all the workers in the bargaining unit whether or not they belong to the union, and bargaining unit members are not required to belong to the union unless the contract specifies membership as a condition of continued employment.

Table 1. Employed Workers Belonging to or Represented by Unions in Major Occupational Groups, 1984

Occupational group	Total employed (thousands)	Percent belonging to unions	Percent represented by unions
Managerial and professional	20,817	15.8	20.2
Technical, sales, and administrative support	29,135	11.2	13.8
Service occupations	13,066	15.1	17.2
Precision production, craft and repair	11,188	30.1	32.5
Operators, fabricators, and laborers	16,213	33.1	35.2
Farming, forestry, and fishing	1,775	5.5	6.4
Total	92,194	18.8	21.6

Source: The Bureau of National Affairs, Inc., "BLS Survey On Union Membership, Wages," *White Collar Report*, Vol. 57, February 20, 1985, pp. 173, 175.

sentation levels are lowest in business and personal services, farming, and finance.

The figures in Table 2 show that, if unions are to play a major role in determining the terms and conditions of employment of American workers, they must expand their representation in growth industries. The work forces in these areas are increasing rapidly while those in most well-organized industries are stable or declining. The number of computer specialists, health technicians, bank tellers, and office machine operators has increased steadily, while that of locomotive engineers, postal clerks, precision machine operators, telephone installers and repairers, and construction laborers has declined. Changing technology and shifting product markets and production locations will continue the trend. The significance of these changes is illustrated by the restaurant industry, in which the number of employees—many of them part-time workers—increased during 1977–81 by more than the total number of workers in basic steel and motor vehicles combined.

For unions to organize successfully in these areas, they will have to make structural changes. Consolidations will occur as they did in the past in response to changing environments. Overlapping union jurisdictions and the nonaffiliation of large international unions with the AFL-CIO result in wasteful duplication of organizing efforts and opportunist raiding of already organized bargaining units by rival unions. In chemicals, for instance, 22 unions together represented about 125,000 workers in 1974. Five of these were not

Table 2. Employed Workers Represented by Unions in Selected
Industries, May 1980

Industry	Thousands of workers	Percent of employed workers
Railroads	474	81.8
Postal	509	73.7
Automobiles	582	61.2
Primary metals	686	58.4
Communications	714	49.7
Paper	369	49.1
Public utilities	594	43.1
Aircraft	286	42.4
Food processing	628	37.5
Local government	703	36.9
Educational	2,767	34.3
Petroleum	75	34.1
Mining	286	32.1
Construction	1,574	31.6
Rubber and plastics	205	29.6
Electrical equipment	599	26.9
State government	253	26.0
Chemicals	320	25.8
ALL INDUSTRIES	22,493	25.7
Apparel	326	25.1
Printing	290	20.2
Federal government	347	19.3
Hospitals	692	17.7
Textiles	117	14.9
Entertainment and recreation	127	14.1
Personal services, except private household	229	13.9
Welfare and religious	207	13.4
Medical, except hospitals	229	10.0
Retail trade	1,363	9.8
Professional services, except medical and educational	137	6.5
Insurance and real estate	153	5.5
Agriculture	51	3.5
Banking and other finance	38	1.6
Private household service	7	0.6

Source: Courtney D. Gifford, *Directory of U.S. Labor Organizations: 1982–83 Edition*
(Washington, D.C.: The Bureau of National Affairs, Inc. 1982).

AFL-CIO affiliates. Table 3 shows the number of unions which shared representation in seven partially organized industry groups. The falling ratio of union organization reflects job losses in heavily unionized industries and geographic regions coupled with union inability to win enough elections in new bargaining units to offset the job losses. In 1950, unions won three out of four NLRB elections; by the mid-1970s they were losing more than half. Seeber and Cooke analyzed the data on certification elections and found that the most important reason for labor's declining success is grow-

Table 3.   Distribution of Union Representation in Selected Partially Unionized Industry Groups, 1974

Industry group	Number of unions	Number of AFL-CIO unions
Printing and publishing	19	13
Chemicals	22	17
Food and beverages	26	17
Wholesale and retail trade	22	13
Transportation services	37	28
Service	45	27
Government	64	39

Source: Bureau of Labor Statistics, U.S. Dept. of Labor, Handbook of Labor Statistics, 1978, Bulletin 2000 (1979), pp. 502–503.

ing employer resistance to unionization. Other contributing factors are the movement of jobs into locations and sectors that are traditionally hostile to collective bargaining and to the decreasing size of election units.[5]

Congressional hearings in 1979 produced evidence that antiunion management consultant firms are involved in two-thirds of all NLRB representation elections. One firm had assisted employers in nearly 700 separate elections during the preceding two years and had defeated unions in nine out of 10 contests. Workers are intimidated in these campaigns by illegal firings and threats to discipline union supporters. The incidence of such acts has risen sharply with the increased employer use of outside consultants to maintain a "union-free environment." Unfair labor practice charges brought by unions in 1957 resulted in the reinstatement of fewer than 1,000 workers who had been illegally discharged; in 1980 the number of charges was nine times the 1957 figure and the number of reinstated workers reached 10,000—1.3 workers for every election. The overall odds were 1 in 25 that a union supporter would be discharged illegally during the campaign.[6]

While there is evidence of increasing dissatisfaction with unions by many American workers, a survey of unorganized workers suggests greater support than is indicated by NLRB election outcomes. When nearly 1,000 nonsupervisory workers were asked in a 1977 U.S. Labor Department poll whether they would favor collective bargaining if given the opportunity to vote in a representation

[5]Ronald L. Seeber and William N. Cooke, "The Decline in Union Success in NLRB Representation Elections," Industrial Relations (Winter 1983).

[6]U.S. Congress, House, Pressure In Today's Workplace, Subcommittee on Labor-Management Relations of the Labor and Education Committee, (Washington, D.C.: 1980).

election, 33 percent said they would. About four of every 10 blue-collar workers voiced their support (compared to 28 percent of the white-collar employees), as did two of every three minority workers; 40 percent of the women workers and 35 percent of those in the south indicated approval of unions. Nevertheless, those polled revealed certain reservations. Many of them viewed unions as a last resort to remedy unsatisfactory working conditions rather than as a preferred solution. This sentiment was especially strong among white-collar employees.[7]

Economists and Economic Bargaining

Economists in market societies must take into account the impact of unions. Some perceive unions as unwanted obstacles to the wage and employment outcomes of a free labor market. But most regard them—if not enthusiastically then at least with tolerance—as natural institutions in the market economy. They accept the need to understand unions, and so theorize about and measure the economic impact of collective bargaining.

Market Theory. Market theorists treat labor like any other factor of production. The demand for labor is a derived demand, which means that it is determined by the demand for the final product and the production method that is used. The greater the derived demand for labor, the more the union can raise wages without losing jobs as a result of higher labor costs. In other words, employer demand for the labor is not very sensitive to changes in its price (wage).

The British theorist Alfred Marshall enumerated four conditions under which the demand for union labor is insensitive to wage increases. Demand will be more insensitive to negotiated labor cost increases:

(1) The more essential union labor is in the production process,

(2) The more that the prices of products made by union labor can be raised without losing sales revenues,

(3) The smaller the ratio of the cost of union labor to total costs of production, and

(4) The faster that prices and wages rise for the additional ma-

---

[7]Thomas A. Kochan, "How American Workers View Labor Unions," *Monthly Labor Review* (April 1979).

chines and workers that could be substituted for union labor in the production process.

The first condition implies that there are no good substitutes for union labor. Translated into economic bargaining relationships, it means that skilled workers who cannot be replaced by less-skilled employees have potential bargaining power because they are indispensable to the final product. Marshall used a hypothetical strike by plasterers against building contractors to illustrate the concept of derived demand. Printers and tool-and-die makers are other historical examples of irreplaceable skills and consequent union bargaining power. Introduction of new machines and processes, which enable unskilled or nonunion operators to do the work, erodes this power. Cold-type printing technology, prefabricated building materials, and computerized machining pose the same threat.

The second condition involves the extent to which products made under nonunion conditions are substitutes for union-made goods. As long as there are no such products, union labor has bargaining power. To illustrate the point, when the Bell Telephone service companies of AT&T used only telephones made by AT&T's Western Electric equipment manufacturing subsidiary, unions representing Western Electric's production workers negotiated with the knowledge that labor costs could be increased without losing sales to other telephone equipment manufacturers. Union bargaining strength was diminished, however, when government deregulation exposed Western Electric products to competition from nonunion equipment makers.

The third condition has to do with the proportion of union labor costs to total production costs. The smaller the ratio the more an employer can increase union labor costs without charging higher product prices. Individual building trades unions have been able to negotiate high wages in part because no one craft accounts for a substantial part of total construction costs, even though the total labor cost is a large part of overall cost.

The final condition has the least effect on union bargaining power. It concerns changes in the cost of substitutes for union labor in the production process. An employer dissatisfied with the high cost of union labor might turn to machine or human substitutes. If this is technologically possible, the employer might find also that as machines or other workers are substituted for union labor their costs rise so fast that it soon becomes inefficient to continue the substitutions. The lack of obvious examples to illustrate this relationship suggests that it is not a common occurrence in real situations.

Marshall's conditions imply economic constraints on how much unions can raise labor costs before the employer begins to eliminate union jobs. The theory says that high-priced union labor eventually will experience a decline in demand. In the long run, therefore, as employers and consumers make technological and other adjustments to high labor costs, union power diminishes.

Quantitative Analysis. The economic impact of unions and bargaining can be estimated quantitatively as well as theoretically. Wage differences between union and nonunion workers are measured by industry and occupation to determine whether workers covered by union contracts fare better than those not covered. Quantitative studies show definite statistical relationships between unionization and high wages, but the causal relationship is not very clear.

Unionized workers have higher earnings than nonunion workers by industry and occupation. Economists differ, however, about how much of the differential is due to unionization. Some attribute it to differences in personal characteristics between union and nonunion workers, such as education and training levels, or to productivity differences among workers. Another argument for minimizing the effect of unions is that high wages themselves may lead to unionization and therefore be the causal factor.

Complicating the issue of wage differentials is the problem of isolating and measuring the union "threat effect." The threat effect occurs when nonunion employers match union wage levels (and negotiated increases) in order to avoid becoming unionized. It is difficult to determine the importance of this threat because employers seldom acknowledge that it is a motivating factor.

Because it cannot be measured accurately, the threat effect causes economists to understate the full impact of unions on earnings. Only years after the fact, for example, did Mesta Machine Company, the nation's largest manufacturer of machines for the steel industry, concede that its historical practice of keeping pace with unionized steel wages had been part of a "human relations" strategy of avoiding the union. The steelworkers union was unable to organize Mesta until 1967, three decades after most of the industry was under contract.[8]

Quantitative studies of wage differences estimate the wages of union workers to be 10 to 30 percent higher than they would be in

---

[8]Thomas F. O'Boyle, "Turnabout in Fortunes of Mesta Machine Is History With a Moral," *The Wall Street Journal*, January 3, 1984, p. 31.

the absence of collective bargaining. The earliest quantitative studies, which covered the decades before and immediately following World War II, found a 10 to 15 percent union impact. More recent findings raise the estimated range to 15 to 30 percent; moreover, the widest differentials measured are for the 1970s.[9] These studies were made before the wave of concession bargaining by unions in the 1980s.

Variations in the range of union wage impact result from industry differences and business cycles. Union impact has been greatest in construction, transportation, and printing and least in industries with largely unorganized work forces or problems of long-term economic decline. Union workers also fare better than nonunion workers in recessions and during periods of rapid price inflation.

Studies conducted in the 1970s show that unions benefit nonwhite male workers proportionately more than they do other groups of workers and that they are especially effective in protecting the job security and earnings of younger and older workers. Unions also reduce earnings differentials between skilled and less-skilled workers and between white-collar and blue-collar employees, and they introduce new kinds of compensation systems that benefit workers, such as automatic cost-of-living adjustments and regular upward wage revisions.[10]

Another area of interest to economists is the union impact on income distribution. At issue is whether unions increase labor's share of national income. According to the evidence, they do not. An exceedingly small increase has occurred in the ratio of national income that goes to wage and salaried employees, and most of it can be traced to shifts in the relative importance of different sectors of the economy—such as the long-term decline of small farming in America—rather than to unions and collective bargaining.

Market economists try to explain this inability of unions to increase labor's overall income share even though they negotiate higher earnings for union members. Since a minority of eligible employees in the United States actually work under union contracts, economists reason that negotiated wage increases cannot determine overall income distribution. Again, this conclusion minimizes the

---

[9]Albert Rees, *The Economics of Trade Unions*, revised edition (Chicago: University of Chicago Press, 1977), pp. 70-5.

[10]These findings are summarized in Thomas A. Kochan, *Collective Bargaining and Industrial Relations: From Theory to Policy and Practice* (Homewood, Ill.: Richard D. Irwin, Inc., 1980), pp. 338-39.

importance of union threat effects. In addition, market economists theorize that high pay levels and large wage increases eventually are self-defeating, either because employers eventually offset rising labor costs by substituting machines for workers or because negotiated wage increases cause higher product prices and discourage consumer purchases. Finally, it is argued that the income gains of union workers come at the expense of nonunion workers. High union wages result in fewer workers being employed in unionized industries; workers who cannot find jobs in the unionized industries must compete with each other for work in nonunion industries— which drives down nonunion wages.

These conventional explanations for organized labor's inability to redistribute income lead to an anti-union conclusion. Economic bargaining gives rise to market forces of supply and demand that not only prevent workers from increasing their overall income share (while holding down the wages of nonunion workers), but also cause high-paid union workers to lose jobs to machines and shrinking product sales.

Another issue in the economic impact of unions is inflation. For unions to cause inflation, negotiated wage settlements must be greater than productivity and must spread across the economy from one industry to another. Quantitative studies show no such effect. Wage patterns do tend to cluster around certain industries and occupations, but they do not generally move into other areas of the economy and create inflationary spirals. Similar wage movements in unrelated industries are caused instead by broad economic trends including inflation. Negotiated wage increases are an effect and not a cause of inflation. Economic bargaining is not the dynamic force behind inflation; it is the institution by which labor responds to inflation.

Unions can prolong inflation, however, by negotiating "catch up" wage increases. Wage settlements that compensate union members for losses in purchasing power due to earlier price increases can sustain an inflationary momentum by providing more spendable dollars to workers as consumers. If increases in their incomes match price increases, workers are not hurt by inflation; if they do not, workers "pay" for inflation through lower standards of living.

Statistical studies indicate that union attempts to match price increases with negotiated wage increases prolong inflation. Unions respond slowly to changes in the rate of inflation. They customarily negotiate future contract terms and conditions on the basis of recent experiences and current expectations of their members. A time lag occurs between increases and decreases in the rate of inflation and corresponding shifts in union economic bargaining priorities. Negotiated cost-of-living adjustments and deferred wage increases reflect worker expectations of continued price increases.[11]

Case Studies. A third approach in the analysis of economic bargaining is the case study. That is the method used in this book. Case studies rest on empirical evidence and a theoretical frame of reference, but they are not quantitative in nature. Instead, they draw together a variety of information sources which cannot be expressed or measured quantitatively, such as organizational structures, behavioral patterns, and social constraints.

Economic bargaining experiences in several industries and firms in the private sector are described and analyzed in subsequent chapters. The descriptions emphasize economic institutions, objectives, and outcomes. The basis of analysis is an institutional model of comparative union-management bargaining power.

The method is to examine the economic bargaining environment in a variety of settings. Individual cases involve an industry, firm, or single plant. The purpose is to determine and explain relative union-management bargaining power. This involves identifying and defining the conditions under which bargaining power exists, and then determining whether these conditions are present in the selected cases. Conditions favorable to union power are those that give employers the ability to pay higher negotiated labor costs and unions the ability to make employers pay.

When an appropriate case has been selected for study, as much information about the case is collected as is practicably permissible. The bargaining power model is then used to distinguish the relevant from the less important material and to arrange the information according to specified categories of analysis. The final step involves making a determination of union bargaining strength depending on the presence or absence of the power variables. The following list identifies the broad areas of investigation in economic bargaining case studies:

(1) The structure, behavior, and performance of unionized firms and industries,

---

[11]For a discussion of these quantitative findings and the implications that follow regarding the economic advisability of trade unions from the neoclassical economics perspective, see Albert Rees, *The Economics of Trade Unions*, rev. ed. (Chicago: University of Chicago Press, 1977).

(2) Labor productivity,
(3) The extent of unionization,
(4) Economic bargaining structures, and
(5) Bargaining relationships among unions.

The ability-to-pay, ability-to-make-pay framework of analysis is a static method. It identifies relative bargaining power at a point in time. From it, we can estimate bargaining power now or at some historical point; we also can compare or contrast relative power at different times. But we cannot explain changes in power over time. In order to do that—to make the analysis dynamic—we have to consider the things that cause the underlying conditions and therefore affect the distribution of power. This is a complex but more valuable analysis which involves three broad areas of change in the market economy:

(1) Changes in organizational structures,
(2) Changes in technology, and
(3) Changes in public policy.

Changes in organizational structure affect the strategic importance of the prevailing structures and practices. A change in the operating structure of a corporate employer, for example, can alter the prevailing sources of union strength—the extent to which workers are unionized, the economic bargaining structure, or relationships among unions. When it takes such changes into account, the case study is more perceptive and discerning than when it consists of static assessments of relative union-management strength.

The analysis is more complete when it is expanded from the study of a single bargaining relationship to include many cases. One industry or firm may not represent the general trend in economic bargaining. It would be a mistake therefore to base generalizations on the single case. Investigation of several cases increases the likelihood that the analysis accurately describes reality. The object is to find patterns of economic bargaining experiences from among the several case studies. When such patterns are discerned, tentative generalizations can be made about all economic bargaining relationships. A large number of cases, accurate individual investigations, and skillful integration and interpretation of the evidence increase the reliability of the findings.

Like all systems of social science inquiry, the case study method is both rational and intuitive. A unique feature of the method is that it never ends—it is not final and definitive in its conclusion—because its subject never stops changing. For this reason, case studies are associated with that part of modern economics called evolutionary or institutional.

The strength of the case study approach is its close proximity to the subject matter, or its empirical realism. An inherent weakness is the difficulty in conducting enough cases to warrant analytical generalizations. Another is the danger of subjective bias by the investigator in the selection, research, and interpretation of specific cases. At its best, however, the case study method gathers, organizes, and assesses a considerable amount of detail about the institutional world of work, unions, and economic bargaining.

Key Words and Phrases

job security	industrial system
bargaining power	public policy
production process	National Labor Relations Act
distribution of income	National Labor Relations Board
managerial prerogative	"union-free environment"
common law precedent	unfair labor practice
factor of production	derived demand for labor
labor market theory	deregulation
neoclassical theory	wage differentials
mobility	compensation systems
complete knowledge	income share
deductive theory of wage and employment levels	institutional labor practice
	empirical evidence
free market	evolutionary economics
unregulated system	institutional economics

Review and Discussion Questions

1. What is the difference between the neoclassical (labor market) theory of wages and employment and the union theory?

2. How and when does the author say it was "demonstrated that America could no longer have both industrial stability and nonunion workplaces?" Would you say that this statement still holds for today?

3. What has been the trend in union membership as a percentage of the total labor force? Which sections are gaining? Which are declining?

4. British economic theorist Alfred Marshall said that demand for union labor would not be affected by negotiated labor cost increases under four conditions. What are they?

Chapter Resources and Suggested Further Reading

The management case for unilateral control of the workplace is discussed in Reinhard Bendix, *Work and Authority in Industry: Ideologies of Management in the Course of Industrialization* (1956). The classic statement of management control in practice is Frederick W. Taylor, *Scientific Management* (1947). A critique of management control is Harry Braverman, *Labor and Monopoly Capital: The Degradation of Work in the Twentieth Century* (1974).

Histories of worker experiences in America under nonunion—or market—conditions include David Brody, *Steelworkers in America: The Nonunion Era* (1969); Cletus E. Daniel, *Bitter Harvest: A History of California Farmworkers, 1870-1941* (1981); Hannah Josephson, *The Golden Threads: New England's Mill Girls and Magnates* (1949).

Two statements by market economists in opposition to unions and collective bargaining are Henry C. Simons, *Economic Policy for a Free Society* (1948); Milton Friedman, "Some Comments on the Significance of Labor Unions for Economic Policy," in David McCord Wright, ed., *The Impact of the Union* (1956). A criticism of the pure market theory of wages is Lester Thurow, *Generating Inequality* (1975).

Standard works by market economists on the impact of unions are H. Gregg Lewis, *Unionism and Relative Wages in the United States* (1963), and Albert Rees, *The Economics of Trade Unions* (1977). Of the two, Rees is written more for the general reader.

A summary of quantitative analyses of economic bargaining is George Johnson, "Economic Analysis of Trade Unionism," *American Economic Review* (May 1975). A useful survey, written in a nontechnical style, is Thomas A. Kochan, *Collective Bargaining and Industrial Relations: From Theory to Policy and Practice* (1980). More technical in its approach is Daniel J. B. Mitchell, *Unions, Wages and Inflation* (1980).

The case study method is described and evaluated in Paul Diesing, *Patterns of Discovery in the Social Sciences* (1971). Historical and recent examples of union bargaining case studies using various philosophical and methodological approaches include Jacob H. Hollander and George E. Barnett, eds., *Studies in American Trade Unionism,* (1912), Reprint, (1970); Harry A. Millis, ed., *How Collective Bargaining Works* (1945); Harold M. Levinson, *Determining Forces in Collective Wage Bargaining* (1966); Gerald G. Somers, *Collective Bargaining: Contemporary American Experiences* (1980); Andrew Zimbalist, *Case Studies on the Labor Process* (1979).

Economic methods and theories, from Adam Smith to the institutionalists, are discussed in Paul J. McNulty, *The Origins and Development of Labor Economics: A Chapter in the History of Social Thought* (1980). Alfred Marshall's derived demand analysis is in chapter six of his *Principles of Economics*, 8th ed. (1982), which was originally published in 1920.

2

The Sources of Union Bargaining Power

This chapter identifies and describes the sources of union bargaining power in the private economy. A union is likely to have bargaining power if employers have the ability to pay higher wages and benefits and provide good working conditions and if the union has the ability to make the employers pay. Selected bargaining experiences are described in order to demonstrate the relationship between structure, technology and public policy, and relative labor-management bargaining power.

Employer Ability to Pay

The market environment in which employers do business is important to the bargaining potential of unions for two reasons. One concerns the product market where employers sell goods and services. The other refers to the labor market where employers hire workers to transform materials into saleable products. Revenues obtained from product markets provide the resources for money payments in labor markets. The larger the revenues the greater the possible payments to labor.

Union and management therefore have a mutual interest in promoting and maintaining product market performance because they both stand to gain from it. But they have no such mutual interest in rising labor costs. To employers labor costs are deductions from revenues; to workers they are purchasing power, economic security, and better working conditions. Bargaining disputes therefore involve terms and conditions in labor markets, not the results experienced in product markets. A union engaged in a bitter strike over negotiated wage increases later cooperates with the struck em-

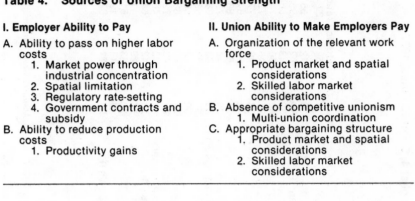

Table 4.   Sources of Union Bargaining Strength

I. Employer Ability to Pay	II. Union Ability to Make Employers Pay
A. Ability to pass on higher labor costs	A. Organization of the relevant work force
1. Market power through industrial concentration	1. Product market and spatial considerations
2. Spatial limitation	2. Skilled labor market considerations
3. Regulatory rate-setting	B. Absence of competitive unionism
4. Government contracts and subsidy	1. Multi-union coordination
B. Ability to reduce production costs	C. Appropriate bargaining structure
1. Productivity gains	1. Product market and spatial considerations
	2. Skilled labor market considerations

ployer to protect threatened sales markets. The union applauds an expansion of the firm's market share, but not a reduction in labor costs as a result of labor-displacing machinery.

Table 4 identifies four product market conditions that improve an employer's ability to pay labor cost increases by passing them on to consumers as higher prices. These conditions allow firms to increase prices without losing market shares to rival firms. This occurs for one of two reasons. In one instance conditions are such that all firms charge the same or similar prices, and therefore do not compete on the basis of differences in labor costs but through advertising and other forms of nonprice competition. In the second situation, the firms in an industry can pass on labor cost increases through government rate-setting processes or under the terms of exclusive supplier contracts.

Industrial Concentration and Administered Pricing. Industrial concentration refers to the share of sales accounted for by the largest firms in an industry. An industry is considered concentrated when the largest four firms account for half or more of total sales.[1] Table 5 shows that in 1972 the top four firms had 73 percent of the tire and tube industry and 77 percent of the passenger car tire product class within that industry. Particular product lines often are more concentrated than their industries. Basic steel was not highly concentrated at the four-firm level, but its sheet and strip mill product class was.

Industrial concentration persists despite profit levels which would otherwise attract new firms, increase product supply, and

---

[1]The market share of the leading firms is expressed as the dollar value of their product shipments as a percentage of total industry shipments.

Table 5. Concentration Ratios in Selected Industries and Product Classes, Largest 4, 8 and 20 Firms, 1972

Industry or product class (P)	Firm concentration ratio 4	8	20	Industry or product class (P)	Firm concentration ratio 4	8	20
Motor vehicles	93	99	99+	Hardware	35	42	55
Trucks (P)	84	97	99+	Motor vehicle hardware (P)	NA	89	95
Cereals	90	98	99+	Bakery	32	43	56
Cigarettes	84	NA	100	Soft cakes (P)	48	60	74
Tires and tubes	73	90	98	Cotton textile	31	48	72
Auto Tires (P)	77	93	100	Cotton sheets (P)	28	46	77
Aircraft	69	87	98	Oil refining	31	56	84
Military aircraft (P)	74	94	99+	Gasoline (P)	31	55	86
Transformers	58	74	89	Pharmaceuticals	26	44	75
Power transformers (P)	67	86	97	Central nervous system drugs (P)	43	63	88
Beer and ale	52	70	91	Meatpacking	26	39	53
Canned beer and ale (P)	59	77	96	Beef (P)	30	42	58
Internal combustion engines	48	69	89	Paper mills	24	40	66
Truck and bus diesel (P)	96	100	100	Writing paper (P)	32	49	72
Radio and TV sets	46	69	85	Men's and boys' suits and coats	19	30	46
Household TV (P)	66	93	100	Men's suits and coats (P)	28	42	64
Steel mills	45	65	84	Newspapers	17	29	41
Sheet and strip mill products (P)	54	77	98	Daily and Sunday (P)	20	33	51
Bars, plates, etc. (P)	59	70	85	Letterpress printing	9	13	19
Construction machinery	41	53	70	Magazines and periodicals (P)	59	71	82
Scrapers, graders, etc. (P)	48	60	82				

Source: U.S. Department of Commerce, Bureau of the Census, Concentration Ratios in Manufacturing: 1972 Census of Manufacturers (Washington, D.C.: 1975).

lower product prices (and profits). This is because of natural and human barriers preventing the entry of competitive sellers. Among the former are limited mineral reserves and shipping ports; among the latter are heavy advertising and product styling costs, patent control, prohibitive financial requirements, and exclusive buyer-seller arrangements.

Administered pricing accompanies concentrated structure and barriers to entry. When a few companies dominate the industry or product class they have discretion over product prices and output. They are "price-makers" rather than "price takers." An administered price differs from a competitive one in that it is made by executive decision. Prices are set to achieve a predetermined target rate of profit on investment. These profit levels are not necessarily exorbitant, but are predictable. U.S. Steel, for example, historically averaged an 8 percent rate of return in its basic mills while General Motors until recently was able to get 15 to 20 percent. Both were lead firms in their industries. Under administered pricing the largest firm is responsible for industry standards on labor costs, product quality, acceptable forms of nonprice competition, and other practices essential to industry stability.

Industrial concentration ratios are important to product market power but do not tell the whole story. They overstate the market power of domestic auto manufacturing companies, for example, because the figures do not take into account the domestic market share held by foreign sellers, which in 1981 was about one-quarter of the U.S. auto market. Concentration ratios also exaggerate the power of major tire producers by neglecting the countervailing market power of auto producers, retail chains, and other large buyers which use their volume-buying capacity to obtain significant price discounts.

By contrast, low concentration ratios in newspapers, drugs, and oil refining understate actual market power. Most newspapers sell in limited geographic regions rather than nationwide. Most cities in the United States have only a single local paper. Market power is therefore much greater than the ratio suggests; individual publishers have considerable discretion over price and product in the absence of local competition. Pharmaceutical companies sell in national markets but frequently avoid competition in specific product markets because exclusive patent and brand name rights exclude rivals. Major oil companies are vertically integrated, meaning they own and operate facilities at each stage of petroleum production. Therefore, even though the four largest refiners had only 31 percent of the market in 1972, they and a few other integrated majors exerted effective control over the entire industry because thousands of nonintegrated oil companies were dependent on them for the purchase or sale of resources and services.

Corporate Consolidation. The primary cause of industrial concentration is corporate consolidation, not internal expansion. Big companies get that way more often by buying up competitors than by expanding their sales through better products at lower prices. Corporate combinations are of three types:

(1) Corporate *consolidation*, in which a number of firms simultaneously are brought together under common ownership, as occurred in the formation of U.S. Steel and other industrial trusts;

(2) Corporate *merger*, in which the assets of two previously independent firms are combined under common ownership, as in the 1892 merging of Edison General Electric Company and Thomson-Houston Electric Company to form General Electric; and

(3) Corporate *acquisition*, in which the stock of one company is purchased or traded by another company, as in Continental Oil's acquisition of Consolidated Coal.

The word "merger" is commonly used in place of "consolidation" and "acquisition" in industrial organization discussion. Three great merger waves in American business history are responsible for the present high level of industrial concentration. They occurred around the turn of the last century, again during the 1920s, and then beginning in the late 1950s.

Mergers produce five types of corporate industrial structures: horizontal, vertical, diversified, holding company, and multinational.

Horizontal merger combines firms that previously competed in the same sales markets. Acquisition of Drewrys, a local brand of beer, by a regional brewer named Associated Brewing Company, which also had several other acquired breweries, is an example of horizontal merger.

Vertical merger integrates firms that previously bought and sold from one another in their production and distribution activities. U.S. Steel was created through the combination of some 785 separate plants having both horizontal and vertical relationships in each stage of iron and steel production: ore ranges, coke ovens, railroads and ore carriers, steel furnaces and fabricating mills.

Diversified merger brings together firms that do not have direct market relationships and linkages. Acquisition of Hartford Fire Insurance Company and the Avis car rental agency by International Telephone and Telegraph (ITT), a huge conglomerate corporation, illustrates this type of consolidation.

Holding company merger places a previously independent firm under the ownership of a company that itself does not make and sell products or services but simply owns companies that do so. AT&T until recently consisted of subsidiaries in regulated industries, including the 22 Bell phone companies, and in unregulated sectors, such as Western Electric, the equipment manufacturing arm of AT&T.

Multinational merger combines firms doing business in more than one nation. Acquisition of the U.S. cookie manufacturer Keebler by the British firm United Biscuit was a multinational combination. The effects of each of these corporate merger outcomes on unions and collective bargaining are described and analyzed in subsequent chapters.

Spatial Limitation. Some industries have an ability to pass on uniform increases in labor costs even though they are not highly concentrated—building and construction, maritime shipping and longshoring, and interstate trucking. Harold Levinson attributed this condition to "spatial limitations of the physical area within which new entrants can effectively produce." High labor costs can be passed on in higher prices because unionized employers have little fear of nonunion employers coming into the industry. Prospective competitors would have to locate in an area already occupied by unionized employers or would have to come in at a stage of production which is unionized so effectively that they could not do business without recognizing the union and paying negotiated standards. "Under this type of industrial structure," Levinson says, "the union need only achieve a high degree of organizational strength within the limited strategic areas involved in order to be protected against the undermining effects of new nonunion entrants or of runaway shops, irrespective of how easy entry into the industry itself might be."[2]

Product and technology characteristics explain the situation in some industries. In construction, a building cannot be assembled in Alabama and located in New York. Low wages and benefits in the

---

[2]Harold Levinson, "Unionism, Concentration and Wage Changes: Toward a Unified Theory", *Industrial and Labor Relations Review*, (January 1967), p. 202.

Alabama trades cannot bring down high standards in New York as long as New York unions have organized their labor markets and negotiate uniform labor costs among all the employers. In longshoring, there are only so many seaports in which ships can be loaded and unloaded. Because unions have thoroughly organized the Atlantic, Gulf, and Pacific coasts and have established uniform labor costs, there is no threat from nonunion stevedoring companies.[3]

Regulatory Rate-Setting. In interstate trucking the Interstate Commerce Commission (ICC) was authorized to license carriers engaged in long-distance trucking and the Teamsters union (IBT) had organized all or most of those carriers and negotiated a master freight agreement covering their drivers. A spatial limitation existed within which labor cost increases could be passed on in the form of regulated freight rates. The usual practice was for the carriers to determine freight rates through industry boards and then submit them to the ICC for approval and enforcement. Employers accepted the IBT's consolidation of bargaining structures nationwide. According to Pierson, they saw the union as an "essential link in the process whereby trucking firms could move together in securing ICC approval of rate increases."[4]

Railroads, intercity buses, airlines, and AT&T's long-lines telephone system are other examples of economic bargaining under federal regulations. Urban mass transit systems, power utilities, and branch or local telephone companies are under state and regional control agencies. Like the federal regulatory bodies, state agencies have been inclined to permit employers to compensate for negotiated labor cost increases with rate hikes. According to one interpretation of labor relations in mass transit, "the single most important factor in wage agreements has been their acceptability to the public regulatory commission."[5]

Theoretically, the practical restraint on higher wages and benefits in such cases is the desire of regulated firms to stay competitive with employers who sell substitute services. Interstate for-hire trucking companies do not want their shipping fees to rise much higher than the costs to shippers of buying and operating their own

---

[3]In the East, the International Longshoremen's Association (AFL-CIO) negotiates similar regional and port contracts; in the West, the International Longshoremen's and Warehousemen's Union (Ind.) negotiates a coastwide master agreement.

[4]Frank Pierson, *Unions in Postwar America: An Economic Assessment* (New York: Random House, 1967), p. 116.

[5]Darold T. Barnum, *From Private to Public: Labor Relations in Urban Mass Transit* (Lubbock, Tex.: Texas Tech University, 1977), p. 129.

trucks. Negotiators for unionized carriers may be secure in the knowledge that higher labor costs will be passed on to shippers, but they also know that substantial wage hikes can make for-hire non-competitive with private carrier or rail freight services.

Regulatory rate-setting is less a source of employer ability to pay now than in the past because of recent deregulation.

Government Contracts and Operating Subsidies. Cost-plus contracts and operating subsidies to private industry are another means of improving employer ability to pay. Aerospace firms, for instance, have used the reimbursement guarantees of cost-plus defense contracts to hire excess numbers of top-ranked graduating engineers and scientists for these projects, subsequently keeping the best and letting the others go. Whether they also paid higher hourly labor costs than they might otherwise pay is uncertain, but it is reasonable to believe that the net effect of cost-plus pricing was to introduce an ability-to-pay element into contract negotiations in certain industries.

Operating maritime subsidies enhanced employer ability to pay in that industry. When the level of federal subsidy peaked in the mid-1960s, operating subsidies designed to make the American merchant fleet competitive accounted for 72 cents out of every dollar in wages received by seamen.[6] The government also maintains maritime employment by requiring that federally subsidized shipments be made in American vessels.

Productivity. Employers also increase their ability to pay by raising productivity levels, which allows them to provide higher wages and benefits without raising prices. Worker productivity is defined as a positive change in the amount or value of output-per-hour-worked. Large increases in output normally signify falling costs of production per unit of output because production costs, including labor, are not rising as fast as output is increasing.

Workers can share in these gains. If a product can be produced with 5 percent fewer hours of labor than it took the year before, the employer can increase the earnings of all hourly workers by 5 percent without increasing prices or reducing profits. Increasing productivity has made these workers 5 percent more valuable, and the 5 percent pay increase is offset by the 5 percent fewer hours of work that are needed to get the same output.

Employers in concentrated industries are most likely to achieve sizable productivity increases because they use large amounts of

---

[6]"Of Ships, Subsidies, and Seamen," *Monthly Labor Review* (October 1965), p. 111.

capital equipment in their production processes. The term "capital intensive" is used to describe industries characterized by high ratios of capital equipment to labor. Steel mills, paper plants, telephone companies, and oil refineries all are capital-intensive industries. With the exception of steel in recent years, they are also high productivity industries. Each is also a high wage industry.

The role of productivity in collective bargaining is discussed more fully in Chapter 3. It is sufficient for now to say that labor and management can agree more easily on improvements to the employer's product market position than on costs of production and labor market productivity. Higher revenues pay for wage and benefit improvements; lower production costs through productivity can too, but at the cost of fewer production jobs.

Union Ability to Make Employers Pay

Employer ability to pay higher labor costs depends on markets and production processes. Union ability to make employers pay depends on organizational achievements.

Unions must, among other things, match the economic structures of employers. Robert Hoxie recognized this imperative even before it was demonstrated by the CIO in the 1930s. "The union organic structure shows a tendency to parallel the capitalistic," he observed, "a union unit to meet each capitalist unit."[7] As Table 4 indicates, this means that unions must organize the *relevant* workers, must eliminate *competitive* unionism, and must establish *appropriate* bargaining structures. Each of these is an attempt to "parallel" industry organization. Unions do not determine the structure and behavior of industry, they accommodate themselves to the industrial environment.

Organization of the Relevant Work Force. Unions must organize the relevant work force if they want bargaining power. In craft industries this includes workers capable of doing the skilled work, because to leave them unorganized is to expose the unionized trade to substandard rates.

Industrial unions, for their part, must follow the work wherever it is being done. Where products are made in a single workplace, the union only needs to organize locally. However, production at several locations requires organization of every workplace to

---

[7]Robert F. Hoxie, *Trade Unionism in the United States* (Chicago: University of Chicago Press, 1917), p. 99.

avoid having products made where the union is weakest or nonexistent. Production by several firms in numerous locations prompts the union to organize workers in each plant of every firm.

The implication is clear: an employer's ability to knit fabric, assemble autos, or make tons of steel outside the scope of the union contract or negotiated pattern undermines established standards.

Movement of union textile mills from northern to southern states before and after World War II changed the relevant work force so much that the unions never recovered their organizational base. Movement of General Motors parts production facilities to southern states forced the United Auto Workers (UAW) to follow. The union could not rest until it had organized the new relevant workers. When GM opened eight southern parts and subassembly plants during 1973-77 the UAW claimed the company had a "southern strategy" aimed at undermining GM-UAW national wage and benefit standards. GM executives denied the accusation, saying they had been attracted to the south by low energy costs, not cheap labor. Local plant management nevertheless fought UAW organizing drives at parts plants in Mississippi and Georgia with a determination that GM had not displayed against the union in decades. Initial employee elections went against the UAW in both plants, despite National Labor Relations Board findings that in Mississippi the management violated labor laws.

At the next national contract negotiations UAW officials insisted that GM agree to a "neutrality" clause pledging noninterference with future organizing campaigns. After initial opposition, the company agreed. Shortly afterward the UAW won a close election at a subassembly plant in Louisianna; subsequent victories in Georgia added momentum to the union's effort. But in three elections it failed to win an Alabama steering-gear plant.

The rise of mini-mill, nonunion steel companies, mainly in the south, has forced the Steelworkers union to launch new organizing drives. A sustained campaign was waged against Florida Steel, one of the nation's fastest-growing producers with 17 mills in three southeastern states. Despite some election wins by the union, it has not been able to get a contract at Florida Steel.

The term "relevant work force" means something different in construction situations than it does in manufacturing. Building trades must organize all the workers with certain occupational skills rather than all the workers in a given location. If builders can obtain only union labor, then union standards must be observed. In practice, construction workers in different segments of the industry experience different levels of unionization. While residential building has been largely nonunion, commercial and industrial construction is much more unionized, and engineering projects and road building are also heavily organized, especially where federal funding is involved.

An historical example of power based on unionization of the relevant work force is the San Francisco Building Trades Council during the years before World War I. Craft unions in the Bay Area had organized to the extent that a tradesman found working at a job site without a union card from the council was immediately taken off the job. Union members were fined a day's wages if they consented to work alongside nonunion labor. Council officers could enforce union standards because they had the power to discipline recalcitrant individuals and affiliated locals. It is astonishing, however, that they never engaged in collective bargaining with the employers. Council members instead decided on changes in economic terms and job conditions based on local union proposals. Contractors were then informed of the new standards and union labor was withheld from those which failed to cooperate. The result, concluded an historian of San Francisco labor relations, was that the council enjoyed "unquestioned success in securing higher wages, shorter hours, and better conditions of employment for its members than otherwise might exist."[8] Complete organization of the relevant work force thus gave Bay Area trades the kind of unilateral power normally enjoyed by nonunion employers that offer workers jobs on take-it-or-leave-it terms.

By contrast, at about the same time a carpenter's business agent in Georgia described the effect of not having the relevant work force organized. Here it was because of union refusal to take in black carpenters. "We are always in competition with them," he complained. "The contractors prefer them because they can get them cheap . . . The reason is that they are not well organized and can be hired for less wages . . . The mere fact that all of the boss builders in the south are advocating leaving the negroes out of the unions is a good reason why we should organize them."[9]

Union failure to follow production to new geographic locations invariably weakens its bargaining power because nonunion products eventually replace union ones. Skilled workers in New Jersey

[8]Ira Cross, "The San Francisco Building Trades," in John R. Commons, editor, *Trade Unionism and Labor Problems* (Second Series) (Boston: Ginn and Company, 1921), p. 487.
[9]Herbert Gutman, *Work, Culture and Society: Essays in American Working-Class and Social History* (New York: Knopf, 1976), p. 198.

silk mills struck spontaneously in 1911 over deterioration of wages, benefits, and working conditions resulting from the opening of non-union shops in Pennsylvania. The Pennsylvania mills were built purposely by the owners around the turn of the century to employ low-wage, unskilled labor using the new labor-saving multiple-loom machinery. Employers would not have been able to introduce the skill-destroying machines in New Jersey without a fight from the union.

Initially the mills did not compete. But when the Pennsylvania region showed larger profits and higher productivity than New Jersey, the employers introduced multiple looms into the Jersey mills. The resulting job losses, lower wages, and work-related grievances prompted a New Jersey strike. It lasted six months, ending with some temporary wage improvements but no resolution of the job-displacement issue. Six months later the workers, now only partially unionized, were out again. This time their strike ended in violence and the total defeat and destruction of the union.[10]

Absence of Competitive Unionism. The second organizational condition that enables the union to make the employer pay is the absence of competitive unionism involving the relevant work force. When two or more unions negotiate competitively the power of each is diminished. They are vulnerable to whipsaw tactics in which one is played off against the others. When this happens unions often try to reconcile their differences in order to coordinate activities and present a united front against industry.[11]

Perhaps the most dramatic example of this involves unions representing General Electric plants after World War II. In 1946 the major GE union at that time, the United Electrical Workers (UE), inflicted a two-month, costly strike upon the major electrical products firms in its successful effort to make GE match the auto and steel pattern being negotiated by CIO unions. Out of that experience GE executives, who referred to the strike as being "little short of a debacle," determined to isolate future economic bargaining from the dominant industrial settlement trends.

The remedy they devised came to be known as "Boulwarism,"

---

[10]Graham Adams, Jr., *Age of Industrial Violence, 1910–1915: The Activities and Findings of the United States Commission on Industrial Relations* (New York: Columbia University Press, 1966), pp. 75–100.

[11]Competitive is distinguished from rival unionism. The former pits two or more unions against one another in economic bargaining because they represent parts of the same relevant work force; the latter refers to unions representing different groups of workers within the same firm or industry and the resultant rivalry among them to improve on one another's separately negotiated contracts, a practice known as "leap-frogging."

named after GE's then-director of marketing Lemuel Boulware. After he was put in charge of industrial relations, Boulware substituted "take-it-or-leave-it" company proposals for "give-and-take" collective bargaining. He also initiated corporate marketing of its "fair, firm" contract offer directly to union members instead of through their unions.

Boulwarism was successful during the postwar period chiefly because union representation in GE plants became fragmented. In 1949 UE stopped paying dues to the CIO because of allegations that it was Communist-dominated and because of raids upon its bargaining units by other CIO unions; it was later expelled from the CIO. A rival organization, the International Union of Electrical Workers (IUE), was chartered by the CIO to replace it, with ensuing splits at GE plants and elsewhere. Some AFL affiliates, notably the electricians' union (IBEW), also took away UE bargaining units. Soon there were 13 separate international unions representing more than 150,000 GE workers and negotiating about 60 different contracts. IUE now dominated union represention at GE, but no union could claim independent bargaining power against the company. Their segmented negotiating structure and GE's nonintegrated production process kept them weak. Individual GE plants operated independently of others and several of them manufactured the same electrical products.

Boulwarism undermined union bargaining initiative and enabled GE to substitute its own agenda and terms. The unions were played off against one another by selecting that union whose leaders were most in need of a contract settlement, offering them one slightly superior to the "fair, firm" offer made to everyone else, reminding them that they alone could not win a strike against GE, negotiating the company's desired settlement, and then presenting that to the other unions as the best they could get. GE thus initiated and formulated the ultimate settlement pattern.

The eventual result of this new approach by GE management was to create wide wage differentials both within the company and, because it is the industry's lead firm, between the industry and other manufacturing sectors that were organized by CIO unions. From near parity at the end of the war, the wages and benefits of electrical workers fell behind those of auto workers by $2–$3. Wages in electrical products were 98 percent of those in all durable goods manufacturing industries in 1947, but only 91 percent in 1966. Fringe benefit standards also lagged in electrical products but the differences are not easily measured. Finally, GE's unions had not negotiated union security clauses in 1966, although unions in other basic goods industries had long enjoyed such provisions in their master agreements. In 1969 UE reported wide differences in average hourly earnings among its unionized GE plants.

Differentials of this magnitude and persistence are intolerable for unions representing workers in large profitable corporations. They therefore resolved to plan and undertake coordinated actions against GE. In the 1966 round of bargaining a committee of international union representatives met to formulate common contract demands. Each union subsequently tried to hold out until all of them were prepared to settle for something better than GE's "fair, firm" offer. They were moderately successful.

The momentum carried into the 1969 round, however, when the coordinating unions conducted an effective strike and forced even greater contract improvements. In addition, a federal appeals court decision, handed down two days after the strike started, sustained an NLRB finding that Boulwarism constituted illegal employer refusal to bargain in good faith. Further erosion of the GE strategy occurred in 1970 and 1973 negotiations. Since then, GE has come to the bargaining table just like other major industrial employers. Yet its success demonstrates the damage to union bargaining power of competitive unionism.[12]

Another labor response to competitive unionism is to organizationally consolidate separate bargaining units. An example is the formation in 1969 of the United Transportation Union (UTU) from four large, separate operating railway brotherhoods. In announcing the decision to amalgamate, presidents of the four unions said the action "brings to fruition" the dream of Eugene Debs, a turn of the century labor leader who organized an unsuccessful industrial or multi-craft railway workers' union. They might have added that Debs' failure occurred in part because of the opposition he got from their unions. In any event, given the economic state of the industry, the consolidation was essential, they said, because:

> This shrinking industry no longer makes it possible for the traditional unions to meet the demands of the times. We have united to save our energy for constructive purposes.
> . . . We invite cooperation, a joint effort and consolidation with other railroad unions and other transportation unions.

---

[12]Despite the gains made by the coordinating unions after 1966, wage differentials between electrical products and all durable goods continued to widen, at about the same annual rate of 3 percent, between 1967 and 1979; this was probably due to substandard cost-of-living formulas in GE contracts during these years of rapid inflation.

. . . We will now be able to apply our united strength to the problems of our members and our industry, and end the battle of craft versus craft, and workingman versus workingman.[13]

Union mergers in the metal mining industry, where the Steelworkers absorbed the Mine, Mill and Smelter Workers, and in the brewing industry, where the Teamsters acquired most Brewery Workers local unions, further illustrate the consolidation response. In each instance a larger organization had enfeebled the bargaining effectiveness and drained the resources of the smaller one. Net union strength presumably was increased by the merger.

Appropriate Bargaining Structure. The third organizational requirement for unions shown in Table 4 is to establish an appropriate structure. Unions must negotiate contracts which cover the relevant work force either directly, as in industrywide agreements, or indirectly through strong settlement pattens among companies. Because the relevant work force includes workers producing goods or services that sell in competition, a union aim is to expand the bargaining structure or pattern to include them all. To obtain the greatest union impact during strikes, bargaining structures should be sufficiently centralized to ensure that economic terms and conditions affecting the relevant work force are negotiated at the same time. This structure removes the relevant work force from economic competition.

Because unions want to stabilize labor costs at the level of employer competition, the appropriate level of centralization differs from one industry to another, depending on market organizations and production processes. In construction, a contract covering all the skilled tradesmen employed in a given labor market is sufficient; in longshoring an agreement is needed that includes all coastal ports.

In manufacturing, the contract should cover all plants making the same products. Six contracts in six separate locations with staggered expiration dates undermine union bargaining power. A strike at one plant has minimal impact because inventory reductions, additional shifts, or overtime production at other plants can allow the employer to recover production being lost at the struck location.

Events in the glass industry demonstrate the importance to unions of consolidated multiplant bargaining structures. In the late 1960s Libbey-Owens-Ford Company (L-O-F) operated 10 flat glass plants in different geographic locations. The Glass and Ceramic

---

[13]*Labor*, December 14, 1968, pp. 1, 4.

Workers Union (GCW) held a multiplant contract that covered eight of them and single agreements covering two others which had been constructed after the original multiplant unit was established. L-O-F refused to combine the three separate bargaining units into a single unit for all 10 plants. GCW successfully petitioned the NLRB for the rights of workers at two separate plants to determine in elections if they wished to be included in the multiplant contract. They voted for a single unit.

Hoping to extend the consolidation principle to PPG Industries, another multiplant glass producer, GCW then asked the Board to allow self-determination elections there. Of PPG's 16 plate glass plants, GCW had a multiplant contract covering nine of them and separate agreements in three others. Workers at the remaining four were represented by other unions. This time, however, the Board refused to order consolidation elections at the three plants in which GCW held separate contracts.

These examples of union attempts to consolidate bargaining structures in order to bring relevant workers under single contracts explain why unions try to develop industrywide and companywide structures in concentrated manufacturing industries.

Sometimes the union prefers to negotiate contracts on a companywide rather than a industrywide basis because the former is more appropriate to the structural environment.

Perhaps the union believes it can play off one company against another in order to get a better pattern of settlements. By striking or threatening to strike one of several competing companies—as in the auto or tire industries—the union forces the target company to take into account the fact that in a strike it will lose sales to competitors.

Where the industry contains a large number of competitive firms, the union normally prefers to bargain with an association of employers on either a nationwide or a geographic areawide basis. The choice of which structure the union prefers depends on the scope of the product market, which in turn defines the relevant work force to be brought under standard contract terms.

Labor relations in bituminous coal were dominated historically by fluid national product markets and changes in the relevant work force. No individual or group successfully monopolized, cartelized, or otherwise controlled the production and marketing of soft coal, which was abundant and deposited in many locations. Even large mining companies did not control supplies the way big companies often did in basic manufacturing.

Coal mining was divided into three distinct segments. First, large northern operators, led by Consolidated Coal Company, sold to power utilities and other volume buyers in addition to smaller wholesale coal suppliers; second, most integrated steel companies owned and operated so-called "captive mines" as internal sources of raw material for their coke ovens; third, independent coal producers, mainly southern operators, supplied the remainder of the market under short-term contracts and usually at prices below those charged by northern producers.

Industry fluctuations were inevitable. Rising prices encouraged new mines and expansion of existing operations, which increased supply, brought prices down again, and bankrupted marginal operators. Eventually, bad times gave way to good, and the cycle was repeated. To counter this process, the United Mine Workers (UMW), an industrial union founded in 1890, negotiated the Central Field contract to include operators in several Midwest states and western Pennsylvania.

Coal was both the most frequently shipped commodity and an important cost of production for coal-fired steam locomotives. It was thus in the financial interests of the carriers to ship great quantities of coal from southern nonunion mines to the northern industrial users. This practice increased rail shipping revenues and also brought down the prices of coal and reduced the local railroad operating costs. Rail owners imposed freight rates favoring southern coal shipments and encouraged shipments from mines selling coal at the lowest prices. The effect was to bring downward price pressure on union operators and prompt them to resist UMW contract demands.

New coal fields were later opened in West Virginia by banking, steel, and railroad interests. UMW efforts to organize them failed, encouraging the largest unionized employers to repudiate the Central Field contract. Consolidated Coal and Pittsburgh Coal inspired other coal operators to revoke their union agreements and install the open shop. John L. Lewis, UMW president from 1920 to 1960, then imposed autocratic rule inside the union on the grounds that an organization that spoke with one voice could hasten the adoption of industrywide bargaining in order to stabilize markets to the mutual benefit of both capital and labor. This did not happen until 1950 when the Bituminous Coal Operators Association was organized and negotiated an industrywide contract with the UMW.

Commercial printing is an historical example of employer association bargaining in a nonconcentrated industry. The international union became involved in local bargaining because labor relations had become more formalized and the international was thus more responsible for the actions of its locals. The employers then responded with their own association to counter union consolidation.

Shortly before the turn of the century the International Typographical Union (ITU) established a national defense fund to assist striking locals. It soon became apparent that individual locals got into stoppages without first informing the international union, but then requested strike benefits. Union headquarters was responsible for maintaining the strike fund but had little control over expenditures. So the union's constitution was changed to give the international union the power to decide which strikes qualified for funds. By 1904 headquarters authority was complete, due largely to the unsuccessful outcomes of expensive local strikes. After that the international threatened to withhold funds from striking members unless certain provisions were included in all locally negotiated contracts. International approval thus became a means of standardizing negotiated terms and conditions throughout the industry.

At the same time, local printing firms were strengthening their national trade association, the United Typothetæ of America (UTA). The UTA had earlier rejected ITU offers to negotiate with the union as the representative of the entire industry, but in 1904, the year ITU headquarters consolidated its control over strike funds, it began to establish labor policy for member shops in all union labor matters except wages, which remained subject to local conditions.

In the nonconcentrated service industries that market nationwide, unions prefer to negotiate industry contracts with employer associations. Industrywide master agreements in long-distance trucking are a good example of union success in this regard.

Teamster policy has been to consolidate the economic provisions of regional and metropolitan contracts into a national master freight agreement. This began in earnest with the 1957 election of James Hoffa to the union's presidency. Over the next decade Teamster conventions gave Hoffa control over internal union policymaking bodies and national contract negotiations. By 1967 all major economic issues in interstate trucking were being resolved at the national level. The union also established industry contracts for auto haulers, oil tankers, and other special freights, and companywide pacts for moving vans and at United Parcel Service, all of which were patterned after its trucking settlements.

In regional nonmanufacturing industries, unions want areawide contracts which cover all firms. The old retail clerks and meatcutters unions, now combined as the United Food and Commercial Workers (UFCW), negotiated such contracts with associations of retail grocery chains. The Hotel Employees and Restaurant Employees try to do the same with area hospitality establishments, but they are generally less successful than UFCW because of various disadvantages for unions in the hospitality industry.

Areawide association bargaining dominates the building and construction industry. Typical of construction labor relations in large cities is the multilayered bargaining structure in Washington, D.C. As of 1980, the Washington building trades council, representing 26 separate locals of 14 international unions, negotiated contracts with the Washington Construction Employers Association (WCEA). The WCEA represented 16 different groups of contractors with which hundreds of area firms were affiliated. The Construction Contractors Council with 40 affiliated contractors, for example, was a WCEA member.

In addition to negotiations between union and employer associations, bargaining occurs within the specialized trades over matters uniquely relevant to them. For example, the Carpenters' District Council, which consists of several locals having jurisdiction in the Washington vicinity, has a separate agreement with the same Construction Contractors Council that is affiliated with the WCEA. Since the geographic area covered by their contract is wider than in the WCEA agreement, several dozen contractors are listed, half of them also being included in the WCEA agreement.

For effective bargaining power the unions must keep the Washington-area contractors under the terms of these contracts. A contractor who drops out of the employers' bargaining unit could operate below union scale and pose a competitive threat to both union contractors and workers. Another potential problem for the parties is the threat of outside contractors obtaining work inside the geographic coverage of the contracts and then operating under nonunion conditions.

Heavy construction often entails another kind of bargaining structure appropriate for large national contractors. These firms work on major projects in various labor market areas almost at random. An appropriate bargaining structure for the union in this setting is a companywide national contract negotiated by the international union. Pierson describes these as agreements in which "the national contractors agree to use union help wherever their projects might be located througout the country and to abide by the locally bargained rates and work rules." In exchange for this commitment to work as a union shop, the national contractor wants assurance from the international union that its operations will not be hampered by area work stoppages. Therefore, Pierson notes, "[t]hough it is not written in the agreement, the international unions also accept the responsibility of protecting the national contractors from overzealous locals and from possible discrimination by local unions in favor of local contractors."[14]

In recent years unions have had to respond to conglomerate and multinational corporate structures. Because unions relate to specific industry structures, a multi-industry conglomerate structure puts them at a bargaining disadvantage. To some extent, all the production workers of a conglomerate employer are part of the relevant work force, even though they are in separate unrelated manufacturing and service divisions. A single union cannot hope to organize workers in so many industries, therefore it must cooperate and coordinate its activities with unions which represent workers employed by the same conglomerate.

The multinational dimension compounds the problem for unions. Overseas production removes the relevant work force beyond the grasp of U.S. unions and requires them to build alliances and operating relationships with foreign labor movements if they are to offset the resulting structural disadvantage. Chapter 8 describes union experiences with these new corporate structures.

Union Bargaining Power and Union Democracy

A final issue remains regarding the relationship between union bargaining power and the structural and institutional environments within which bargaining occurs—the impact of centralized bargaining on internal union government. Union bargaining strength often rests on centralized authority and decision-making processes. The internal issue is whether union bargaining power and union democracy are compatible. Specifically, does the union's bargaining power in centralized markets preclude rank-and-file political participation? Can unions be both strong and democratic?

Some observers and practitioners of bargaining believe that centralized bargaining institutions do in fact erode democracy, not because union leaders become political tyrants, but because responsibility and power inside unions travel upward when bargaining be-

---

[14]Frank Pierson, *Unions in Postwar America: An Economic Assessment* (New York: Random House, 1967), p. 102.

comes formal, technical, legalistic, and concentrated. With fewer areas of discretion in the negotiation process, it is argued, local leaders and members are less inclined to be activists. The union loses its enthusiasm and energy at the grass roots level.

Richard Lester, an early proponent of this view, described the loss of internal union political activity and traced it mainly to the evolution of economic bargaining. Managerial centralization imposes centralization inside unions; concentrated structures and complicated issues require the emergence of "professional" union officers and staff negotiators; unity and support for national negotiating policies become internal union imperatives. Forceful presentation and defense of opposing views on bargaining matters are decried as being divisive and disruptive. Dissent is stifled because the union is in battle; like an army in the field, it does not tolerate debate.

Professional union and management representatives meanwhile try to avoid unrelenting conflict because it is mutually destructive. They establish new and often informal avenues of communication and cooperation. As a result, writes Lester, "collective bargaining institutionalizes conflict by gradually building up orderly processes, joint machinery, and other administrative restraints against unruly or precipitate action." Smoother, more stable labor relations are realized but, he fears, these mature bargaining relationships discourage organizational vitality.

George Brooks, a former international union staff member who shares this view, attributes the corrosive effect to differences of interest and outlook between union members and officers. Unions are vehicles to obtain immediate job improvments but also have their nonorganizational purposes and priorities. To Brooks, the members mainly are interested in the *content* of the negotiated settlement and are "notoriously indifferent to the means by which the settlement is achieved, although they have a profound reluctance to put their jobs on the block . . ." By contrast, union staff and officers may be interested in contract content "in a subsidiary sense," but they are more concerned "in the fact of settlement itself." Their stake is in the union as an organization. Therefore, "the organizational objectives of the union" in an ongoing bargaining relationship receive the union negotiators' greatest attention "whether the settlement is in one amount or another."

Other writers argue forcefully that any sacrifice of union democracy and vitality due to centralized bargaining is exaggerated and must be weighed against bargaining gains. Clark Kerr acknowledges internal centralization but reminds us that "unions do make a major over-all contribution to a democratic society" because they "create a two-party legislative system governing the life of the workplace," without which "the rules would be set exclusively by the employer."

The labor historian Philip Taft dismisses the problem more vigorously. Unions are always in a state of seige, he says, so they cannot indulge the luxury of town-hall democracy. Leaders should be free of time-consuming restraints while making crucial bargaining choices. "If the labor or product market in which a union operates undergoes a change," he explains, "the leaders may try to adapt the union's structure and operations to the new needs." Accommodation is essential to the well-being of the members. Therefore, Taft argues, it "may require less localism and more centralized control, and changes may be resisted by powerful individual and local groups."[15]

This is not an idle academic debate. It reflects the strife inside unions undergoing change. Taft could have been anticipating the case of interstate truckers, for instance. In the process of consolidating contracts, Hoffa strengthened his governing power and curbed the area councils and big-city locals. When he came under attack for this at the union's 1966 convention, Hoffa defended union centralization as a response to growing integration by the industry:

> Yes, there are those who continually harass this international union and attempt to divide us by stating that the General Executive Board is taking away the autonomy of the local unions and their ability to negotiate their own agreements. Yet I defy a single member . . . to point out a single instance where master agreements, contract agreements with companies across the United States, have taken away a single power of autonomy of a local union in this international union. We recognize we can no longer go it alone. We recognize we must have coordinated activity and must deal with corporate structures as we find them in industries. We can no longer just travel down the road blindly and wonder where we are going and hope we do not stumble.

---

[15]Richard A. Lester, *As Unions Mature: An Analysis of the Evolution of American Unionism* (Princeton, N.J.: Princeton University Press, 1958), p. 32.; George Brooks, *The Sources of Vitality in the American Labor Movement*, Bulletin No. 41 (New York State School of Industrial and Labor Relations, Cornell University, July 1964), p. 9.; Clark Kerr, *Unions and Union Leaders of Their Own Choosing* (Santa Barbara, Calif.: The Fund for the Republic, 1957), p. 7; Philip Taft, *The Structure and Government of Labor Unions* (Cambridge, Mass.: Harvard University Press, 1962), p. 244.

Later in the proceedings a local officer rose to address the delegates in support of Hoffa and the international union. His statement echoes Taft:

> [Local autonomy] is a beautiful thing, but we cannot afford it if in fact we are giving it up. We cannot protect the big city local . . . if Sealtest or Borden's or Beatrice [Foods] or anyone else can come within 150 miles of Louisville . . . and build a brand-new automated plant out in the country area that is not organized or is poorly organized and back ship [dairy products] to my town, it doesn't matter what my contract says. It doesn't matter if everybody has autonomy . . . we've got voting machines all over the damned hall [but] if nobody is working, then we are dead.[16]

Centralization of bargaining power did produce economic gains for truckers. "Aside from the construction trades," concludes Levinson, "the Teamsters have done at least as well or better than other strongly unionized sectors of the economy, including the trucking industry's major competitor, the railroads." Teamster wages rose 40 percent between 1958 and 1967, while unionized railroad workers received an average 33 percent increase, steel workers obtained 24 percent, and auto workers got 39 percent.[17]

Elsewhere, union centralization probably resulted in inferior bargaining settlements. In the West Coast paper industry two unions, the Pulp, Sulphite, and Paper Mill Workers and the Paper Makers (which have since merged), jointly negotiated a multiplant agreement covering all the West Coast mills of national and regional paper companies. For 30 years they conducted strike-free labor relations. The unions never had to strike over economic demands. They simply adopted the pattern established on the coast by a militant union which represented lumber and sawmill workers employed by the same companies.

But then changing technology suddenly destroyed the sawmill workers' bargaining power and a power vacuum was created in the bargaining relationship. Either the paper mill unions or the employers had to fill the void. The latter took the initiative and substituted lower southern wage rates in paper for the West Coast patterns that had paid the highest salaries in the industry.

---

[16]International Brotherhood of Teamsters, *Nineteenth International Union Convention*, 1966, pp. 130, 569.

[17]Harold Levinson, "The Trucking Industry," in *Collective Bargaining and Technological Change in American Transportation*, Harold Levinson, Charles Rehmus, Joseph Goldberg, and Mark Kahn, eds. (Evanston, Ill.: Transportation Center at Northwestern University, 1971), p. 31.

Dissatisfied with the performance of the international union officers who controlled West Coast contract negotiations, dissident locals in the two organizations began to challenge the centralized structures. In the Pulp, Sulphite, and Paper Mill Workers, locals found they could not elect an international vice president for their region who was sympathetic to local bargaining objectives. Vice presidential officers were elected at national conventions, where delegates from every region voted for the candidates in each region. Most delegates were neither knowledgeable nor concerned about West Coast issues and would not vote for candidates running in opposition to the international union slate. The dissidents shifted their tactics by advising the rank and file to reject inferior settlements, but the companies and the unions agreed that in the next round of negotiations the internationals would assume direct control over the proceedings.

West Coast local leaders then resorted to the unpleasant, infrequent and difficult task of replacing both international unions with an independent regional union. After a bitter election campaign, in which the dissidents emphasized the erosion of economic standards in their region, the rank and file voted out the two unions by a 57 percent majority and endorsed the Association of Western Pulp and Paper Workers.

Centralization of bargaining authority had been consistent with satisfactory economic performance just in the short run. When environmental change required timely union responses, the internationals chose to preserve existing practices at the expense of bargaining effectiveness. In the long run the strategy failed.[18]

---

[18]Years after the breakaway it was uncertain whether the Western Association had successfully re-established union wage leadership on the West Coast. Initially the union asked the employers to negotiate industrywide contracts on economic issues, as in the past, and local supplemental agreements covering working conditions. Instead the 16 companies insisted on negotiating economic issues on a mill-by-mill basis at their 44 locations in three states. *Monthly Labor Review* (April 1969), p. 81. The union proceeded to whipsaw the mills, settling with those most vulnerable to strikes and then extending the pattern to the others. In this way it was able to re-establish industry wage differentials in favor of the West Coast. The employers responded with a strike insurance system; changing technology also added to their bargaining power. In the 1978 bargaining round, Crown Zellerbach, for example, settled early for a contract at its most productive mill but held out for better terms at seven older mills. High-level mechanization enabled other companies to continue production despite the strikes. Sporadic and overlapping stoppages occurred from July 1978 through May 1979. *Business Week*, October 2, 1978, p. 29; *Wall Street Journal*, May 10, 1979, p. 32. Unsuccessful in its whipsaw tactics, in 1981 the union accepted joint bargaining with the six major producers for a contract affecting 38 percent of the industry. The parties settled without a strike. Union negotiators recommended rejection of the industry's final offer on grounds it failed to offset inflation but the members voted acceptance. *Monthly Labor Review* (June 1981), p. 56.

In neither interstate trucking nor West Coast paper did the dissidents wish to dismantle centralized bargaining structures. Presumably they recognized the strategic significance of centralization, and instead wanted to establish leadership accountability and responsibility and member involvement and ultimate decision-making authority in contract bargaining. In this view there is not a contradiction between consolidated bargaining and union democracy.

Summary

Union success in negotiating economic standards generally depends on employers' ability to pay higher labor costs and unions' ability to make employers pay. Employer ability to pay depends on the ability to raise prices in product markets and the extent to which labor cost increases are offset by increased productivity. Union ability to make employers pay depends on the ability to establish advantageous bargaining structures and institutions. Unions have to organize completely the relevant labor force, eliminate competitive unionism, and establish appropriate bargaining structures.

Elimination of competitive unionism and the existence of favorable bargaining structures enhance union power. But they can also create conditions that eventually undermine union power—institutionalized and excessive labor-management cooperation and the deterioration of internal union democracy and vitality.

Key Words and Phrases

product market	spatial limitation
labor market	relevant labor force
concentration ratio	Boulwarism
administered pricing	appropriate bargaining structure
"non-price" competition	conglomerate firm
barriers to entry	

Review and Discussion Questions

1. Why do unions have a stake in promoting a strong market for the products or services of their employers?

2. Does the union have the same stake in productivity? Why or why not?

3. Give some examples of "nonprice competition."

4. Give examples of "concentrated" and "nonconcentrated" industries.

5. What fact causes the concentration ratio in the automobile industry to be overstated? In the rubber industry?

6. Generally speaking, what effect has deregulation had on union bargaining power?

7. Why is it necessary to enhance union bargaining power, both to organize the relevant labor force *and* to attain the "appropriate" bargaining structure?

8. What effect does the multinational corporation have on a union's "relevant labor force" and "appropriate bargaining unit?"

9. From what you know of union members' attitudes, are they more interested in contract settlements or union democracy?

Chapter Resources and Suggested Further Reading

The development of industrial concentration and administered pricing concepts can be traced in the following works: Gardiner Means, "Notes on Inflexible Prices," *The American Economic Review* (March 1936); Joe S. Bain, *Industrial Organization* (1959); J. Kenneth Galbraith, *The New Industrial State* (1967); A. D. H. Kaplan, Joel B. Dirlam, Robert F. Lanzillotti, *Pricing in Big Business* (1955); John M. Blair, *Economic Concentration* (1972).

For a summary of the data on the relationship between high concentration ratios and product market power, see William Shepherd, *The Economics of Industrial Organization* (1979). An analysis of market power in oil is John Blair, *The Control of Oil* (1976). The relationship between wage levels and rates of wage increases and industry concentration is discussed in Arthur Ross and William Goldner, "Forces Affecting the Interindustry Wage Structure," *Quarterly Journal of Economics* (May 1950); Martin Segal, "Union Wage Impact and Market Structure," *Quarterly Journal of Economics* (February 1964); Leonard Weiss, "Concentration and Labor Earnings," *American Economic Review* (March 1966); Thomas Kochan and Richard Block, "An Interindustry Analysis of Bargaining Outcomes: Preliminary Evidence from Two-Digit Industries," *Quarterly Journal of Economics* (August 1977).

The sources of union bargaining power—which become the determinants of union wage policy—are identified and debated in John Dunlop, *Wage Determination Under Trade Unions*, (1950), Reprint (1966), in which Dunlop argues that pure economic variables explain union bargaining power and policies, and Arther Ross, *Trade Union Wage Policy* (1953), where Ross introduces the internal union political element into the determination of economic bargaining. An attempt to reconcile the economic and political approaches of Dunlop and Ross is Harold Levinson, *Determining Forces in Collective Wage Bargaining* (1966). For a discussion of the "spatial limitation" concept, see Harold Levinson, "Unionism, Concentration and Wage Changes: Toward a Unified Theory," *Industrial and Labor Relations Review* (January 1967). Also see Daniel J. B. Mitchell, "Union Wage Policies: The Ross-Dunlop Debate Reopened," *Industrial Relations* (February 1972).

Information on the UAW's attempts to organize GM plants in the South is from, *Wall Street Journal*, September 7, 1976, p. 2, and *Washington Post*, December 21, 1976, p. C-24, and December 24, 1976, p. A-2. The steering-gear plant finally was unionized on the basis of signed authorization cards in 1982. This left only one GM plant unorganized in the South, a small Delco-Remy facility in Mississippi, *AFL-CIO News*, September 11, 1982, p. 3.

Economic bargaining in the electrical products industry is discussed in Neil Chamberlain, Donald Cullen, David Lewin, *The Labor Sector*, 3rd ed. (1980); James Healy, ed., *Creative Collective Bargaining* (1965); *UE News*, November 17, 1969; David Lasser, "A Victory for Coordinated Bargaining," *American Federationist* (April 1967). Data on earnings differentials at GE during 1947-66 are reported in Michael Newman, "Communism, the UE, and the CIO" (1982).

Bargaining unit determination in the flat glass industry involved these cases: *Libbey-Owens-Ford Glass Co.*, 169 NLRB 126, 67 LRRM 1096 (1968); *Glass & Ceramic Workers v. NLRB*, 463 F.2d 31, 80 LRRM 2882 (3d Cir. 1972); *Libbey-Owens-Ford Glass Co.*, 202 NLRB 29, 82 LRRM 1417 (1973); *PPG Industries, Inc.*, 180 NLRB 477, 73 LRRM 1001 (1969).

Events in the soft coal industry are described in McAlister Coleman, *Men and Coal (1943)* (1969); Hoyt Wheeler, "Mountaineer Mine Wars: An Analysis of West Virginia Mine Wars of 1912-1913 and 1920-1921," *Business History Review* (Spring 1976).

Typesetting is discussed in George Barnett, "Collective Bargaining in the Typographical Union," in Jacob Hollander and George Barnett, eds., *Studies in American Trade Unionism* (1912). The Teamsters union achievement of national bargaining in trucking is explained in Ralph and Estelle James, *Hoffa and the Teamsters: A Study of Union Power* (1965).

In addition, other collective bargaining industry studies are recommended for their readable style and discussion of the institutional variables in collective bargaining: William Serrin, *The Company and the Union: The "Civilized Relationship" of the General Motors Corporation and the United Automobile Workers* (1973); Robert Ozanne, *A Century of Labor-Management Relations at McCormick and International Harvester* (1967); David McCabe, *National Collective Bargaining in the Pottery Industry* (1932); Elizabeth Baker, *Printers and Technology* (1957); Joel Seidman, *The Needle Trades* (1942).

Case studies of the relationship between bargaining structure and internal union democracy include Charles P. Larrowe, *Shape-Up and Hiring Hall: A Comparison of Hiring Methods and Labor Relations on the New York and Seattle Waterfronts* (1955); Robert Christie, *Empire in Wood: A History of the Carpenters' Union* (1956); Garth Mangum, *The Operating Engineers: The Economic History of a Trade Union* (1964).

Collective bargaining developments in the West Coast pulp and paper industry that led to the breakaway movement are traced in Harold Levinson, *Determining Forces in Collective Wage Bargaining* (1966). The story of the Pulp, Sulphite dissidents is told in Harry Graham, *The Paper Rebellion: Development and Upheaval in Pulp and Paper Unionism* (1970). Russell Allen shows the relationship between the collective bargaining developments and the growth of internal opposition in Pulp, Sulphite in his review of Graham's book: *Industrial and Labor Relations Review* (April 1972).

3

Standards in Economic
Bargaining

Economic bargaining involves both economic and political variables. Three generally accepted criteria measure the economic environment: the cost of living, productivity, and profits. Together these standards define the minimum and maximum economic limits within which bargaining settlements can occur over time. Another standard, comparability, implies the political and institutional environments that determine the range of short-term settlements, given the economic boundaries.

Economists differ over the relative significance of the economic and political forces in bargaining. John Dunlop, a former U.S. Secretary of Labor, took the position that the American trade union substitutes collective for individual worker action in order to achieve specified economic goals. "An economic theory of a trade union requires that the organization be assumed to maximize (or minimize) something," he reasoned. "Although not the only possible objective, [union] maximization of the wage bill may be regarded as the standard case."

Dunlop's explanation rests on conventional market theory. Union negotiators make rational economic choices between higher wages and job security because they cannot have both at the same time. The highest possible wage that can be negotiated will result in a loss of jobs; if the union wants maximum employment it must settle for less than the highest wage it could negotiate. If union policy is to obtain the highest total wage bill, as Dunlop says, then the organization will accept the combination of hourly compensation and number of employed members which produces the highest money amount.

This situation is where the economic standards of bargaining become important. In making the wage calculation, the union considers both employer ability to pay and employment needs, each of which is suggested by profit and productivity information. The cost of living, which is external to the economic situation of the employer, is relevant to union wage policy because it determines the actual purchasing power of the negotiated increases.

Arthur Ross has an opposing view to that of Dunlop. To him, union policy is more complicated than wage bills. Union workers want to establish wage parity with comparable work groups more than they seek to maximize anything. Moreover, union negotiators cannot maximize the wage bill if they want to. They cannot predict future employment levels at different wage amounts, nor can they trace current changes in employment to earlier wage changes.

Ross's foundation of union wage policy is comparability, which is not a market concept. It arises instead from the social perspective of the union worker and is expressed in the political life of the organization. Workers in one group compare their wage increases with those in other groups. Political pressures result, and the group's leaders are compelled to negotiate equivalent increases. Ross calls these wage relationships the "orbits of coercive comparison."

Harold Levinson combines Dunlop's economic and Ross's political variables with a third category he calls "pure power." By this he means the extent of union organization and other, less tangible factors such as worker militancy, aggressiveness of union leadership, and management resistance to union demands. Despite being difficult to isolate and quantify, these variables must be considered. They decide union size, financial resources, cohesiveness, and other determinants of union policy.

Levinson studied bargaining outcomes in key West Coast industries after World War II. He found in each case that the process was "extraordinarily complex," but always involved more than either wage maximization or coercive comparisons. More information is needed, he concludes, "before a more complete theory of wage determination under collective bargaining can be developed." Purely quantitative studies are inadequate, however, because they fail to explain satisfactorily the intricate web of economic settlements. There is an "essentially qualitative" aspect to "some of the most important variables," Levinson concluded. He conceives the "pure power" criterion in order to evaluate the significance of nonquantifiable factors such as management resistance, bargaining histories, and leadership qualities.

This chapter examines the four standards of economic bargaining. Each is discussed separately according to its conceptual basis, its historical development and application, and its recent importance as both a negotiating statistic and a bargaining tactic. However, this approach involves something of an artificial separation since, in practice, economic bargaining simultaneously involves the entire range of economic, political, and institutional forces. The importance of a single standard cannot be determined without reference to the others, but to describe and interpret them requires that they be considered individually.

Cost of Living

Unions try to protect members against the effects of inflation by negotiating cost-of-living adjustment clauses (COLAs), or escalator clauses, in their contracts. These provisions contain pay adjustment formulas designed to compensate workers during the life of the contract for any losses in real earnings (purchasing power) due to consumer price increases.

The incidence of negotiated COLA clauses rises and falls with the rate of inflation. Accelerated inflation rates during the Korean War brought the ratio of workers protected by such provisions in 1952 up to nearly one-half of workers covered by major contracts. With a subsequent slowdown of price increases, the coverage fell sharply. Renewed inflation during the Vietnam War escalation of the late 1960s boosted the ratio to 41 percent. With continued inflation, the trend remained upward. The ratio rose to more than one-half in 1979. As the severe recession which followed drove down prices, union interest in cost-of-living clauses waned. COLAs were modified and in some instances eliminated altogether in exchange for other benefits.

More important than falling inflation rates or shifting union priorities was a move in the early 1980s towards union concession bargaining under the threat of worker layoffs and plant shutdowns. This trend resulted in frequent elimination or reduction of cost-of-living clauses. A 1983 survey by The Bureau of National Affairs, Inc., showed that 48 percent of the contracts analyzed contained escalator clauses.

The Distribution of COLA Clauses. The ratio of workers covered by COLAs varies among industries and unions. It is highly concentrated in primary metals and transportation equipment manufacturing, where union policy is to negotiate escalator clauses, and in the trucking and communications industries. Nearly half of the workers covered by escalator clauses in 1978 worked under contracts negotiated by four unions—Auto Workers, Communications Workers, Teamsters, and Steelworkers.

COLAs are less important in construction than in manufacturing. The inflation of the 1970s did prompt some building trades to incorporate escalator clauses into their agreements, but by 1978 only 9 percent of major construction industry contracts still had them. Railroad brotherhoods have vacillated on the matter, letting COLAs expire when inflation recedes and renegotiating them when it resumes.

The Development of COLA Clauses. Unions anticipate inflation in their economic bargaining in either of two ways. One approach is to negotiate short-term agreements, each of which tries to compensate for previous inflation. An infrequent variation of this response involves negotiating a long-term contract with no scheduled deferred wage increases but with provisions allowing the union to reopen the contract and renegotiate wage levels. A more popular strategy is negotiation of long-term contracts with automatic adjustments for future price increases, either as deferred wage increases or as COLA provisions that periodically adjust wages to compensate for inflation. In periods of rapid inflation, unions commonly combine deferred wage increases and COLA adjustments.

Escalator clauses originated with the emergence of multiyear contracts in the 1950s. The integration of COLA provisions and long-term contracts represented a shift in union bargaining tactics. Negotiating objectives of the unions after World War II consisted initially of annual wage increases and fringe benefit improvements, but this approach became unpopular with the rank and file members in 1947, when a sharp rise in inflation wiped out most of the previous year's wage gains. A long-term contract negotiated by Sinclair Oil and the Oil Workers Union seemed to be a better approach in that it contained both a scheduled wage increase and regular cost-of-living adjustments.

In addition, it became apparent that if unions accepted multiyear contracts, large employers would negotiate comprehensive economic "packages" to offset inflation and compensate for productivity increases. Long-term contracts thus assured industry of uninterrupted production over lengthy time periods, making it easier for management to decide product price and output levels and reducing the amount of time and anxiety involved in contract renegotiations. As a result, the three-year agreement, which was nearly nonexistent in 1948, by 1957 accounted for roughly one-third of all contracts. Within a decade, it had become the standard.

Negotiating Escalator Clauses. Escalator clause language specifies how the wage adjustments are to be made. Whether a particular COLA compensates workers fully for cost-of-living increases is determined by three provisions: the adjustment formula, the frequency of adjustments, and possible limitations on the amount of the adjustment.

All escalator clauses are based on the Consumer Price Index (CPI), which is the standard measure of price inflation. There is more than one index from which to choose, however. Since 1978 the U.S. Department of Labor has published the Urban Wage Earner and Clerical Worker Index, which applies specifically to workers covered by COLA clauses. It measures changes in the prices of goods and services typically purchased by workers and weights them according to their relative importance in family buying patterns. Most labor contracts use this figure, although contracts covering workers in certain metropolitan areas can choose to use the CPI published for that city.

The COLA formula determines the size of the wage adjustment. It specifies the amount of increase in the CPI that results typically in a one-cent-per-hour compensation in wage payment. Unions naturally try to negotiate adjustment formulas that pay more money for given CPI increases; how successful they are varies among industries and organizations. A General Electric-International Union of Electrical Workers (IUE) escalator clause negotiated in the mid-1970s called for an additional cent-per-hour for each three-tenths of one *percent* increase in the CPI. By contrast, basic steel and auto contracts effective at the same time provided for an additional penny for every three-tenths of a *point* increase in the CPI. The distinction here is between percentage and point changes in the CPI. A given increase in prices results in a greater point increase than percentage rise in the CPI. Auto and steel workers therefore were compensated more under their contracts than electrical products workers were under the GE agreement for the same increases in the CPI. (Appendix A of this chapter explains the calculations behind these adjustments.)

Another contract negotiated during the 1970s combined percentage and absolute wage adjustments. Under the AT&T Long Lines Department-Communications Workers of America (CWA), agreement, every 1.0 percent increase in the CPI raised workers' pay rates by 0.6 percent of their weekly base earnings rounded to the nearest 50 cents, plus an additional 50 cents per week. Only a small proportion of escalator clauses differentiate adjustments according to individual earnings. Some employers prefer to negotiate percentage rather than across-the-board, cents-per-hour payments in escalator clauses. Over time, across-the-board increases narrow earnings differentials, which forces employers to pay more for new hires and unskilled workers than they otherwise might.

To reverse this leveling effect, Boeing Company negotiated a two-tiered wage structure in 1983 with the Machinists union in Seattle. The change was initiated by Boeing in response to years of across-the-board COLA payments. Pay differentials between skilled and less-skilled hourly Boeing workers had declined from 50 percent to 25 percent. The 1983 agreement dropped the old escalator formula and quarterly adjustment schedule and substituted fixed percentage increases annually. It also discontinued across-the-board wage increases based on productivity improvements and permitted substantially lower hourly rates for newly hired employees. Machinists leaders recommended against these terms, but the Boeing members approved them by a three-to-one margin.[1]

COLA Adjustment Formulas. Unions that have negotiated high hourly wages must negotiate equally high COLA adjustment formulas in order to keep workers abreast of inflation. A 5 percent rise in the CPI erodes the real value of a $10 hourly wage by 50 cents, and that of a $5 wage by 25 cents. Assuming a CPI figure of 200, the bargaining unit with a $10 average hourly wage therefore would need an adjustment formula of one cent per hour for each 0.2 point increase in the CPI for its members to be fully compensated. By contrast, a bargaining unit with a $5 hourly rate would need an adjustment formula of one cent for each 0.4 point increase in order for workers to be fully compensated.

Escalator clauses were uncommon in the 1950s, but they did protect effectively against inflation. The GM-UAW 1948 COLA increased hourly earnings one cent for each 1.14 point increase in the CPI, a formula that yielded wage adjustments proportionate to average hourly wages in the auto industry at that time. A 1959 study showed that negotiated COLA clauses generally resulted in full compensation. During 1968–74 however, the CPI rose at an annual

---

[1] Roy J. Harris, "Boeing Accord Attacks Narrowing Pay Gap Between Skilled and Less Skilled Workers," *The Wall Street Journal*, October 19, 1983, p. 33. The concessions made Boeing a more profitable company. During 1984, the company posted higher profits on lower sales revenues, which it attributed to increased interest earnings, cost cuts, and greater productivity. "Boeing's Net Rose 11% in 2nd Period as Sales Fell 13%," *The Wall Street Journal*, July 31, 1984, p. 41.

average rate of 6.3 percent, while annual COLA payments in major contracts averaged 3.1 percent. By 1977 COLA increases averaged little more than half the rate of inflation.

The frequency of cost-of-living adjustments determines how often covered workers are compensated for rising prices. In the mid-1970s, most COLA adjustments occurred either every three months (46 percent of those effective in 1975) or once a year (38 percent), but more workers were covered by annual rather than quarterly clauses.

Another reason many escalator clauses do not fully compensate workers for inflation is that they limit adjustments. These restrictions are mainly in two forms: exclusion of the first contract year from cost-of-living adjustment, and ceilings or "caps" on the total compensation amount. Of several hundred major contracts with COLAs surveyed in 1975, one-fourth provided for no adjustment in the first year, and another quarter limited first-year compensation to a fixed amount. Based on the average amount, a production worker would have lost 41 cents per hour to inflation that year.

Ceilings or "caps" on escalator clauses often occur during periods of rapid inflation. Unions may agree to such restrictions in order to negotiate a first COLA clause into the contract or to relieve employers of the financial burden of established clauses. Basic steel and auto contracts in the mid-1970s did not contain such ceilings; electrical products and men's clothing did.

Union strategy in negotiating COLAs is to seek the strongest adjustment formula and most frequent adjustments and to bargain for minimal restrictions on payments. Unions also want the adjustment money considered as a part of hourly base wages for purposes of determining fringe benefits and other calculated payments. These provisions increase the total money value of COLAs. Unions also may try to freeze all or part of the increase into the wage base, so that wages cannot be reduced if the CPI declines. Finally, they want escalator clauses to specify that cost-of-living adjustments apply to all hours worked, not just to regularly scheduled work time.

Management does not attach the same importance to cost-of-living as do unions. A 1978 survey of labor relations practices in 688 large U.S. firms found that nearly two-thirds of them did not consider inflation among the top three management criteria in wage bargaining. Only 3 percent ranked the cost-of-living factor as the most important standard.[2]

---

[2]Thomas A. Kochan, *Collective Bargaining and Industrial Relations: From Theory to Policy and Practice* (Homewood, Ill.: Richard D. Irwin, 1980), p. 217.

Productivity, Jobs, and Earnings

Labor productivity is defined as a change in output per hour of labor over a specified time. Higher productivity enables an employer to obtain the same quantity of a product with fewer labor hours because output is greater for each hour worked.[3] Productivity is therefore a basis for higher pay.

If fewer total labor hours currently are needed to produce last year's output, more can be paid for each hour of labor this year. A 3 percent increase in the firm's productivity, for example, permits a 3 percent rise in the incomes of everyone associated with the firm's production process. Such a pay raise can occur without raising the firm's cost for a unit of production. The higher earnings are offset by additional revenue from the greater output, assuming product prices stay the same. As an alternative to rising incomes, the 3 percent productivity could be used to reduce product prices by that amount. (See Appendix B of this chapter for a numerical illustration of productivity calculation.)

Job and Skill Displacement. Increasing productivity is generally desirable—there is no controversy about that—but its beneficial effects in specific cases are questionable. Employers and workers may take opposing views about introducing machines to improve productivity. To the employer they mean progress: lower unit costs of production and possibly higher profits. To the workers they might mean more pay and less hard, dirty, and dangerous work. However, they also might reduce existing jobs or create new ones that require less skill for lower wages or are repetitive and monotonous.

Machine technology alters established work routines, and for that reason may be resisted by labor. Turn-of-the-century glovemakers, most of them immigrant workers, told why they opposed the introduction of machines that combined two previously separate job tasks into a single process which was faster but specialized and routine. "You shrink from doing either kind of work itself, nine

---

[3]Productivity and production should not be confused. Production is the amount of output produced; productivity is the efficiency with which it is produced. While productivity rates and production levels normally move in the same direction, productivity can increase or decrease independent of changes in production. In the tire industry, for instance, labor productivity rose substantially during 1928–31 due to the introduction of new machines and production methods, but the total volume of tire production dropped sharply because of the economic depression. The result was a 41 percent reduction in production labor requirements, three-fourths of which was attributed to increased productivity with the remainder accounted as lower tire output. Bruce Minton and John Stuart, *Men Who Lead Labor* (New York: Modern Age Books, 1937), p. 207.

hours a day," one of them said. "You cling to the variety. . . . *Here* is a luxury worth fighting for!"

With the knowledge that workers will resist disruptive technology, employers are tempted to install new processes quickly and unilaterally. A print cloth manufacturer surreptitiously displaced the skilled workers who operated machines that were called "mules." "On Saturday afternoon after (the workers) had gone home," the mill superintendent later boasted, "we started right in and smashed a room full of mules with sledge hammers. . . On Monday morning, (they) were astonished to find that there was no work for them. That room is now full of ring frames run by girls."[4]

New production methods also can erode union ability to negotiate higher wages in new job classifications. This situation occurs where the effect of technology is to eliminate the highest paid group. According to the United Food and Commercial Workers, it is happening now in the retail food industry. In 1980 the union surveyed the impact of "boxed beef" technology on the distribution of fresh meat and, ultimately, on the number of jobs in central cutting centers and retail meat counters.

Boxed beef differs from whole beef in that it is cut and wrapped at the slaughtering plant and sent directly to retail stores as prepackaged meat for display. It is no longer deboned and trimmed in cutting centers or retail meatcutting departments. During 1972–80, the union found, eight of 42 surveyed cutting centers were closed and seven others converted to boxed beef warehouses, eliminating 28 percent of the union jobs in these firms. Exact figures are not available on the number of meatcutter jobs destroyed in retail food stores by boxed beef technology, but the union estimates it to be about 5,000. Because meatcutters earn 10–15 percent more than other retail store employees, these job losses deprive the union of its wage leader in retail food contract negotiations.[5]

Industry Productivity Performances. Productivity rates among industries are uneven, due mainly to differences in the ratios of capital and labor used in production. In Table 6, 16 selected manufacturing and service industries are ranked according to their annual rates of productivity during 1947–78.

Productivity gains are highest in industries where the produc-

---

[4]Herbert G. Gutman, *Work, Culture, and Society in Industrializing America: Essays in American Working-Class and Social History* (New York: Alfred A. Knopf, 1976), pp. 23 and 39.

[5]William Burns, "Changing Corporate Structure and Technology in the Retail Food Industry," in Donald Kennedy, Charles Craypo, and Mary Lehman, *Labor and Technology* (University Park, Pa: Labor Studies Department, 1982), pp. 50-2.

tion process can be mechanized or automated. The more it resembles a continuous flow of output, the greater is its productivity potential. Energy plants and transmission systems generate and carry electric power in capital-intensive, nearly continuous flow processes; gas utilities process and distribute their product in a similar method. Both industries require huge fixed investments and use high ratios of nonproduction to production workers. Telephone service companies integrate electronic terminal, switching, and transmission devices in a highly capitalized continuous-flow process. Introduction of electronically automated switching systems, to cite one of many recent innovations in telecommunications, resulted in large productivity increases but also the loss of thousands of telephone operator jobs.

Above-average productivity in transportation industries results from equipment changes that increase freight capacity with the same or less labor. A shift from steam to diesel engines in rails had this effect. Larger aircraft increased productivity for airlines, espe-

Table 6. Annual Rate of Productivity Increase for Production Workers and Annual Rate of Output Increase, Selected Industries, 1947–78

Industry	Production worker annual rate of productivity increase (%)	Annual rate of output increase (%)
Gas and electric utilities	6.4	7.0
Telephone communications	6.2[a,b]	8.1[b]
Petroleum refining	5.5	3.4
Air transportation	5.1[a]	12.3
Railroad transportation	5.0	0.5
Household appliances	4.8	5.1
Paper and pulp mills	4.2	4.1
Tires and tubes	4.0	4.1
Soft coal	3.5	0.8
Motor vehicles	3.5[c]	5.4[c]
Nonfarm private sector	2.1[d]	3.5[d]
Steel	2.1	1.3
Hotel and motel	1.9[a,b]	3.4[b]
Retail food stores	1.8[a]	2.2[b]
Footwear	1.2	−0.4
Eating and drinking places	0.7[a,b]	3.1[b]

[a] All employees
[b] 1958–78
[c] 1957–78
[d] 1950–79

Source: U.S. Labor Department, Bureau of Labor Statistics, *Handbook of Labor Statistics*, Bulletin 2070 (December, 1980), Table 105.

cially in the heavily traveled, long-distance routes and larger engines and trailers had the same effect in interstate trucking.

Assembly line methods in mass production industries listed in Table 6 usually have yielded steady productivity gains. Such increases depend on improved machinery, work reorganization, faster work paces, and automation. The growing use of robots instead of hourly auto workers to spot-weld and spray-paint vehicles is a harbinger of the future for assembly-line industries.

The figures in Table 6 show how the interaction of productivity and production affects blue-collar employment. The number of employed coal miners fell by 60 percent during this 30-year period because annual productivity increased 3.5 percent and yearly output only 0.8 percent. In rails, where output increases lagged far behind productivity gains, hourly employment fell by 64 percent.

The reverse effect occurs when productivity gains are modest and output increases large. Production jobs in eating and drinking places rose 179 percent during 1964–78, an absolute increase of 2.2 million workers. Airline fares increased so rapidly that the work force more than quadrupled during this time, despite rapid productivity increases.

Productivity as an Economic Bargaining Issue

Productivity as an economic bargaining standard is linked to union responses to new technology. Unions might prefer that production methods stay the same, but this is unrealistic. As a practical matter, labor often must negotiate tradeoffs involving the new technology, such as higher earnings for the remaining workers in exchange for accepting the new process. It is easier to make such agreements during times of economic prosperity than in periods of decline. Productivity is thus a union-initiated bargaining item when the economy is expanding and a management issue when the reverse is true.

Unions and Technology. Political economists at Johns Hopkins University studied changing technology and unions during the early decades of this century. George Barnett was foremost among them. He made case studies of the impact of machines on jobs and earnings in several industries and of the success or failure of union responses. Union typesetters were threatened by the linotype, stonecutters by the stone planer, and hand-glassblowers by bottle-making machines.

Barnett constructed five tests to determine how much new machinery will displace existing jobs: (1) how rapidly the machine is introduced; (2) how quickly skilled workers can leave the affected industry for other jobs; (3) how much the new process reduces the price of finished products and therefore creates more jobs by increasing consumer demand; (4) what ratio of total jobs the machine can replace; and (5) how useful existing skills are in operating the new machines.

Barnett's framework permits an explanation of the impact of mechanization and automation in particular industries. It goes beyond theoretical generalizations to examine real structures, attitudes, and behavioral relationships in the process of technological change.

Of the three unions Barnett studied, the International Typographical Union fared the best. ITU policy was not to fight the machine; instead the union encouraged employers to allow displaced typesetters to become linotype operators at no loss of pay or control over working conditions. The Glass Bottle Blowers union initially opposed but then accepted bottle-making machines and, like the Typesetters, encouraged craft workers to become machine operators. However, the union also organized new operators who never had been skilled bottleblowers. Not only did the union survive, it grew in membership along with the rapidly expanding glass container industry.

Only the Journeymen Stonecutters union tried to resist the machine. It did so for internal union reasons and because stone planers transferred work from building construction sites, where the union was strong, to quarries, where it was on unfamiliar ground and was resisted by the workers. The union failed to organize the relevant work force during a period of crucial change and declined as an effective force.

Current Union Policy. More recent studies show that unions normally consent to job-displacing new technology, if not immediately then over time, with the understanding that union members will not be displaced indiscriminately. The first comprehensive report of the impact on productivity of industrial unionism was issued in 1960. Based on extensive interviews with management and on written contracts and grievance settlements, Slichter, Healy, and Livernash concluded that, except in a few industries where craft traditions remained strong, unions and collective bargaining did not deter the use of labor-saving technology. The chief effect was that employers had to use labor more efficiently than in the past, when it was a relatively cheap and subordinate factor of production.

An extensive survey of actual union responses to changing technology on the job was made during 1977-79 by McLaughlin and Miller. They interviewed nearly 100 union and employer negotiators and neutral participants who had been involved in labor relations disputes over new technology. These included local and international officials of 16 unions in construction, printing, transportation, various metal manufacturing industries, entertainment, banking, retail, and public employment.

Based on the results of these interviews as well as a review of the literature on labor and productivity, McLaughlin and Miller identified several union responses to technological change, ranging from unqualified opposition to active encouragement. The most common response, they found, is "willing acceptance," in which the union does not actually oppose introduction of new technology. The second most frequent response is temporary opposition, where union negotiators resist the change until they become convinced either that members of the bargaining unit will not be hurt or that they will receive adequate compensation. The innovations then are accepted with or without negotiated adjustments. Only rarely does a union choose to compete against the new method.

McLaughlin and Miller also found that the economy is the principal external factor in determining union responses. During prosperous times, when alternative jobs are available, unions are more amenable to concessions. The implication of this attitude is that productivity gains are more likely to occur under expansionary rather than restrictive national economic policies.

Such findings support a statistical analysis of unions' impact on productivity by Brown and Medoff. Their study measured relationships between industry productivity levels and ratios of unionization. Productivity was defined as an increase in the value added to products by labor during the production process. They found union labor to be 20 to 30 percent more efficient than nonunion labor across industry lines. The authors attributed this relationship to low employee turnover, high worker morale related to high earnings and superior fringe benefits, and employee involvement in workplace decisions through union activities and the collective bargaining agreement.

Bargaining Over Productivity. Productivity bargaining involves differences that arise over management's desire for flexibility in the use of labor and labor's demand for job security. When management tries to increase control it usually infringes upon the "web of rules" that governs production in union shops. Killingsworth used this term to include the "customs, practices, unwritten understandings and *de facto* restrictions as well as formal contractual provisions which govern the creation, elimination and combination of jobs and which prescribe work methods, crew sizes, work assignments, and the procedures for changing them."[6] Changing technology requires labor and industry to accommodate their conflicting interests over job security and managerial control.

Killingsworth examined bargaining responses to technological change in five industries. Ranked according to the increasing degree of restrictive union work rules he found in the early 1960s, they were auto, rubber tire, basic steel, West Coast longshoring, and rails. He found substantial differences between them because of various environmental settings. In each instance, however, the adjustment was ongoing.

Unions in auto and tire manufacturing had few restrictive work rules. Instead they placed emphasis both on the economic security for employees adversely affected by new technology and on equitable distribution of the effects of technology. Rubber workers differed from auto in one important respect: they practiced a "subterranean approach" to job preservation, including wildcat (unauthorized) work stoppages, slowdowns, and other informal means of withholding efficiency.

Master contracts in basic steel contained clauses on local working conditions which restricted management control over crew sizes except in the event of major equipment or process changes. Established practices in particular mills also impeded managerial flexibility. While the overall cost of these work rule restraints probably was not great, Killingsworth concluded, they irritated and frustrated local management. In 1959, the industry decided to challenge the Steelworkers on these provisions, prompting the longest strike in the industry's history, but without resolving the matter.

In West Coast longshoring the union acknowledged that restrictive practices were harmful to the industry. Union leaders convinced the membership that to persist in them would jeopardize both jobs and existing conditions by depriving members of access to the machine-related occupations that someday would displace production labor. The parties negotiated a "productivity agreement" in which accumulated work rules were completely abolished and the

---

[6]Charles C. Killingsworth, "Corporate Approaches to Problems of Technological Change," in Gerald Somers, Edward L. Cushman, and Nat Weinberg, eds., *Adjusting to Technological Change* (New York: Harper & Row, 1963).

industry financed early retirement and economic security for displaced workers. The compromise arrangement went into effect in 1961; by 1966 the dockowners had saved an estimated $100 million in return for $29 million in worker benefits.[7]

The web of rules was more elaborate and restrictive in rails than in longshoring. Here, Killingsworth found, extensive working rules served as a substitute for direct supervision in an industry where the workplace is mobile.

As the railway brotherhoods had gained bargaining rights and a substantial degree of economic power, they negotiated work rules including rigid separation of craft classifications and job duties. Some rules—like that requiring the presence of coal firemen on diesel engines—were clearly counterproductive. The unions nevertheless refused to give them up. They did this in part because of the concessions they had made previously to preserve work rule language in the contracts. The members viewed these rules as job property rights in lieu of foregone wages and benefits. Even so, in the two decades after Killingsworth's report, most railway brotherhoods had to relinquish established practices due to industry pressure, adverse public opinion, Congressional action, and arbitration awards.

Productivity and Concession Bargaining. Since the mid-1970s, productivity has become a management issue in economic bargaining. The failure of American industry to compete with foreign producers at home and abroad is popularly attributed to lagging productivity. Management negotiators cite this in their demands for work rule changes giving them greater control over the workplace.

Workers have become more responsive over time to these demands, because if they do not accept them management may relocate production operations. A survey by The Bureau of National Af-

---

[7]An anecdote narrated in Larrowe's biography of West Coast longshore union leader Harry Bridges suggests that economic bargaining is more an art than an exact science. It took three years to negotiate the productivity agreement, during which Paul St. Sure, the chief industry negotiator, agreed to finance the continued investigation and experimentation necessary for progress in the talks. As Larrowe tells it:

> In 1959, after the discussions had been going on for a year and a half, it was apparent that they would continue for perhaps another year or so. "To buy time," St. Sure has recalled, "I offered the union, on behalf of the employers, $1 million for another year's delay for discussion and experimentation. When I made the offer, Mr. Bridges asked, 'Where did you get the million?' I said, 'It's a nice round figure and I didn't want to insult you by offering you less than a nice round figure.'
>
> "He came back the following day and said, 'The figure is $1,500,000.' So I said, 'Where did you get the million and a half?' He said, 'From the same place you got the million.' So we settled on that."

Charles P. Larrowe, *Harry Bridges: The Rise and Fall of Radical Labor in the United States* (Westport, Conn.: Lawrence Hill, 1972), p. 353.

fairs, Inc., of 91 concession bargains in 1982 found 31 instances of work rule changes in more than a dozen cases. By 1983 substantial changes had been negotiated in steel, auto, rails, meat packing, airlines, construction, tires, and petroleum.[8]

Two cases in other industries illustrate the trend. Under the threat that their work would be subcontracted to nonunion firms, several hundred union loggers accepted work rule changes by Crown Zellerbach on the Pacific Coast and agreed to base future wage increases entirely on productivity gains. In New York, Xerox said it had been "hit very hard by competition from Japan," and persuaded the union at its largest domestic manufacturing plant to accept company plans to subcontract work as a cost-saving measure. In return, Xerox agreed to transfer any displaced employees to other jobs at existing pay rates.[9]

Profits

Negotiated wage and benefit increases do not come mainly at the expense of employer profits; they occur in conjunction with them. The factors that enable firms and industries to make profits also enable them to pay higher labor costs. Employers who can pass on labor cost increases by raising prices and reduce labor costs by mechanizing their production processes can afford to negotiate higher earnings and benefits.

New unions might squeeze employer profits in the initial rounds of economic bargaining, as empirical evidence suggests. Established unions might negotiate increases that cut into employer profits for a while, usually during periods of rapid economic expansion when labor is scarce and employers are unwilling to risk production stoppages. However, unions do not permanently transfer profits into the hands of workers. As a standard used in economic bargaining, therefore, profits offer tangible evidence that employers can pay and provide symbolic justification for union demands.

On the other hand, when profits are falling or negative the union is constrained to relax its demands or even to exempt struggling employers from established standards and conditions. This

---

[8]The Bureau of National Affairs, Inc., *Labor Relations in an Economic Recession: Job Losses and Concession Bargaining* (Washington, D.C.: 1982), pp. 11–12; "A Work Revolution in U.S. Industry," *Business Week*, May 16, 1983, p. 100.

[9]"Loggers Tie Pay to Productivity," *Business Week*, November 29, 1982, p. 35; "Clothing Workers Improve Security in New Xerox Pact," *AFL–CIO News*, May 28, 1983, p. 6.

can happen whether or not labor costs are a major cause of the poor performance, because failure to agree casts the union as irresponsible. Employers that are losing money may ask unions to sever negotiated wage changes from cost-of-living and comparability factors and instead to link them to future earnings. They may propose profit-sharing formulas in which wages vary with financial performance or stock ownership plans which rescind scheduled wage increases in exchange for ownership shares in the company.

Obtaining Reliable Profit Data. A procedural issue in bargaining is the union's ability to obtain reliable profit information. In publicly owned corporations, where shareholder financial statements and required government reports are readily available, this is not a great problem, since the union has access to profit data apart from that which the employer provides. The parties may differ over the figures' meaning, but the information is there for either to cite. By contrast, privately owned companies do not have to publish financial figures. Unions try instead to obtain information from other sources, such as civil records and articles in the business press.

Inadequate information is also a problem when unions negotiate single-plant contracts with multiplant employers. Figures seldom are available on that basis. Stockholder statements normally do not disaggregate financial data beyond the division level, nor do required government forms specify information at the plant level. Unions are thus dependent on information supplied by the employer, a dependency which hurts the union when a multiplant company demands concessions based on allegations that a specific operation is unprofitable.

Professional Football. Industry revenues have been a central issue in contract negotiations between professional football players and club owners. The National Football League (NFL) represents the owners in economic bargaining and the National Football League Players Association (NFLPA) negotiates for roughly 1,500 players. Since the late 1960s the union has tried to bargain a larger share of increasing club revenues. A series of player strikes and owner lockouts between 1968 and 1975 culminated in the lengthiest stoppage in U.S. professional sports during the 1982 season.

Football is the most profitable professional sport in America. Economist Barbara Bergman estimated that professional sports received a combined $1.2 billion in revenues in 1982. Of that amount, football would get roughly $600 million; the players would get about $140 million, and other team expenses would total $160 million, leaving $300 million for the owners.

Despite playing fewer games than other sports, football made more money because of lucrative NFL television contracts with national networks. Due to the popularity of the game, club royalties rose sharply with each round of TV bargaining. The 1978 four-year contracts were worth $800 million, or roughly $5.5 million annually for each team, more than twice the amount owners received under the previous agreement. The 1982 contract was estimated at more than $2 billion over five years, or about $14 million annually per team.

A majority of football teams are owned by wealthy individuals and families. This makes it difficult for outsiders, including the NFLPA, to obtain reliable information on revenues and profits for individual clubs. The union has alternative sources: court records and hearings and data supplied by its members. From these figures, the NFLPA estimated average club receipts of $15.6 million and average player salaries of $83,800 for 1981. Assuming an average roster of 53 players, which includes the injured players kept on club payrolls, average total player cost would be $4.4 million, or 28 percent of gross receipts. Additional payments to players were thought to have brought their share to about 32 percent, although in the 1982 negotiations the NFL claimed it was 44 percent. In either case, this is a much smaller ratio than occurs in other professional sports, especially in basketball, where player salaries average 60 to 70 percent of club revenues.

Player earnings differ widely both among and within professional sports. In 1981 the average baseball player made $250,000 from the sport and the average basketball player $215,000, compared to the estimated $84,000 in football. Within football, nearly a 100 percent difference separated the lowest and highest paid positions. A six-year veteran quarterback averaged $153,000, while an offensive lineman with an equal number of years in the league averaged $79,000.

Salary differences inside football reflect the relative availability and value to owners of players in various positions, but differentials among the sports reflect dissimilar labor markets. In baseball, the free agent draft gives owners who are willing to spend money the chance to acquire a competitive advantage. They can purchase the contracts of superior players who are both eligible and willing to move to another team. The effect has been to bid up average player salaries, those of stars and journeymen alike. In basketball, inter-league competition for quality players, between the established National Basketball Association and its short-lived rival American

Basketball Association, lifted salaries rapidly before the two leagues were merged.

Before 1977 football had no free agentry, and interleague competition ended with the World Football League's demise in 1976. The union claimed that competitive bidding before that had raised player salaries in the NLF to 67 percent of gross revenues. Afterwards, it said, the ratio fell to one-third.

The free agent system negotiated by the NFLPA in 1977 had not had the effect that it did in baseball of drawing clubs into expensive bidding. Of more than 100 players who became free agents in 1978, including outstanding performers like Chicago Bear running back Walter Payton, only six received offers from other clubs, and Payton was not among them. No player actually traded uniforms that year as a result of free agentry. The main reason was the draft rules adopted by league owners. Under them the receiving club had to make sizeable compensating payments to the player's former team and, in the case of high-salaried players, lost first-round picks in future college player drafts.

With free agentry not having its intended effect, and without a rival league, the union developed an alternative strategy. It would increase the players' share without also widening their salary differentials and putting them in competition with one another for larger slices of the bigger salary pie. Football salaries are determined through separate negotiations between the player, usually assisted by his agent, and the club, subject to the minimum salary schedule in the NFL-NFLPA contract. Private settlement of salary disputes threatens the NFLPA because it excludes the union from the most important economic transaction between workers and management.

Union officials and player representatives therefore endorsed a novel economic demand. They asked the NFL for a fixed percent of gross revenues to be earmarked for player salaries and benefits. This lump sum would be used to replace individual player-owner negotiations with a leaguewide salary schedule based mainly on years of playing experience. This approach drew immediate fire from the owners, stunned the fans, and alienated some of the high-salaried players. Quarterbacks as a group had never given the union much support, but now several of them vowed to cross NFLPA picket lines if the union struck over the issue.

The NFLPA's actual wage demand was a 55 percent share of the gross club revenues to be allocated according to a negotiated salary schedule and supplemental payments based on player seniority. The first serious economic counterproposal was made by the owners in early September, after the player representatives had voted to strike. Its worth was estimated by the league at $600 million but it left intact individual salary bargaining. The union turned it down and called a strike effective the third game of the season. The players believed they had the power to win because the league could not replace them without losing fan interest. "We are the game" became their strike slogan.

The dispute lasted longer than observers had predicted it would or the experiences of other sports strikes suggested. By early November, however, individual owners began conceding the need to reach agreement while the scheduled season could still be salvaged. On the other side, players from six NFL teams voted support for the league's September offer "in principle." Settlement was reached eight weeks after the strike started. The football season was resumed a few days later and the players soon ratified the pact.

The five-year contract gave the union control over how the owners would spend $1.6 billion of revenues in player salaries, benefits, and economic security guarantees. However, it did not specify a percentage share of revenues nor did it adopt uniform pay scales based on seniority. Estimated worth of the economic package was 46 percent of NFL gross revenues over the life of the contract. The contract also linked future player bonuses and severance payments to seniority and provided sizeable increases in minimum salaries for rookie players which could narrow future pay differentials. Finally, it gave the union the right to approve or reject agents hired by players to represent them in individual bargaining.

Comparability

Comparability in economic bargaining usually means that workers in one group have come to expect their union to match or exceed the gains made by workers in comparable groups. Where comparability is an overriding consideration, strong settlement patterns result. Conditions peculiar to a given plant, firm, or industry, cannot offset the importance of economic parity. Relative bargaining power thus depends on union ability to establish and maintain strong patterns and the countervailing power of employers either to break patterns or negotiate less costly ones.

Comparability in Post-World War II Economic Bargaining. Pattern bargaining among firms and industries became prominent after 1945. Most of the nation's basic industries had been organized in the 1930s and during the war. The CIO industrial unions were ready after the war to test their power. They wanted to take labor costs out of competition by negotiating similar economic packages throughout their respective industries and to narrow pay differentials among firms within industries.

Strong interindustry patterns resulted. Postwar government policy fostered the spread of settlements across industry lines. Unions imposed terms that matched the "going patterns" and employers increased prices to adjust for higher labor costs. Spreading wage patterns became a justification for union demands, usually a more important standard than profits and productivity.

During 1945–48 unions in basic manufacturing industries negotiated annual rounds of similar economic gains. Patterns also were negotiated in transportation and coal mining. Table 7 lists companies and industries in which these patterns developed.

Each pattern round began in secondary industries—clothing, textiles, shoes, oil refining or longshoring—and spread to basic industry. Negotiators postponed their agreements until either steel or auto had settled along the lines of the developing pattern. That contract then became the "key" bargain for establishing the national pattern.

In 1945–46 the key bargain finally was established in basic steel. It called for an 18-to-18½ cents-per-hour wage increase. Wartime price controls were still in effect, so when the Truman Administration permitted the steel companies to increase product prices to offset higher labor costs, rather than get them back through productivity gains or increased output, pattern bargaining independent of industry performance was legitimized.

The 1947 round yielded an increase of 15 cents per hour in wages and six paid holidays. Again the pattern was set in steel. In the third round, 1947–48, a two-year GM-UAW pact which contained productivity and cost-of-living formulas set the pace. Although economic recession in 1949 frustrated the emergence of a clear pattern, several industries adopted similar health and welfare plans, and the $100-per-month pension benefit became a basic manufacturing standard.

Interindustry patterns faded after the 1940s. The trend favored decentralization. Long-term contracts resulted in staggered expiration dates, and formula bargaining put some industries on different projections.

The 1948 GM-UAW agreement inaugurated long-term contracts in postwar labor relations. At first skeptical, UAW negotia-

Table 7. Total Value of Wages and Fringe Benefits Negotiated in Selected Companies and Industries, 1945–49

| | Total value of negotiated wages and fringe benefits | | | |
Company or industry	Wages	Pensions	Paid holidays	Health/Welfare
Nonmanufacturing:				
Soft coal	62¢	(1950)[a]	–	20¢/ton
Sinclair Oil	65½¢	(1950)	6½	contr.[b]
Anthracite coal	50¢	(1950)	–	20¢/ton
Pacific longshoring	67¢	(1951)	–	3¢
Nonoperating rail unions	65¢	by law	by law	by law
Atlantic longshoring	63¢	$35/mo.	–	3¾¢
Manufacturing:				
General Motors	44¢	(1950)	6	contr.
American Woolen	45¢	–	6	non-contr.
American Viscose	45¢	(1950)	6	contr.
U.S. Steel	46½¢	$100/mo.	(1952)[c]	contr.
ALCOA	43¢	$100/mo.	(1950)	contr.
Ford Motor	42½¢	$100/mo.	6	contr.
Armour	44½¢	(1952)	8	(1952)
Chrysler	43¢	(1950)	6	contr.
Northern cotton	42¢	–	6	non-contr.
General Electric	42¢	(1950)	6	contr.
Rubber	41¢	$100/mo.	6	contr.
Anaconda	42¢	–	6	contr.
Int'l Harvester	40½¢	(1950)	6	contr.
Women's clothing	42¢	yes	6½	non-contr.
Men's clothing	40¢	$100/mo.	6	non-contr.

[a] Indicates the year in which the union negotiated $100/month (or $125/month), contributory).
[b] Designates whether plan is employee contributory.
[c] Indicates the year in which the union negotiated six paid holidays.

Source: Harold Levinson, *Collective Bargaining in the Steel Industry: Pattern Setter or Pattern Follower?* (Ann Arbor, Mich.: Institute of Labor and Industrial Relations, 1962), Tables 4, 5 and 6.

tors later agreed that adjusting wages automatically on the basis of productivity and cost of living would minimize economic strikes like the union's 113-day walkout two years earlier. In 1950, despite an unimpressive yield from its escalator clause, the UAW accepted an unprecedented five-year GM contract which retained both the COLA adjustment and the productivity formula. Ford and Chrysler followed the GM lead with comparable pacts. Negotiators elsewhere showed little interest in the Big Three approach until the Korean War accelerated inflation. Long-term contracts with escalator clauses then became fashionable.

Negotiated economic packages among key industrial unions

occurred at different times but did not vary widely in content over the next few years. A comparison of wage increases during 1948–55 at General Motors, U.S. Steel, and B. F. Goodrich shows no significant differences between the three. Despite industry variations in profits, productivity, and output expansion, the comparability factor kept them reasonably matched, although increases at B. F. Goodrich started to lag behind the others in the 1950s.

Intraindustry Patterns. Pattern bargaining became more prevalent within industries than between them. Unions tried to extend contract settlements in concentrated industries from large producers to suppliers and fabricators. Once established, key bargains were pattern targets in negotiations with secondary companies. Unions nevertheless showed pragmatism in this regard. Where economic conditions permitted, the key settlement was matched by smaller firms; where they did not, the union normally reduced its demands rather than risk hurting the employer and threatening jobs.

Strategic bargaining requires negotiators to identify and defend the comparative standard most advantageous to them. Company representatives select lower-paid groups of workers for comparison; union negotiators pick high-paid groups. Employers doing business in high-wage industries that are located in low-wage geographic regions will prefer local wage standards. Their unions, however, will emphasize industry averages in justifying wage demands.

Employers resist paying labor costs above the industry average. Allis-Chalmers closed its electric power transformer manufacturing plant in Pittsburgh, displacing more than 1,000 hourly and salaried workers, rather than operate under a wage and benefit pattern from another industry. The UAW had negotiated its farm equipment pattern at the Pittsburgh plant, presumably because Allis-Chalmers was mainly a farm machinery producer, rather than accept the lower pattern in electrical products.[10]

It is difficult for unions to establish strong patterns in nonconcentrated industries. Price competition among producers is common and this encourages individual firms to try for labor cost advantages by breaking the pattern. Workers also are likely to be geographically dispersed and therefore more difficult to organize into strong bargaining structures.

Textile Industry. Textiles illustrate union inability to establish pattern bargaining in a nonconcentrated industry. Years ago textile

---

[10]Allis-Chalmers, *Annual Report, 1974,* "Chairman's Letter to Stockholders."

employers moved south from New England, in large part to escape organized labor, even though the unions had made economic bargaining concessions to keep them in the north. Two unions, the Textile Workers Union (TWU) and the United Textile Workers (UTW), which have since merged, competed for representation rights in the mills. They negotiated key contracts with lead employers that became pattern settlements for entire regions. American Thread, for example, was a pattern setter for some 75 New England mills employing about 25,000 workers.

However, if neither union was strong in a given area, nonunion employers could establish the pattern. Dan River Mills repeatedly undermined both unions by granting unilateral wage increases in its southern plants. During a 1951 strike in some mills, the company forced a 2 percent wage increase on the union. This became the pattern for textile-clothing settlements throughout the south. As a result, the union was decertified and its rival later chosen to represent the same employees. By 1965, however, the new union had negotiated a total of only 55 cents in wage increases. That year the company refused to meet its wage demands and again made a small unilateral wage increase which became the regional pattern.

In 1974, the workers struck Dan River for nine weeks over modest wage and benefit improvements and union security provisions. Once more the company granted an increase that had not been negotiated, this time after the union had called off its strike without a settlement. Even before that, however, management had been getting normal production levels by using a reduced work force six days a week.

Meatpacking. A host of unfavorable trends in meatpacking forced the United Food and Commercial Workers (UFCW) to make economic concessions in the industry master agreements. Loss of markets by leading firms and their eventual acquisition by conglomerate corporations undermined the historical bargaining structures. The sudden dominance of firms opposed to master agreements, like Iowa Beef Processors, further weakened the union's ability to negotiate intraindustry patterns based on comparability. Economic recession and unstable cattle and hog production in the early 1980s caused heavy layoffs and a number of packing plant closings, which demoralized union workers and made them vulnerable to concession pressures.

While the UFCW was not averse to temporary economic givebacks under these conditions, the union wanted to handle them in an orderly manner that would preserve industry standards, even at lower levels. The UFCW wanted to keep labor costs from becoming a competitive factor among employers in their efforts to hold product markets. In addition, a uniform wage and benefit base would make it easier for the union to regain what it had given away when the industry recovered. In late 1981, therefore, UFCW agreed to a 44-month wage freeze and a shorter suspension of cost-of-living payments in a pattern-setting agreement in pork processing. Concessions then spread to other pork processors and into beef packing during 1982.

Subsequent actions by the old-line firms made it impossible for the union to maintain even the concession pattern. Greyhound Corporation, Armour's parent owner which had initiated the 1981 union concessions, revealed it was selling out to Con Agra, a diversified basic food supplier, because the UFCW would not take further concessions. Con Agra then announced that Armour operations would be curtailed unless it negotiated "satisfactory terms and conditions of employment at each of the plants." About the same time Wilson Food filed for bankruptcy and unilaterally cut wages up to 55 percent. UFCW struck Wilson for three weeks before signing a new agreement which cut the base wage rate by 25 percent and reduced benefits.

By mid-1983 only one-third of the union's members in meatpacking were still working under the master agreement, down from 55 percent when the 1981 concessions were made. Anticoncession strikes and plant closings were frequent occurrences. Relations between the UFCW and some of its locals soured as the union tried to hold the line on plant-level givebacks in order to preserve the integrity of the master agreement. An Iowa local was put under trusteeship after it negotiated exceptionally large concessions to keep open an Oscar Mayer plant.[11]

Summary

Analytical Methods. Economists differ on the relative importance of economic and political variables in determining union wage policy. The issue is whether unions try to maximize the total economic cost of labor, as stated by John Dunlop, by estimating the probable effects of wage increases on the number of union workers

---

[11]Joann S. Lublin, "Effort to Save Pay Scales in Meatpacking Brings Lewie Anderson Many Spats, Not All With Firms," *The Wall Street Journal*, August 4, 1983; "Problems Continue in Meat Processing Industry," *Monthly Labor Review* (September 1983).

employed. Arthur Ross and others reject this explanation as being too simplistic and instead emphasize the political variables in labor-management relations. A middle approach by Harold Levinson incorporates both the economic and political conditions and adds an institutional dimension to the approach.

The analysis in this book takes into account union wage policy as determined either by economic or political considerations, but it puts greater emphasis on the external environment's impact on union bargaining power. To that extent, the analysis used here is an extension of Levinson's institutional power variable.

Dunlop and Ross wrote during the time that organized labor was asserting itself after decades of subordination to industrial employers. They understandably assigned major importance to unions and union policy as the determinants of economic bargaining outcomes; they put the issue of relative bargaining power almost exclusively within the framework of union objectives and choices and took the external environment more or less as a set of given structures, processes, and rules.

Recently, however, unions have lost momentum and initiative largely as a result of fundamental changes in the bargaining environment. It seems appropriate now to attach greater importance than did these early observers to the aspects of the bargaining relationship that are more influenced by capital than labor. These include the organization and behavior of business enterprises, the development and introduction of new product and production technology, and the enactment and enforcement of laws regulating or deregulating product and labor markets. As a result, the approach used here is similar to the work of institutional economists, especially Robert Hoxie and George Barnett, who wrote during the decades around the turn of the century, before organized labor in America had found a way to unionize mass production industries permanently.

Against this backdrop of institutional power variables, certain standards of economic bargaining are identified and used to interpret and evaluate the terms and conditions negotiated by the parties.

Economic Bargaining Standards. Four standards in economic bargaining are profits, productivity, the cost of living, and comparability. It is difficult to know the extent to which industry profits are diverted to union members as a result of wage and benefit increases. Under competitive product markets, more of the negotiated labor cost increases would come out of profits than they would where market power or public policy enabled firms to pass on labor cost increases as higher prices. In either case, profits are a rough indicator of employer ability to pay. They alert the union to the employer's ability to pay and can be used to solidify the rank-and-file.

Productivity is a controversial standard in wage bargaining. It was used historically to justify union wage demands, as a way of assuring that workers shared in the benefits of an expanding economy. It has lately become a management issue. With the decline of American industry at home and abroad, employers want unions to help raise productivity levels. Specifically, this means abandoning accepted work rules and permitting new machinery and production techniques.

Union negotiators instinctively resist this change. Either they are not persuaded by management's claims or their members refuse to give up existing standards. Under the threat of a plant shutdown, production relocation, or even corporate bankruptcy, unions have agreed to various types of "productivity bargaining."

The cost of living is an important standard in wage bargaining during periods of economic expansion and rising prices. Erosion of workers' real earnings results in political pressure on union negotiators to bargain compensating payments through escalator clauses. They are found in roughly half of all major contracts but their frequency varies among industries and occupational groups. They compensate partially for the effects of inflation.

Comparability is another wage standard. Union ability to negotiate pattern settlements is a rough measure of its bargaining power. Strong patterns override differences among individual employers to impose uniform standards based on key settlements.

Unions normally exercise restraint in deciding how far they will try to extend the pattern. The further an employer is removed from the industry's pattern-setting core, as in the case of independent auto parts suppliers, the more inclined the union is to exempt the firm from meeting the pattern. Signs of union weakness in this regard are the inability to impose patterns on major producers or the necessity to submit to the wage patterns of nonunion firms or those which negotiate with independent unions.

Economic bargaining standards are not objective measurements that identify appropriate or equitable terms of settlement. They serve two other functions. First, the cost-of-living, productivity, and profit standards indicate the economic boundaries within which settlements are consistent with prevailing economic conditions. What is actually negotiated depends on the relative bargaining power of the parties at that time, not on what cost-of-living, profit, and productivity figures warrant or on what might be considered just and equitable.

Second, the comparability standard indicates anticipated settlements. It depends on other bargaining outcomes that are considered appropriate bases of comparison. Like economic standards, comparability does not determine the bargaining outcome. It only suggests alternative results. The actual outcome again hinges on power variables.

Key Words and Phrases

productivity	escalator
cost of living	free agent
profitability	orbits of coercive comparison
comparability	givebacks
disaggregate	

Review and Discussion Questions

1. Name and define the four generally accepted standards in economic bargaining.
2. Name and explain the basis of union wage policy according to Arthur Ross.
3. What effect did "free agentry" have on professional baseball players? Football players?
4. How does the author of the book explain union wage policy?

Chapter Resources and Suggested Further Reading

Sources used in the introduction to this chapter are John Dunlop, *Wage Determination Under Trade Unions (1944)* (1966); Arthur Ross, *Trade Union Wage Policy* (1956); Harold Levinson, *Determining Wage Forces in Collective Bargaining* (1966).

For the section on the cost of living, the sources are H. M. Douty, "Cost-of-Living Escalator Clauses and Inflation," (1975); Victor Sheifer, "Cost-of-Living Adjustment: Keeping Up With Inflation?," *Monthly Labor Review* (June 1979); Jack Stieber, "Evaluation of Long-Term Contracts," in Harold Davey, et al., eds., *New Dimensions in Collective Bar-*

gaining (1959); Robert Ferguson, *Cost-of-Living Adjustments in Union-Management Agreements* (1976).

The discussion on productivity and economic bargaining draws upon George E. Barnett, *Chapters On Machinery and Labor (1926)* (1969); Sumner Slichter, James J. Healy, and Robert Livernash, *The Impact of Collective Bargaining on Management* (1960); Charles Brown and James Medoff, "Trade Unions in the Production Process," *Journal of Political Economy* (June 1978); Doris McLaughlin, assisted by Christine Miller, *The Impact of Labor Unions on the Rate and Direction of Technological Innovation* (February, 1979).

The section on negotiating over revenues in professional football is based on Barbara R. Bergman, "Why the Football Union Can Hit Hard," *The New York Times*, September 19, 1982; Roger Noll, ed., *Government and the Sports Business* (1974); "NFL's $2 Billion TV Deal," *Chicago Tribune*, February 27, 1982, which lists the NFLPA figures on industry income and average player salaries for 1981; Frederick C. Klein, "Pity the Poor Professional Football Players," *The Wall Street Journal*, August 3, 1979; "The NFL Players Out of Time," *Business Week*, November 29, 1982.

Sources on comparability as an economic bargaining standard include H. M. Douty, "Wage Policy and the Role of Fact Finding Boards," *Monthly Labor Review* (April 1946); Harold Levinson, *Determining Forces in Collective Wage Bargaining* (1966); J. W. Garbarino, "The Economic Significance of Automatic Wage Adjustments," in Harold Davey, et al., eds., *New Dimensions in Collective Bargaining* (1959); George Seltzer, "Pattern Bargaining and the United Steelworkers," *Journal of Political Economy* (August 1951); Harold Levinson, "Pattern Bargaining: A Case Study of the Automobile Workers," *Quarterly Journal of Economics* (May 1960); G. P. Shultz and C. A. Myers, "Union Wage Decisions and Employment," *American Economic Review* (June 1950); U.S. Department of Labor, Bureau of Labor Statistics, "Wage Chronology: Dan River Inc., January 1973–June 1974," (1975).

Appendix A

Inflation and Wages

What is the exact impact of inflation on the purchasing power of wages and exactly how much of a wage increase is needed to compensate fully a group of hourly workers for past inflation? The following numerical example answers both questions in a hypothetical situation.

Assume an existing three-year contract became effective October 1, 1977 and expires September 30, 1980. Contract renegotiations are underway in September 1980, when the latest available Consumer Price Index (CPI) figure for Urban Wage Earners and Clerical Workers is for July 1980. To determine the percentage increase in the CPI during the life of the contract the procedure is as follows:

		CPI
(1)	July 1980	248.0
	October 1977	−184.5
		63.5

That is, between October 1977 and July 1980 the CPI increased 63.5 points, from 184.5 to 248.0. The next step is to convert the point increase to a percentage increase by dividing the point increase by the CPI figure in the base period, October 1977.

(2) $63.5 / 184.5 = .344$, or 34.4%

Multiplying the average hourly wage of the bargaining unit effective October 1977, which is assumed to have been $6.50, by the percentage increase in the CPI between October 1977 and July 1980 gives the exact amount by which the average hourly wage rate has lost purchasing power. This indicates the difference between "money wages" and "real wages" as a result of the 34.4% inflation during the period. In other words, what impact did the slightly more than one-third increase in prices since October 1977 have on the purchasing power of the average wage?

(3)	Average hourly wage, October 1977	$6.50
	Percentage rise in CPI, October 1977—July 1980	× .344
		$2.236

Thus, inflation has eroded the real value of the $6.50 average hourly wage by $2.24. The $6.50 now has a real purchasing power of $4.26. To fully compensate the average member of the bargaining unit for price increases since October 1977, the average wage rate would have to be raised by $2.24 to $8.74. How much has the average wage increased under the contract since October 1977? Assume that the two deferred wage increases effective October 1978 and October 1979 raised the $6.50 rate to $7.30, the current average hourly wage in the bargaining unit. Therefore:

(4) Current average hourly wage $7.30
     Average hourly wage, October 1977   −6.50
                                                                                          $0.80

(5) Amount needed for full compensation $2.24
     Average hourly wage increase
     since October 1977   − .80
                                                                                          $1.44

An increase of $1.44 is needed to restore the purchasing power of the average hourly wage in the bargaining unit to its October 1977 level. That is, for the union to restore the October 1977 purchasing power of the hourly wage it would have to negotiate a 19.7% wage increase ($1.44 / $7.30).

Appendix B

Productivity and Wages

A numerical example illustrates the productivity concept. Assume 500,000 units of product "x" are manufactured in 1980 using 200,000 hours of production labor and that each unit of "x" sells for $5. In 1981, however, 515,000 units of "x" are produced using the same amount of production labor, 200,000 hours, and selling at the same price, $5. The higher output could have resulted from harder work, better machinery, a new production method, or some combination of these things. In any event, productivity in this instance is measured by output times price divided by hours for the base year (1980), compared with the same calculation for the current year (1981):

(1) $\dfrac{\text{Output} \times \text{Price}}{\text{Hours}}$ is the basic ratio in the computations; therefore:

(2) (1980) $\dfrac{500{,}000 \times \$5}{200{,}000}$ = $\dfrac{\$2{,}500{,}000}{200{,}000}$ = $\$12.50$ output per hour

(3) (1981) $\dfrac{515{,}000 \times \$5}{200{,}000}$ = $\dfrac{\$2{,}575{,}000}{200{,}000}$ = $\$12.875$ output per hour

(4) $\dfrac{\$12.875 - \$12.50}{\$12.50}$ = .03, or 3 percent productivity gain during 1980–81

Production workers as well as other income recipients in the production process now can receive a 3 percent wage increase without increasing product prices as a result of the 3 percent productivity gain:

	1980	1981
Productivity	500,000 per year	515,000 per year (with 3 percent gain)
Labor cost	$1,000,000 (assume $5 per hour)	$1,030,000 (assume 3 percent increase: $5.15 per hour)
Other costs	$1,250,000	$1,287,500 (assume 3 percent increase)
Profits	$250,000	$257,500 (assume 3 percent increase)
Total sales price	$2,500,000 ($5 × 500,000)	$2,575,000 ($5 × 515,000)
Price per unit of X	$5	$5

This example simplifies the productivity calculation. It assumes only one product is manufactured and that its price and the number of production hours remain constant from one year to the next—obviously unrealistic conditions. But the relationship between higher productivity and the ability to pay higher wages without raising product prices is shown with precision. In reality all the variables are changing simultaneously; that is why reliable figures on workplace productivity are difficult to calculate.

4

Craft Bargaining

Unions representing craft workers ordinarily have considerable bargaining power. Industries that employ large numbers of skilled workers often are able to pay higher labor costs because "spatial limitations" or government regulation encourage cost pass-through practices. Some industries are even more able to pay as a result of above-average productivity gains resulting from the growth of output or job mechanization.

Craft Unions

Craft unions typically have the ability to make employers pay higher labor costs, for reasons that are both internal and external to the union. Internally, strong identification with a specific trade or craft and a commitment to protect the job motivate skilled workers to unionize the relevant work force and to build exclusive, self-sufficient craft organizations. Externally, specific craft labor is essential to continued production. Assuming that the union has organized its relevant work force, striking craft workers are irreplaceable.

Craft bargaining power is nevertheless vulnerable to environmental change. Economic and political changes undermine spatial limitations and other market sources of employer ability to pay. Structural changes redefine the relevant work force, bring separate crafts into jurisdictional conflict, and make obsolete existing bargaining units. Corporate reorganization can add new workers to the established work force—workers who perform the same production tasks but are not covered by the union contract. New technology can lessen industry dependence on a particular craft. Government deregulation can reduce ability to pay by exposing union employers to competitive entry by nonunion firms.

80

Craft bargaining is associated with a variety of industries. Table 8 identifies some of them according to product and structural type. The largest group is nonconcentrated nonmanufacturing, where localized production and marketing practices encourage craft bargaining among small employers. But a gradual disappearance of craft distinctions and the expansion of bargaining units to include unskilled jobs displace craft structures in many manufacturing and service sectors. Only those industries designated by asterisks in the table still exhibit craft bargaining, and in some of them it is disappearing.

Narrow craft bargaining never flourished in concentrated manufacturing industries. The craft-based Amalgamated Association was expelled from the steel industry after it chose to strike unsuccessfully against the newly formed U.S. Steel Corporation in 1901 rather than be ousted piecemeal from the mills of previously independent companies. In the paper industry, the original AFL limited its membership to skilled machine tenders and beaters, even though such a narrow craft base was impractical. An industrial union was created through a series of mergers and replaced the craft organization as an AFL affiliate in 1903.

Some nonconcentrated manufacturing industries practiced craft bargaining until technology or membership opposition made industrial bargaining imperative. With a mix of skilled and un-

Table 8. Selected Private Sector Industries Characterized Historically by Craft Bargaining, According to Type of Industry and Organizational Structure

	Industry Type	
Organizational structure	**Manufacturing**	**Nonmanufacturing**
Concentrated	Glass bottle Iron and steel Paper	Railroad* Airlines* Intercity bus* Motion picture*
Nonconcentrated	Printing* Garment Baking Machine tool Meat cutting	Construction* Health care* Offshore maritime Mass transit Power utility Trucking Eating and drinking places

*Industries characterized by craft bargaining structures.

skilled, native and immigrant, and radical and conservative workers, the men's clothing industry was able to keep labor divided and escape widespread organization by any single craft or industrial union until the Amalgamated Clothing Workers of America (ACWA) made impressive organizing gains. ACWA was born in 1914 as a protest against the craft conservativism of the United Garment Workers (UGW), an earlier AFL affiliate controlled by skilled garment cutters. UGW had relied on the union label rather than direct job action to organize and bargain with the industry.

The break occurred when UGW leadership and strikers in Chicago made unprecedented bargaining gains but were then undermined by the union's failure elsewhere. They and others first tried to reform the UGW. Failing that, they left and made the ACWA the dominant union. Although led by skilled tradesmen, ACWA adopted industrial union tactics in organizing and bargaining, a more consistent approach than craft unionism to the industry's structure and technology.

Transportation

Craft unions have had considerable bargaining success in the concentrated nonmanufacturing industries listed in Table 8. Three reasons can be cited: (1) craft skills are essential in transportation; (2) interconnecting service operations—"hub-and-spoke" systems in airlines, and coast-to-coast integrated services in rails and intercity buses—foster corporate consolidation and companywide bargaining units; (3) spatial limitation through government regulation gave the crafts historical bargaining power.

After having been defeated in strikes against cooperating railroads and consolidated carriers in the decades following the Civil War, the railway crafts rose to prominence within the American union movement. They performed as well as any labor organization at the bargaining table during the period when craft unionism dominated. Hoxie attributed their success to centralized internal decision making (which he considered to be an essential structure for any union dealing with major corporations), to the pure collective bargaining objectives they pursued in place of broad social and political goals, to their cooperative and conservative approaches to labor-management relationships, and to their ability to shut down rail operations through strikes. As Table 9 shows, in the post World War II period, the railway brotherhoods continued to negotiate above-average increases, higher even than those in the unionized

Table 9. Annual Rates of Change in Hourly Earnings in Selected Industries, 1953-76

Industry	Annual percentage change				
	1953-58	1958-64	1964-71	1971-76	1953-76
Telephones	4.1	4.2	4.7	12.3	6.0
Railroads	5.4	2.3	6.5	9.6	5.8
Trucking	4.5	4.2	5.6	8.2	5.8
Steel	5.7	2.6	4.2	11.3	5.6
Building construction	4.2	3.9	7.0	6.4	5.4
Motor vehicles	3.6	3.9	5.7	8.5	5.4
Tires	4.1	3.8	4.3	6.7	4.7
Electrical equipment	4.0	2.9	4.8	7.1	4.6
Men's and boys' suits	2.5	3.3	5.5	6.5	4.5
All industries	4.2	3.2	5.6	7.4	5.0

Source: Adapted from Daniel J. B. Mitchell, *Unions, Wages, and Inflation* (Washington, D.C.: Brookings Institution, 1980), Table 2–7, p. 54.

basic industries. But these gains were accompanied by shrinking employment due to high productivity increases (Table 6, p. 58) accompanying declining demand for rail services which resulted in smaller operating crews and fewer maintenance and repair workers.

This chapter describes craft bargaining in two nonconcentrated but contrasting industry settings, printing and construction. Recent experiences in both reveal at least temporary declines in union bargaining power resulting from long-term changes in industrial organization, technology, and government policy, and from short-term economic recession and unemployment.

Printing

Printing unionism in the United States is as old as the nation. New York printers were organized and struck their employers for standard working conditions in 1776. Printers from major metropolitan areas had twice met and successfully formed national unions before the Civil War was fought.

Printing unions historically have had bargaining power. Employers generally were able to pay and unions had the ability to make them pay. Expanding consumer demand for commercially printed products, increasing newspaper advertising and circulation revenues, and periods of high productivity provided an economic basis for negotiated wage and benefit improvements. Printer skills, exclusive craft unionism, area and companywide contracts, and printer craft militancy gave printing unions strike power. Spatial limitation characteristics among both commercial printing firms and newspapers, together with union success in organizing the relevant work forces, ensured craft dominance. The results were high wages, job security, and substantial union control over production processes. Newspaper typographers, for example, were among the highest paid hourly manufacturing workers; they enjoyed superior fringe benefits and contractual job guarantees and were able to impose and enforce rigid work rules.

Average hourly earnings among print crafts have always varied. According to union sources, the average for all crafts (both union and nonunion) in 1983 as $9.52, compared to $8.84 in manufacturing generally, but among the major printing and publishing occupations average wages ranged from $7.16 for bookbinders (and/or specialty workers) to $10.95 for pressmen (and/or lithographers). For those same craft positions under Graphic Communications International Union (GCIU) contracts the hourly averages are:

All crafts	$12.04
Bookbinders/specialty	9.39
Pressmen/lithographers	13.63

It is estimated that 50 to 60 percent of production workers in newspapers and commercial printing, which together accounted for two-thirds of the printing industry's production work force, were covered by union contracts during 1968–72. The ratio has since declined.

The Development of Printing Unions. The International Typographical Union (ITU), founded in 1852, originally claimed jurisdiction over all work performed in print shops. Newspaper typesetters dominated the organization. They greatly outnumbered members from other printing shops and crafts and generally had more strategic bargaining leverage than the other trades because of newspaper publication deadlines. Typesetters in commercial printing and press operators in commercial and newspaper shops held no important union offices and occupied an inferior place in ITU affairs.

This inequitable standing among crafts changed as a result of new technology. In the 1880s, employers began introducing linotype machines, high-speed printing presses, and stereotype, electrotype, and photoengraved printing plates. Each process modified or eliminated existing skills and required new ones. Mergenthaler's linotype converted typesetting from a hand to a mechanical process and threatened to displace thousands of typesetter jobs. Elsewhere, high-speed presses replaced steam-driven machines and what remained of the primitive hand presses. The new machines elevated the prestige and importance of pressmen, whose jobs now required demanding skills and close attention. Employers now made most of their money from pressroom operations, further diminishing the importance of composition. New printing plate processes completed the specialization of print shop skills and craft demarcations.

So different was the linotype that hand-typesetters faced occupational extinction. Moreover, those who kept their jobs came under the close supervision of machine-paced work. These effects became clear when the West Publishing Company of St. Paul experimented successfully with linotypes in 1889. None of West's typesetters were displaced but the average number of hours they worked was sharply reduced. Altogether, the ITU estimated, 1,450 linotype machines were in use by 1894, directly or indirectly displacing 3,500 printers.

The union had to respond, but ITU president W. B. Prescott urged delegates to the union's 1894 convention to be accommodating. It is clear, he told them, "that hand work cannot begin to compete" with machines, and it would be "futile to attempt to stay the tide of their introduction" by making wage concessions, which he estimated might have to reach 50 percent to be effective. Instead, he advised the union to accept linotypes but have typesetters operate them at union wage scales and under union work rules. His view prevailed and accommodation to the new technology became official ITU policy.

Typesetters survived the linotype because of the ITU's flexible policy and two other factors. First, employers agreed to retrain typographers to operate the machines and were pleased to find that experienced printers made efficient, reliable linotype operators worth the premium pay they received. Second, the new process reduced printing costs and product prices enough for increased consumer demand to enable employers to keep all of their retrained typesetters, and in many instances to hire new hands. It was an exceptional outcome, one in which market conditions were such that labor-saving technology did not result in a net job loss or earnings reduction by the affected craft.

Their survival and subsequent resurgence ensured typesetters of continued control inside the ITU. But their refusal to recognize the emerging print crafts and specialty occupations prompted a series of disaffiliations. First the pressmen left the ITU, in 1889, to form the International Printing Pressmen's Union (IPP), an organization founded on the principle of harmony rather than conflict between labor and capital, and therefore the object of derision from the militant ITU. Three years later the bookbinders left, followed by the stereotypers and electrotypers in 1902, and the photoengravers shortly afterward. Changing technology and craft-exclusive control of the ITU together thus fragmented unionization in the printing industry around the turn of the century.

Economic Bargaining in Printing. Following these defections, each union negotiated separately with area print shops and newspapers, but the ITU held a commanding position. Individual unions normally patterned their settlements after those of the strongest craft, the typesetters. It also represented more workers than the other four crafts combined.

Fragmented bargaining weakened the crafts in confrontations with determined employers. Philip Taft described the consequences of one such incident, the Chicago newspaper strike of 1912. The *Chicago American*, a Hearst paper, imposed unilateral changes in press crew requirements following its unsuccessful demands for work rule concessions from the Pressmen's local. A work stoppage resulted. Claiming this was the first stage of an industry plan to weaken print unions generally, the Pressmen's national president tried to extend the dispute to other Hearst papers. But the heads of rival newspaper crafts, notably the ITU, not only opposed the Chicago pressmen but denounced and disciplined their local leaders who supported them. Isolated, the pressmen eventually surrendered on the *American*'s terms. Hearst went on to become a notoriously antiunion employer, although the industry generally remained unionized.

Craft Cooperation and Consolidation. Some interunion cooperation was achieved with formation of the International Allied Printing Trades Association (IAPTA) in 1911, but in practice the organization's efforts consisted more of union label enforcement than of cooperative organizing and bargaining. Rival crafts could neither resolve jurisdictional disputes nor build bargaining alliances. On one side was the Typesetters' plan for printing trades amalgamation under its leadership; on the other was the Pressmen's proposal for craft federation with individual union autonomy. Neither approach nor any compromise between them was acceptable to both unions.

The IAPTA became inactive, partly because the ITU held half

the votes at Association gatherings. Industry changes following World War II also eroded established craft lines. Lithography, the fastest-growing print craft, had been organized by a CIO union outside the Association and now other CIO affiliates were raiding AFL shops. Another unsuccessful attempt was made to revive printing trades cooperation after the 1955 AFL-CIO merger. Still divided, the crafts had to confront future changes in printing without a coherent response.

Changing industrial structure and technology made traditional union organization obsolete and increasingly ineffective. The result was a series of print union mergers. In 1973 the Printing and Graphic Communications Union (PGCU) was formed by a combination involving the IPP and the Stereotypers and including about 100,000 members. Nearly as large in membership size was the Graphic Arts International Union (GAIU), the result of an earlier merger between the Bookbinders and the Lithographers and Photoengravers. PGCU and GAIU then merged in 1983 to form the Graphic Communication International Union, a consolidated print union committed to an industry rather than fragmented craft approach.

The ITU, with a steadily dwindling membership, meanwhile held merger talks with the Newspaper Guild, a union of reporters, photographers, editors, and commercial employees. But the ITU also was being courted by the Teamsters. This prompted the AFL-CIO to call for the combination of all the printing trades into one organization as a means of improving labor's bargaining power at a time of rapid technological change in the industry. Indeed, the president of the Guild had earlier observed that "the onrush of technology is so swift and so merciless that the forces are in place for a merger of all the print unions." If this does occur, then the fragmentation of print unions that followed changing technology in the last century will be remedied, ironically, by labor's response to current changes in technology as a result of microelectronic innovation.

Printing Technology. Print technology is advancing at an astonishing pace. Operating capital in the average commercial print shop about doubled in value during 1961-71. Even discounting for inflation, this was a dramatic increase in the rate of change.

One explanation for the sudden burst of printing technology after a half century of stagnation is the breakup in the 1960s of a historic duopoly in printing machinery manufacturing. Two firms, Mergenthaler and Intertype, had controlled the industry through patents on key products. Neither was innovative, but both were profitable. This attracted larger, technologically sophisticated producers like RCA, IBM, and Fairchild into the field. They began developing and marketing new typesetting equipment based on electronic, computer, and laser technologies. These advances revolutionized competitive standards and gave rise to an eventual polarization of the industry between technologically efficient and inefficient firms.

Diagram 1 illustrates recent technological changes in printing. Print shop composition now is performed by typists who operate electronic keyboards while seated before visual display terminals (VDTs). A magnetic tape is produced and fed into a computer which makes photocompositions ready for the printing room. Editorial copy is thus transformed directly to printing plates without using the intermediary process of hot metal typesetting. It is the most revolutionary development in the 500-year history of modern printing since Johann Gutenberg's movable type and mechanical press made hand-lettering obsolete.

In addition, preparation departments for prepress work are being eliminated by sophisticated equipment. Electronic color scanners perform the job tasks of process color workers, exotic new cameras displace the stripping operator, computer-driven heliograph scanners do gravure prepress work, and automatic laser platemaking replaces lithography prepress operations.

Inside the pressroom, one kind of machine is replacing another. This reduces crew sizes and results in considerable cost-savings to firms. Unionized shops often agree, however, to retrain displaced journeymen for other jobs—compositors to become phototypesetters, for example—much like obsolete typographers were retrained to be linotype operators in response to that technological change. For unions the problem is more serious where technological change is accompanied by ownership consolidation and the geographic relocation of printing operations.

Commercial Printing

Commercial printing historically was concentrated in several big-city printing centers and consisted mainly of small independent shops. In 1963, the 10 largest print centers contained nearly two of every five firms in the industry, employed one half the printers, and accounted for more than half the industry's revenues. With the industry drawn together in this way, each craft had only to organize

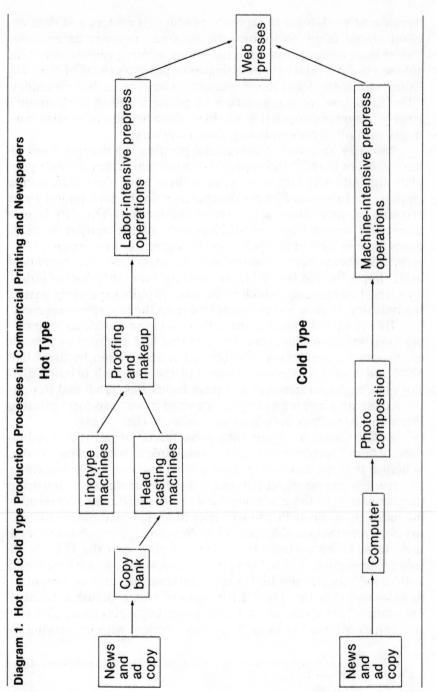

Diagram 1. Hot and Cold Type Production Processes in Commercial Printing and Newspapers

Hot Type

News and ad copy → Copy bank → Linotype machines / Head casting machines → Proofing and makeup → Labor-intensive prepress operations → Web presses

Cold Type

News and ad copy → Computer → Photo composition → Machine-intensive prepress operations → Web presses its relevant work force in separate production centers and then develop stable labor relations with an area employer association. "Most local unions situated in the major printing centers were thus able to obtain a relatively high degree of power because of their position within the local labor market," Gregory Giebel concludes. "The high level of unionization of printers within each union's largely separate jurisdiction enabled them to obtain master contracts with all firms employing their members."[1]

Industry Structure. Commercial printing is a decentralized industry. More than 22,000 separate commercial printing plants populate the industry, and 60 percent of them have fewer than twenty employees. In none of its major branches do the four largest firms account for more than a quarter of the market. The fifty largest letterpress printers controlled 28 percent of the market in 1972, down from one-third in 1963. Certain segments of letterpress, however, are moderately concentrated. In magazine and periodical print shops, the top four firms account for more than half of industry sales. Lithography, which is the most rapidly expanding part of the industry, is even less concentrated than the letterpress segment.

By the early 1980s, however, there was some evidence of growing horizontal consolidation. Print chains had emerged as a result of corporate acquisitions. Established chains owned by firms like NCR and American Can were joined by the multiunit printing divisions of conglomerates such as Litton Industries, GAF and Republic. American Can, for example, acquired more than forty printing firms and American Standard took in more than twenty.

Labor Relations. Print shop consolidations and the introduction of new technologies can erode union bargaining power. Whether they do depends on how unions and employers behave in the new environment. NLRB and federal court decisions illustrate the complexity of these relationships and the difficulty of determining motivation. Scott Printing Corporation, for example, was found to have undertaken a sham sale of its New Jersey composition operations in order to avoid continued bargaining with the ITU. Scott sold the operations to J & J House of Composition, with which it had both a buyer-seller product market relationship and an organizational ownership tie. The NLRB reached this conclusion because the contractual terms of sale had never been observed. The two companies instead exchanged business services without making fi-

---

[1]Gregory Giebel, "Corporate Structure, Technology, and the Printing Industry," *Labor Studies Journal* (Winter 1979), p. 235.

nancial compensation and equipment allegedly purchased by J & J actually never left the Scott plant.[2]

In another case the employer did not violate the law, a federal appeals court ruled, when it substituted "cold type" for "hot type" processes and nonunion operators for typesetters. Island Typographers had warned union bargainers repeatedly of its inability to compete with commercial print shops that used unilaterally installed new equipment and hired trainees from outside the bargaining unit. When the union failed to enforce its union shop clause and waited for more than a year before raising the issue in collective bargaining, it relinquished any subsequent claim of bad faith by the employer. Island Typographical had not acted from an antiunion animus said the court, but for legitimate business reasons.[3]

Organizing problems for unions occur when employers move operations from historic print centers to antiunion locations. When GAIU notified a Corinth, Mississippi, printer of its intent to organize the plant and identified members of the in-plant organizing committee, the company immediately fired or laid off all but two of them. The Board found these actions illegal and ordered the workers reinstated with full compensation. About the same time the W. F. Hall Printing Company of Dresden, Tennessee, was found to have violated the law by responding to a GAIU organizing drive with letters to employees asking them to identify union supporters and promising to discipline the sympathizers.[4]

Yet another danger to print unions was alleged by GAIU president Kenneth Brown in 1978, when he warned the union's executive council that the industry trade organization, Printing Industries of America (PIA), had come under the influence of its "right-wing arm," the Master Printers section. He claimed that PIA was now advising and instructing affiliated printers to frustrate collective bargaining and decertify existing locals. The union and the association previously had worked together to promote stable industry conditions. "Those days are gone," Brown said. Instead PIA holds seminars detailing methods of negotiating to impasse, provokes union strikes, and then encourages antiunion movements among the workers, he charged.[5]

---

[2]*Scott Printing Corp.*, 249 NLRB 946, 104 LRRM 1216 (1980).

[3]*Island Typographers, Inc.*, 252 NLRB 9, 105 LRRM 1455 (1980), sub nom. *NLRB v. Island Typographers, Inc.*, 705 F.2d 44, 113 LRRM 2207 (CA 2, 1983).

[4]*Hall of Mississippi, Inc.*, 249 NLRB 775, 104 LRRM 1541 (1980); *W. F. Hall Printing Co.*, 250 NLRB 803, 104 LRRM 1445 (1980).

[5]GAIU, *Union Tabloid*, (May/June 1978), p. 7.

Economic Bargaining in Chain Shops. Aside from the difficulties of organizing workers following ownership consolidations and production relocations, unions also have problems negotiating contracts with these subsidiaries. Chain-owned print shops are formidable strike opponents because parent companies have "deep-pocket" financial resources to combat union job actions. Two cases demonstrate the shift in bargaining power that occurs.

In May 1974, GAIU struck Kable Printing, a Midwest magazine printing subsidiary of Western Publishing Co., itself a diversified publisher and manufacturer of entertainment products. At issue was Kable's introduction of a new printing operation and use of nonunion workers. (This was one of several disputes involving unions and the printing divisions of Western Publishing.) For years Kable refused to settle with two GAIU locals, during which it maintained partial production with nonunion labor. It then closed the facility. Kable consistently lost money during the stoppage, but the parent company remained profitable and therefore was able to subsidize the struck operations. The dispute lasted six and one-half years and was not settled until late 1980, after Western had sold Kable to Providence Gravure, which maintained friendly relations with GAIU. Providence soon settled with the Kable workers along the lines of its other GAIU contracts and reopened the closed plant.

Printing unions also experience concession demands from individual units of multiplant employers. This occurred in GAIU's 1977 bargaining with the Banta Division of George Banta Company, a privately held concern, in a Wisconsin plant. Banta insisted that the GAIU locals, one representing bookbinders and the other lithographers, accept a longer workweek, reduced cost-of-living payments, and curtailed health benefits. If they refused, warned Banta, the plant might have to be closed for economic reasons. Both locals struck and also brought NLRB charges claiming Banta had instigated an unfair labor practice strike. A subsequent voluntary settlement by the parties and the NLRB resolved the charges, but the company later withdrew from the agreement and had to be ordered by the Board and a federal appeals court to comply.

The Banta dispute split the workers. A number of union members returned to work in the struck facility, but the majority stayed out for the entire seven months. Some union concessions were made in the final settlement, which caused concern in other Wisconsin locals of GAIU that the Banta outcome would establish a precedent for concession bargaining by them. Several Banta strikers were discharged either during the walkout or immediately after, when the company allowed some strikers to return to work but gave job and seniority preferences to those who had deserted the union. The NLRB agreed with the union that this was improper and ordered Banta to abandon its plan and reinstate and compensate discharged unionists who had done nothing to warrant disciplinary action.

An encouraging result of the Banta strike for the union was that it convinced workers they needed to merge their previously independent locals. The merger brought together in a single unit the unskilled, female, and low-paid bookbinders and the skilled, male, high-paid lithographers. Continued separation of these workers following union consolidation at the national level has hampered GAIU effectiveness locally.

Union Responses. Print union responses to environmental change in commercial printing are to prepare members to operate new equipment—rather than try to block its introduction—but to resist employer efforts to escape unionization or weaken standards through structural reorganization and relocation of operations. This policy is reflected in GAIU's model contract, the provisions of which reportedly have been negotiated successfully in a majority of its bargaining units covering lithographers and photoengravers. Employers are required to contribute financially to a training fund for apprentices and a retraining program for journeymen "who may be or are displaced because their jobs were affected by technological changes." According to the union, more than 12,000 printers were trained between 1966 and 1980.

In addition, new or improved machines and processes must be operated by members of the bargaining unit under terms agreed upon by a union-management committee. The union must be notified of such changes 90 days in advance. If the employer fails to comply with all of the contract provisions on technological change, the new "equipment shall not be operated." The employer also recognizes the need for "retraining or rehabilitation of employees in new skills required so that there shall be no layoffs as a result of the introduction of new types of equipment or new processes."

In the matter of chain print-shops, the union may refuse to do work from struck plants owned by the same employer or operated commonly by legally separate firms. Employers are not allowed to use lithographic and photoengraved work produced in any foreign country other than Canada. They also may not transfer equipment in order to escape the contract, or subcontract work where the effect is to reduce the size of the bargaining unit or delay the recall of laid-off members.

The union has also taken steps to organize the relevant work force as a means of maintaining its bargaining power. To combat decertification drives, plant relocations, and the growth of non-union printing operations, delegates to the GAIU's 1980 national convention ratified an increase in dues to finance the addition of several international organizers to work with local unions "in order to stay abreast of the times," as GAIU's president put it.[6]

Newspapers

Daily and weekly newspapers are the third largest source of manufacturing jobs in this country after motor vehicles and steel. While the latter two industries are declining in employment, newspaper jobs are increasing. But the number of blue-collar workers is not growing. While the newspaper industry employed 7 percent more workers in 1980 than in 1977, the number of hourly production workers fell by 2 percent, and from 43 to 39 percent of overall employment in printing.

Changing Technology. New technology is responsible for most of the decline. "The newspaper industry was static" until the 1960s, observed a top official of the publishers association. "Now it is undergoing a complete technological change in virtually every department." The microelectronic system outlined in Diagram 1 enables newspapers to trim labor requirements and cut production costs sharply. It generates type directly from news and advertising copy and assembles entire pages for the pressroom.

Conversion of communications information to an electronic form makes possible national newspapers like *The Wall Street Journal.* The *Journal*'s satellite network converts a newspaper page into a series of electronic impulses; these are transmitted to a satellite which relays them to a dozen *Journal* printing plants across the country. Laser beam technology translates the impulses into press plates, and regional plants print from the plates for distribution the next morning. Satellite transmission gives national newspapers enormous competitive advantage over local and regional dailies because the small lead time they require enables them to run standardized national campaigns by corporate advertisers.

Industry Trends. Newspapers are a statistically decentralized industry but the figures are misleading. In 1972, the top four news-

---

[6]*AFL-CIO News*, August 2, 1980, p. 3.

paper chains accounted for 17 percent of industry sales and the largest 20 firms for 44 percent. This understates the practical level of concentration, however, because most cities are served by one local paper. In 1980, just 34 cities in the United States had competing daily newspapers.

The concentration ratio also is increasing rapidly. The top twenty newspaper chains probably control more than half of the industry. Mergers and acquisitions have created some two hundred publishing chains which own nearly two-thirds of the nation's papers.

Gannett, the largest chain, in 1982 owned 88 daily and 32 weekly papers and also controlled seven TV and 13 radio stations, an outdoor advertising company, and TV production and satellite information subsidiaries. In 1983 it began publishing the nation's first general-interest national daily newspaper—*USA Today*, which has a five-year target circulation of 2.4 million. That goal, if achieved, would give Gannett newspapers more than five million daily readers nationwide.

Chain ownership usually leads to increased advertising and circulation revenues in acquired papers. In addition, labor costs often are reduced through elimination of editorial staff and production employees. Most chains are profitable, productive enterprises which have the ability to pay higher labor costs.

Numerous big-city dailies have failed in recent years, but the largest survivors are prosperous. Thirteen large papers averaged nearly twice the rate of return after taxes in 1976 as that of all *Fortune 500* companies. During 1976–80, publishing was more profitable than industry generally and several of the same chains, including *The Washington Post, Capital Cities Communications, Times Mirror*, and *Gannett*, were among the most profitable.

Consolidation and diversification make chain publishers less dependent on the financial performance of one or a few subsidiaries. As a result they are formidable opponents at the bargaining table. When combined with changing print technology, the effect is to diminish further the established power of unions.

Big-city newspapers increasingly are organized as communications holding companies. The *New York Times* and *The Washington Post* typify the structure. In 1980, the *Times* was one of 29 subsidiaries owned by its parent, the New York Times Company, whose holdings included a chain of Florida newspapers, three book publishers, two TV and radio stations, microfilm and audio-visual suppliers, and newsprint manufacturing mills in Canada. The *Post* is a subsidiary of the Washington Post Company, which is structured like the New York Times Company, but on a smaller scale. It owns, among other properties, *Newsweek* magazine, newspapers in New Jersey and Washington, and newsprint mills. During the 1970s both the *Times* and the *Post* were embroiled in labor disputes with printer unions over technology and job control.

The New York Times. Changes in corporate organization and machine capability at the *Times* reversed the balance of bargaining power long held by the New York print crafts, especially ITU Local 6. In 1970, Local 6 forced the *Times* to accept a 43 percent wage increase over three years and continuation of a previously negotiated ban on job-displacing machinery. To the new publisher of the *Times*, it was, in his words, a "reasonably humiliating experience." He resolved to reverse what he saw as a fatalistic attitude by *Times* management toward union bargaining power and to restore management control over the paper's composition and press rooms.[7]

Technology offered him a way to achieve these ends. By the time union contracts expired in 1973, the environment was quite different from the past. A storeroom full of computerized typesetting machines and a more diversified corporate structure made the paper almost invulnerable to union pressures. If there was a strike the machines could be quickly brought into service. What financial losses the paper might incur during the transition could be easily absorbed by the parent company's other businesses. Whereas in 1970 the *Times* represented 80 percent of the parent company's profits, in 1974 it accounted for 60 percent.[8] Able to make its own demands, the *Times* insisted that Local 6 agree to total automation in return for job guarantees. Union members rejected the proposal, but when the contract expired they chose not to strike.

After several months of talks, neither the ITU nor any other *Times* union had settled. Management meanwhile prepared for a strike by training the paper's nonunion employees in cold type operations. One by one the other unions signed contracts, until finally the ITU accepted an unprecedented 11-year pact. It allowed the

---

[7]Sheldon Zalaznik, "The Evolution of a Pleasant Young Man," *New York Magazine*, May 6, 1974.

[8]In 1976 the New York Times Company made $6.8 million in gross profits from its Florida and North Carolina dailies, a 24 percent rate of return on sales; the same year it realized $10.2 million from the *Times*, down from $23 million in 1973, for a 3.5 percent return. William Jones and Laird Anderson, "Press Concentration," *The Washington Post*, July 24, 1977, p. D-1. The paper accounted for 71 percent of the holding company's revenues in 1974, but only half its profits, and employed five of every six of its workers, *Editor and Publisher*, February 14, 1975.

Times to automate the composing room in return for lifetime job guarantees for printers whose work would gradually disappear, some 800 workers altogether. The settlement became the pattern for ITU contracts with other New York dailies.

As it turned out, the job guarantee solution was not an ideal one for the displaced typesetters. They were assigned different but noncomparable jobs in terms of skill requirements and work satisfaction. Often they became VDT typists and page pasters. The latter involves pasting paper columns produced by automatic composition machines onto page forms. In time, it too will be automated away.

Times management prepared next for a showdown with pressroom employees over the allegedly wasteful manning requirements under their contract. In 1977, a *Times* executive said that, in the event of an impasse in negotiations, the union did not have the power to inflict "an economic strike that would in any way jeopardize the life of the paper, because the outside publications could carry it indefinitely."[9] The following year, as the *Times* was selling the last of its dismantled linotypes to spare parts dealers and third world publishers, talks with the Pressmen's union became stalemated.

With no contract in force, *Times* management and those at the other two New York dailies unilaterally put into effect the manning requirements they wanted. The pressmen struck all three papers and stayed out for nearly three months. In a demonstration of print craft solidarity, they were joined in the walkout by most other unions; more than 10,000 New York newspaper workers were idled. Soon the *Post*'s management broke ranks and ended its strike with an agreement to accept whatever settlement was eventually reached by the other two. This development put pressure on the *Times* and *News* to find a way to get their papers back on the street.

The only way was to compromise. Pressmen agreed to accept the new presses in return for early retirement. In addition, the publishers agreed to guarantee the jobs of more than a thousand union members and to continue existing manning requirements in the press room. Both sides expressed public satisfaction that the New York pressmen's dispute had neither begun nor ended like one in Washington three years earlier.

The Washington Post. Katherine Graham, *Post* publisher and

---

[9]William H. Jones and Laird Anderson, "The Old Gray Lady Gets a Face-Lifting," *The Washington Post*, July 25, 1977, p. D-10.

Washington Post Company president, announced at the 1974 shareholders' meeting that "costs and manpower assigned to production—not editorial extravagance—have held down the *Post*'s profitability in recent years." Introduction of new machines and electronic technology was the answer, she said, if the necessary work rule changes could be negotiated. "The Post will no longer seek peace at any price from the unions," she warned, referring to the paper's history of settling disputes without walkouts but under terms favorable to labor.[10] When a strike was called later by the ITU over technology, it was a brief one and ended in a six-year agreement similar to those in New York—lifetime jobs for 690 *Post* typographers in return for complete automation.

The Pressmen's contract came up next. In view of what would happen, it is curious that relationships between the *Post* and the union had been so harmonious that Pressmen's Local 6 once made Eugene Meyer, Katherine Graham's father and former *Post* owner, an honorary union member. But now the paper prepared for a showdown with the local over manning requirements.

Management came to the table prepared. Among other measures, dozens of the *Post*'s nonunion employees had been trained to operate the latest presses. When the contract expired without a settlement, management scrapped the old work rules and implemented new ones to eliminate jobs and reduce overtime pay for pressmen. The response from the press room was swift and violent. Irate craftsmen partially smashed the presses and went on strike.

The paper continued publication without missing an issue. Until new presses were installed, the paper was printed elsewhere. Meanwhile, the other unions signed contracts with the *Post*, which claimed that 35 strikebreakers were doing the work normally performed by five times that many pressmen. Local 6 lost not only the strike but also its representational status at the *Post*. As operations returned to normal, about 30 of the former pressmen came back on the job after quitting the union.

The Pressmen suffered similar experiences with newspapers elsewhere, though not as violent as at the *Post*. Pressmen's union president Sol Fishko, like his predecessor in the 1912 Chicago news-

---

[10]*Editor and Publisher*, April 13, 1974, p. 11. The *Post*'s new policy began in 1972 when the paper continued publishing during a 16-day strike by the Guild, using executives and other nonunion personnel. In an address to shareholders that year, Graham said of the strike-breaking action: "I think the point has been made. We are determined, and I think our credibility has been established." William H. Jones, "Post. Co. Emphasizes Stand on Cost Control," *The Washington Post*, May 9, 1972, p. D-17.

paper strike, accused publishers of having "an organized plan" to provoke strikes and escape their bargaining obligations. He acknowledged that in such confrontations, the union usually could not enforce established work rules. "Manning used to be sacred with our locals," he told labor writer Abe Raskin, "now nothing is sacred anymore. Each new development makes the presses simpler to operate and our people easier to replace."[11]

Capital Cities Communications. Fishko may have had Capital Cities Communications in mind. One of the most widely publicized instances of conflict bargaining in printing involves a Pennsylvania subsidiary of Capital Cities. Four newspaper crafts in the Wilkes-Barre area struck the paper and eventually started a rival publication.

Capital Cities, then the nation's twelfth largest chain and owner of more than a dozen radio and TV stations, acquired the *Wilkes-Barre Times Leader* in 1978. Within months of the acquisition, local management wanted the unions to give up work rules on manning requirements, overtime pay, and job security. Wages were not an issue. Showing considerable organizational unity, the unions adopted the slogan, "Four Blocks of Anthracite," after the solidity of the region's coal beds, and uniformly rejected *Times Leader* demands. Each called a strike.

Capital Cities sent in strikebreakers from its other newspapers and constructed chain fences around the Wilkes-Barre plant. Predictably, a rash of violent confrontations broke out between union pickets and a security agency hired to protect the strikebreakers and the plant. Capital Cities filed NLRB charges and the unions later agreed under Board stipulation to stop coercing, assaulting, and otherwise harrassing *Times Leader* workers and those of companies doing business with the struck paper, and to bargain in good faith with the paper over a new contract.[12]

A more creative response by the unions was to publish *Citizens' Voice*, a rival newspaper put together by union strikers. A staunch union community, Wilkes-Barre was ideal for such a tactic. Regular readers abandoned the struck daily and subscribed to the *Voice*. Advertisers followed the readers, and the union paper soon claimed larger circulation and more ad revenues than the *Times Leader*. Capital Cities was forced to subsidize the subsidiary. By 1981, it

---

[11]A. H. Raskin, "The Big Squeeze on Labor Unions," *Atlantic* (October 1978), p. 46.

[12]*Wilkes-Barre Printing Pressmen and Assistants Union, Local 137, et al.*, NLRB, Case No. DS-1309, January 24, 1981; *Wilkes-Barre Printing Pressmen and Assistants Union, Local 137, et. al*, NLRB, Case No. DS-1449, February 2, 1981.

conceded that the *Times Leader* was losing about $3 million a year. This was better, however, than the $6.4 million it lost during the first year of the strike. Capital Cities chairman Tom Murphy admitted it had been a mistake to buy theWilkes-Barre paper, but that the strike "is a price we're willing to pay" to change union work rules.

By 1983, all four of the striking unions had been decertified in NLRB elections. Only new employees at the *Times Leader* were eligible to vote in the decertification elections. Union picketing and bargaining activities ceased and the opposing sides settled into a war of attrition over circulation and advertising revenues.

Capital Cities newspapers in Michigan and Missouri also were involved in serious labor disputes. At the *Oakland Press* in Pontiac, Michigan, the Company again used imported strikebreakers; at the *Kansas City Star*, key crafts were unable to renegotiate their contracts and some employee benefits were unilaterally discontinued.[13] In response to these conflicts, the AFL-CIO added Capital Cities to its national boycott list in 1983. Later that year a "corporate accountability" group was organized by the Kansas City typesetters. The group submitted a resolution at the Capital Cities shareholder meeting calling on management to report on its labor policies and practices. Although the resolution was defeated, it reportedly got the largest ratio of the votes in the initial attempt of any such union corporate campaign.

Construction

The construction industry is distributed among a half million building and engineering firms. They range in size from the hundreds of thousands of specialty trades, to a much smaller number of general contractors that manage individual building projects and subcontract work to the trades, to several dozen huge firms which perform general and heavy contracting work, undertake large engineering projects, and provide construction management services. While the industry is known for its structural fragmentation, it is becoming mildly concentrated in heavy construction, where four large companies—Brown & Root, Fleur, Parsons, and Bechtel—control 10 to 15 percent of sales. The top 29 firms account for one-

---

[13]*Oakland Press Co.*, 229 NLRB No. 77, 96 LRRM 1542 (1977); *Local 13, GAIU and the Oakland Press Co.*, 233 NLRB 994, 97 LRRM 1047 (1977).

half. Since heavy construction represents about half of the industry's total sales, these 29 firms control roughly one-quarter of the industry.

The construction work force is larger than that in most industries and occupations. Because of the highly cyclical nature of the building industry, the number of workers fluctuates from year to year. In 1980, 3.5 million construction workers were employed domestically, compared to 3 million in 1977 and 3.6 million in 1979. They worked in more than two dozen basic and specialty trades, and together made up about 80 percent of total construction industry employment, down from 90 percent in the 1950s.

If residential housing is excluded because of its low level of unionization, it is estimated that perhaps three out of every five construction workers were covered by union contracts in the 1960s. The ratios differed widely among crafts, industry sectors, and geographic regions, of course, in response to differences in their environments.

Levels of unionization have generally declined since then, however. A number of industry trends account for this change. Most involve the large wage and benefit differentials and the differences in working conditions that exist between union and nonunion construction labor. When combined with the apparent easy availability of craft labor to work under nonunion terms, the result is a weakening of bargaining power.

Large contractors such as Brown & Root are nonunion operators; previously unionized general contractors affiliate with the Associated Builders and Contractors and declare that they are open shop employers; and many union contractors establish open shop subsidiaries, commonly called "double-breasted" operations, and transfer work out of the unionized subsidiary. These and other initiatives have cut sharply into construction union representation in all parts of the country.

The most common union response to these organizational threats involves cooperative agreements with union contractors and negotiated contract concessions to make them competitive with open shop firms. In early 1984, for example, the Washington, D.C., Building and Construction Trades Council worked out an agreement with the Construction Contractors Council to reduce union labor costs an estimated 20 percent. Nonunion builders, which formerly controlled no more than 25 percent of the work, had captured about 90 percent of all construction in the District. Of the 20 affiliated craft unions, 15 formally participated in this effort to reverse a dramatic decline in organized labor's share of the region's annual $3 billion market construction work.[14]

Local Craft Bargaining in Construction

A case study of two rounds of local contract negotiations in the construction industry illustrates craft bargaining. These talks occurred in 1974 and 1978 and involved the International Brotherhood of Electrical Workers, Local 367, Easton, Pennsylvania, and the Easton Division of the Penn-Del-Jersey Chapter of the National Electrical Contractors Association. Local 367 has jurisdiction over "inside construction" in four counties in Pennsylvania and two in New Jersey, a geographic area that includes both urban and rural labor markets.

Like other construction unions, Local 367 determines its bargaining demands and strategy according to the current state of the industry. Building activities fluctuate widely according to shifts in general economic conditions and changes in federal government monetary and fiscal policies. Construction unions therefore try to bargain substantial wage gains and innovative benefits when activity is brisk, and are content with smaller gains during recessions.

In early 1974 the economic environment for Local 367 negotiators was as good as it had been in years. All of its members were working, and employers were advertising for additional help. A sharp recession would begin later that year, but when the local developed its demands in the winter of 1974, the national unemployment rate for construction was relatively low by historical standards.

Employer ability to pay in construction is related less to contractor profit margins than to the amount of work being done and the corresponding manpower needs of union contractors. Through its own sources, the local was able to document for bargaining purposes more than $100 million in area nonresidential projects either underway or in the bidding process and a soon-to-begin $56 million power plant project; another long-term utility job was still in progress. Finally, in terms of its ability to make employers pay higher labor costs, the union pointed out that nearly half of the projects cited came under Davis-Bacon federal law requirements that hourly labor be paid the prevailing (i.e., negotiated) wage scale. It also re-

---

[14]Peter Perl, "Building Trades Unions Offer Labor-Cost Cut," *The Washington Post*, February 11, 1984, p. A-1.

minded employers that in previous years union members had performed all the prevailing wage work done in the area.

The Easton Division of the tri-state chapter of NECA bargains for all union contractors that are or will be doing work in Local 367's jurisdiction. About 100 firms are affiliated. Actual negotiations are conducted by three-member teams on each side, which bargain the contract and also meet at least once each month to discuss all labor relations matters involving the electrical trade in that area. Nine other IBEW locals represent inside workers in adjacent geographic areas or, in one instance, outside workers in the same geographic region. The outside local does not negotiate independent economic terms, but simply accepts the settlement reached by Local 367 and the NECA branch.

Local 367's three-member bargaining committee is headed by Andrew Cuvo, business manager. He is chief spokesman at the bargaining table. Six months before contract expiration the committee solicits suggestions for bargaining demands from the rank-and-file members. This kind of participation, Cuvo says, gives the committee an indication of what the members will ratify in a final settlement and guards against "panic" among the members to pressure the committee into accepting too little in the settlement during economic hard times. "We do not allow the rank-and-file to dictate to us," he says.

At the local's initial strategy session in 1974, Cuvo indicated he would be principal negotiator and stressed that no disagreement among committee members should be shown at the table—if someone disagreed with the union position on an issue under discussion, his instructions were to shift the talks to another topic and then call a union recess where the matter could be argued privately. Cuvo was adamant on committee members observing this rule. In previous negotiations the union had detected and exploited divisions among association committee members. This time, indeed, Cuvo planned to make use of his knowledge that the association's chief negotiator, a leading area contractor, was bidding on a major project and therefore hoped to avoid labor trouble once the building season started. The contract was due to expire in June.

Overall union bargaining strategy rested on the comparability argument. Contracts negotiated by nine other IBEW locals having adjacent jurisdictions to Local 367 had a 12 percent higher average differential in total hourly compensation than the Local 367 contract. Because seven of them were also due to renegotiate contracts at the same time, the differential would be widened if Local 367 did not make comparable wage gains. Full employment conditions in the trade gave force to Cuvo's suggestions to association negotiators that this wage difference might result in labor shortages. "We argued that with all the upcoming work," he recalled, "we would find it very difficult to supply area contractors with men at the low package rate they were offering."

The local's economic goals in the 1974 talks were substantial. It wanted a two-dollar-per-hour economic package in a two-year contract. This demand represented a 21 percent increase in the current $9.60 average total hourly compensation. The local also was demanding an increase from two to four hours of pay for workers who show up on scheduled work days but find there is no work, as well as an equity wage increase for assistant foremen. Lesser items which the committee was prepared to "trade away" for the priority items included appointment of a small-job foreman where two or more journeymen are working and reverse layoff procedures.

Initial union proposals were inflated above the terms the organization actually expected to obtain. Local negotiators demanded a 25 percent increase in the hourly package in a one-year agreement, substantial increases in wage differentials favoring the foreman classifications, and the "trade away" items.

Following two "skirmish" sessions, members of the employer committee presented counterproposals. They offered a 12.5 percent increase in the hourly compensation package over three years. They also wanted to eliminate a small employer contribution to the apprentice training fund and to renegotiate the entire matter when the fund dropped below a certain amount. Finally, they demanded local union concessions on economic standards for work done in connection with building maintenance contracts, which they argued were needed to make association members more competitive against nonunion bids on maintenance contracts. First, they wanted to pay only 80 percent instead of the full wage for maintenance work, broadly defined, and only time-and-one-half rather than the standard double-time for overtime maintenance work. Second, they insisted on paying a lower hourly wage rate on all projects of less than $50,000.

By the sixth bargaining session, in early June, the association had increased its offer to a 16.5 percent increase in the total hourly package, which would be distributed evenly over three years (53¢–53¢–53¢), plus their initial demands for union concessions.

No one expected the union to agree to these initial terms, so now the serious bargaining began. Agreement was reached at the next session, in mid-June. The union got the hourly package it wanted: $1.80 in wage increases spread over two years, and an additional 35 cents-per-hour in wages for general foremen. In return, however, it agreed that, although regular work on maintenance contracts would pay the full wage rate, overtime work would not receive double-time wages except on Sundays and holidays. It was understood by the parties that if these terms resulted in loss of maintenance contracts to nonunion contractors, a rate of 80 percent of the full-scale formula would become effective on those jobs. Employer contributions to the apprentice training fund would also be reduced by half.

The remaining adjacent locals settled their contract negotiations shortly afterward, following the same general pattern, with the result that the existing differentials in total hourly compensation were maintained. Contracts covering work done east of Local 367 jurisdiction, into New Jersey, provided slightly higher wages; those to the west, in rural Pennsylvania, somewhat lower.

Because of the severity of the 1974-75 recession, the anticipated total number of building projects in the local's jurisdiction did not materialize. Construction employment both nationally and locally fell sharply.

The second round of contract negotiations between Local 367 and the NECA branch occurred in 1978, but in a different environment than in 1974. The national open-shop drive in construction had begun to affect industry negotiations in nearby labor markets. A council of 20 Philadelphia-area construction unions had made substantial concessions in contract bargaining with union contractors. Loss of jobs to nonunion firms had prompted them to accept a multicraft, unprecedented three-year contract which called for a $1.50 wage increase in three 50¢-per-year increments.

These developments encouraged employer associations in adjacent labor markets to ask their unions for similar concessions. They argued that nonunion competition was an increasing threat to both contractors and unions. As a result, one IBEW local close to Philadelphia settled for a $1.10 increase in total hourly compensation over two years. A regional New Jersey-Pennsylvania construction settlement pattern began to emerge when several local unions accepted two and three-year agreements of roughly 70-cent hourly wage increases in each year. Meanwhile, negotiations in other New Jersey units reached impasses over union resistance to comparable concessions. The issue in 1978 area negotiations was whether contractors would impose upon local unions a concession pattern that the industry had originated elsewhere, in place of traditional union pattern bargaining.

The Easton NECA branch came to the table in January 1978 with 29 separate contract demands. Local 367 presented 16 demands. Most employer proposals involved union concessions. Among them were a three-year wage moratorium; elimination of an existing contract provision under which local members working in a New Jersey county received the higher IBEW wage negotiated in that area; elimination of existing wage differentials between subforemen on large and small projects; reduction of the employer annuity fund contribution for new apprentices; and establishment of a secondary wage scale for certain projects that would be several dollars below existing hourly rates.

Union demands included a 10 percent package in each year of a three-year contract (about $1.33 per year) and inclusion of a work preservation clause in the contract that would prohibit union firms from performing work under nonunion conditions, that is, under special subcontracting arrangements or through nonunion subsidiary operations. The last was aimed at suspected "double-breasted" structures which circumvent the union contract.

By mid-April 1978, the parties had met six times. The association's last offer was for 60 cents per hour in wages over three years, contingent upon union acceptance of the same four concessions the employers had proposed in January. The union's final position was for 90 cents in wages for one year (a 6.7 percent increase) and rejection of the contractors' other demands. Informally, however, the parties were not that far apart. The union's "off the record" minimum acceptance level was 65 cents per hour in wages in each year of a two-year agreement and no concessions in other areas. The association's unofficial maximum offer was $1.10 in wages in a two-year contract but with the secondary wage rate concession. Both sides stood firm in their official demands, and the talks stalemated.

With further progress unlikely and the contract about to expire, the parties submitted their differences to the electrical industry's Council on Industrial Relations. The Council was established in the early 1920s primarily to make binding decisions in disputes between local contractors and unions. Its twelve members are divided evenly between NECA and IBEW. All decisions reached at its quarterly meetings must be unanimous. Affiliated contractors and local unions normally are required by their respective organizations to go to the Council in the event of an impasse; there is no internal industry appeal from the Council decisions by either party.

Procedurally, each disputant submits a written statement of its position in the matter, has an opportunity to follow this with oral arguments before the Council, and may offer rebuttal arguments against the position of the other party. Council members may question the parties personally before deciding the case.

In their written submission, the Easton employers defended their long-term proposal as "an essential ingredient for good business management" and in keeping with a general trend in construction. Regarding their demands for wage moderation, they argued there was "a dim outlook for new work in the near future in this area . . . due to inflationary wages and increasing competition from nonunion contractors." These considerations, they said, also justified the secondary wage rate and other specified union concessions. They dismissed the union's demand to prohibit nonunion operations by union contractors on the grounds that it is an issue on which employers are not legally required to bargain.

Local 367's statement offered a "more optimistic" outlook for future job opportunities. Partly on that basis, the union rejected the association's position. It discarded all concession proposals as unacceptable attempts to take away work standards that had been agreed upon by the parties. It defended the union's proposed work preservation clause as something more than a union attempt to preserve jobs. Employers themselves were concerned with "double-breasted" competitors. Individual employers "often complain to this local that they *suspect* another contractor of operating 'double-breasted,' " the union document said.

In his oral argument to the Council, Cuvo criticized the association's attempt to use the Philadelphia settlement as an economic pattern. "I agree with the area contractors' evaluation of [that] multicraft agreement. It is a good agreement for an area that loses practically all of the school and city work to nonunion employers," he observed, "an area where practically every job is plagued by authorized and unauthorized work stoppages and other labor problems." However, he added, the agreement "should not be forced on any local union that controls its work force and has had absolutely no work stoppages for the past six years."

A month after these presentations the Council reported its decision. Wages were increased by $1.40 in a two-year agreement; the hourly package totaled $1.56. All employer proposals to change existing wage and benefit standards were denied, as was the union's work preservation clause. For this reason and because the wage increase awarded by the Council was above the local's unofficial minimum acceptable figure, the union claimed victory in the Council's action.

Summary

Craft bargaining survives mainly in decentralized industries populated by medium and small-sized firms. It also persists in the consolidated service industries characterized until recently by government regulation. Craft unions have natural bargaining power because in most instances employers can neither produce without their members nor easily replace them during stoppages.

Favorable conditions for union bargaining power occur most often in industries featuring "spatial limitations," where geography, regulation, or technology restrict industry production to particular locations or established firms. The relevant work force is clearly defined and easily accessible for union organizing efforts. Employers doing business under these spatial limitations can pay higher labor costs by adding them to product prices.

It must be noted, however, that established craft power is vulnerable to environmental change. Industrial reorganization, technological innovation, or a shift in public policy can undermine union power by disrupting established bargaining structures and procedures. A change in corporate structure may result in a relocation of production operations or in a different relevant work force, one which the union cannot organize. New machines and production processes might de-skill crafts which had been essential to production, or they could blur traditional craft boundaries, jurisdictions, and bargaining structures. A change in public policy toward the industry, such as deregulation or the removal of a protective trade barrier, could expose previously sheltered businesses and unions to low-cost, nonunion competitors.

Printing. Commercial and newspaper printing are related industries in which craft unions have had historical bargaining power. As technology created new production methods, emerging crafts formed their own unions to claim jurisdiction over the expanding operations. The distinctive job culture which evolved around each craft, together with its natural bargaining power, resulted in independent but effective union structures. While a determined employer like Hearst could exploit craft fragmentation and even defeat or contain the print unions for a time, the crafts typically dominated labor relations in major commercial print centers and urban newspapers.

Craft earnings and benefits in the postwar years normally were superior and union work rules often were unassailable by management. Individual crafts negotiated separate agreements with area employers, contracts which typically contained strict working rules on behalf of union employees. Industrial sociologists reported that print craftsmen were among the most satisfied workers and loyal union members.

Toward the end of the 1960s, the environment began to change. A technological revolution swept the printing industry. Some crafts were eliminated while others were raised in importance. In commercial print shops, the crafts associated with "hot type" technology have been adversely affected while those based on "cold type" methods have fared better. The overall effect on craft power is ironical. The structural segmentation that had been a source of union strength became an organizational impediment to flexible union responses. Job attrition contracts negotiated by metropolitan dailies, which now are subsidiaries of large publishing chains, set the pattern for similar arrangements and other concessions in smaller cities and daily papers. Craft strikes against large, diversified employers are no longer as effective as before, because production decisions are centralized and therefore not accountable to local unions and production locations often are moved beyond union reach.

Printing unions adapt to changing conditions by consolidating crafts through organizational mergers, by providing skill retraining to members so that they can keep abreast of new technologies and job opportunities, and by assisting local unions in negotiating model contract language to protect individual bargaining units against hostile environments. They also appear to be more committed to organizing the unorganized than in the past.

Construction. Changing structures and conditions also have undermined the customary bargaining power of construction unions. Like the printers, building trades unions were effective at the bargaining table because of their craft independence and irreplaceable job skills. However, changes outside their scope of influence shifted the balance of power. Open shop contractors claimed increasing shares of the work, as much as 60 percent by the early 1980s. Soaring interest rates sent new construction starts plunging, and unemployment levels in the building industry rose to record highs, further dampening craft bargaining gains. In 1982, for the first time in years, negotiated wage increases in construction trailed those in all industries.

Bargaining in construction is sensitive to current economic conditions and industry trends. This is seen in the two rounds of contract negotiations between an IBEW local and the contractors' organization in the Easton, Pennsylvania, area. The union took advantage of brisk industry activity prior to the 1974–75 recession to negotiate a substantial two-year economic package, but four years later the environment was less favorable. By that time, the open shop movement was becoming a factor in the industry and pressuring unionized contractors to narrow labor cost differentials with nonunion competitors.

This trend presented a problem for the Easton local. Building trades in nearby labor markets had made contract concessions before it started to negotiate. But union resistance at the bargaining table and a favorable award from the electrical industry's joint union-management arbitration committee prevented area contractors from eroding negotiated standards in Easton.

Craft Resistance. Although customarily associated with strong economic settlements, craft unions in printing and construction now represent workers in rapidly changing industries. The first instinct of craft workers and unions is to resist the introduction of new machines, to preserve established union work rules, and to maintain craft integrity and union influence. Craft unions are the standard bearers of an earlier industrial culture. In the end, however, the union's initial response must give way to the power of change. The usual fallback position is to compromise with the new process or structure in order to preserve as many jobs and conditions as possible.

It is to be expected that individuals and organizations will oppose the dismantling of a system that protects their interests in an economic system of competing organized interests. It is especially rational for endangered crafts to resist if it looks as though their interests will not be protected in the new institutional arrangement. To be effective now, the crafts will have to exhibit extraordinary imagination, flexibility, and tenacity. Each is threatened by one or more of the trends in structure, technology, and policy. However, each also has a history to draw upon—unique characteristics that are rooted in job, culture, and experiences.

Key Words and Phrases

nonconcentrated local
  industries
craft solidarity
cold type vs. hot type
chain print shops and chain
  newspapers

"double-breasted" companies
negotiated hourly package
employer bargaining association
Council on Industrial Relations

Review and Discussion Questions

1. Explain why craft unions typically have bargaining power. Identify and describe the kinds of changes in the external environment that weaken craft union power.

2. Would labor in the commercial printing industry have greater bargaining power if one union combined all the workers? Should one union represent workers in both commercial and newspaper printing?

3. Why should a local union in the newspaper industry be concerned whether the employer is part of a chain of newspapers?

4. It was explained in Chapter 3 that productivity gains are a basis for higher wages. Why then do printing unions oppose the introduction of new technology by employers?

5. Are the sources of union bargaining power in the construction industry similar to those of unions in printing? Are there any differences due to dissimilar industry structures and environments?

6. Explain the importance of "double-breasted" construction company organization for union bargaining power. Devise a union strategy in response to this structural change.

7. What role did negotiated work rules play in the construction bargaining case study in this chapter? Did the eventual negotiated outcomes involving work rules accurately reflect relative bargaining power in this instance?

8. Discuss the pros and cons of this statement: small unions do not have the resources to protect their members from the adverse effects of environmental change; therefore *any* national union that has fewer than 50,000 members should merge either with a much larger union or with several other small unions.

Chapter Resources and Suggested Further Reading

Information on early craft bargaining is from Gary M. Fink, ed., *Labor Unions* (1977); Robert F. Hoxie, *Trade Unionism in the United States* (1917).

Discussion of the history of printing unions and collective bargaining is based on George E. Barnett, "Collective Bargaining in the Typographical Union," in Jacob H. Hollander and George E. Barnett, eds., *Studies in American Trade Unionism, (1912)* (1970); George E. Barnett, *Chapters on Machinery and Labor, (1926)* (1969); Philip Taft, "The Limits of Labor Unity: The Chicago Newspaper Strike of 1912," *Labor History* (Winter 1978); Elizabeth Baker, *Printers and Technology* (1957).

Recent developments in printing are described in Gregory Giebel, "Corporate Structure, Technology, and the Printing Industry," *Labor Studies Journal* (Winter 1979); Andrew Zimbalist, "Technology and the Labor Process in the Printing Industry," in Andrew Zimbalist, ed., *Case Studies on the Labor Process* (1979); Theresa F. Rogers and Natalie S. Friedman, *Printers Face Automation: The Impact of Technology and Retirement Among Skilled Craftsmen*, (1980); U.S. Department of Labor, Bureau of Labor Statistics, *Technological Change and Its Labor Impact in Five Industries*, (1977).

The *Western Publishing* case was reported in "Western Publishing Finds Strikers Fight in Corporate Style," *Wall Street Journal*, April 20, 1977, and "Long Printing Strike Ends as New Owner Signs Pact," *AFL-CIO News*, March 7, 1981. The Banta strike and outcome are described in *George Banta Company, Inc. Banta Division*, 236 NLRB 1559, 98 LRRM 1581 (1978), upheld by the 4th Circuit Court of Appeals, 604 F.2d 830, 101 LRRM 3102 (1980); *George Banta Company, Inc., Banta Division*, 256 NLRB 1197, 107 LRRM 1444 (1981); "The Night the Banta Workers Merged," Graphic Arts International Union, *Union Tabloid* (May/June 1978).

GAIU responses to changing structure and technology in commercial printing are identified in Graphic Arts International Union, *Standard Form Contract Manual* (1976); and GAIU, *Background For Bargaining* (1978).

Information on concentration trends in newspapers and the importance of chain ownership structures is from Ben H. Bagdikian, *The Media Monopoly* (1983); William Jones and Laird Anderson, "Press Concentration," *The Washington Post*, July 24, 1977.

The discussion of labor relations at *The New York Times* is based on Harry Kelber and Carl Schlesinger, *Union Printers and Controlled Automation* (1967); Helen Dewar, "Pressmen Reach Tentative Pact in 84-Day N.Y. Newspaper Strike," *The Washington Post*, November 2, 1978. Bargaining and strikes over technology at *The Washington Post* are described in Ben A. Franklin, "Washington Post Firm Over Strike," *The New York Times*, October 12, 1975; Philip Noble, "High Noon at the Washington Post," *New Times*, November 14, 1975; Shirley Elder, "Journalists vs. The Unions at The Washington Post," *Columbia Journalism Review* (May/June 1976). Discussion of Capital Cities Communications and its subsidiaries is based on Sandra Dorr, "Union Busting Returns to Wilkes-Barre," *In These Times*, November 1-7, 1978; Richard L. Hudson, "Whole City

Feels a Newspaper Strike in Wilkes-Barre, Pa.," *The Wall Street Journal*, March 22, 1979; Allan Sloan and Thomas Baker, "Murphy's Law," *Forbes*, March 16, 1981; William Robbins, "Pennsylvania City Divided by Two Newspapers' War," *The New York Times*, July 26, 1983; "Proxy Vote on Labor Policies Gets 'Attention' of Cap Cities," *AFL–CIO News*, May 21, 1981.

Description of the construction industry is from "The Top 400 Contractors," *Engineering News Record*, April 22, 1982; "Surveys Show Open Shop Surge," *Engineering News Record*, September 17, 1981; U.S. Department of Labor, Labor-Management Services Administration, *The Bargaining Structure in Construction: Problems and Prospects*, by Donald E. Cullen and Louis Feinberg (1980).

Information on bargaining between IBEW Local 367 and the Easton, Pa., chapter of the National Electrical Contractors Association was obtained from documents supplied by Andrew Cuvo, business agent, Local 367, IBEW.

5

Craft Bargaining in the Airlines Industry

The preceding chapter described craft bargaining in decentralized, nonregulated industries. This chapter continues the examination of economic bargaining by craft unions but in a historically concentrated and government regulated industry. Air transportation has been characterized by high levels of unionization among most of the major carriers, fragmented bargaining structures along separate craft or occupational lines, and high wages and benefits and secure working conditions. The industry had the ability to pay, and several but not all of the unions had the ability to make the carriers pay.

In the early 1980s, however, air transportation experienced concession bargaining, entry of nonunion carriers into the industry, and novel bargaining solutions to the operating difficulties of some carriers. These resulted mainly from federal deregulation of airlines in 1978 and the subsequent economic recession.

Industry structure, union representation, and bargaining structure and outcomes before deregulation are discussed in this chapter. It then describes and analyses the impact of deregulation and recession on craft bargaining power. It ends with a consideration of new bargaining responses to the changed environment in air transportation.

The Industry Before Deregulation

Until recently the airline industry was closely regulated by the federal government. Fewer than a dozen trunk carriers dominated the industry. Behind them a group of secondary companies acted as local service companies and feeder lines to the major carriers. There were great disparities in operating size. In 1976, United, the largest carrier, flew 2.5 times the revenue passenger miles of all the secondary companies combined and had 1.6 times their revenues.

Each group was also concentrated. The four largest trunk carriers accounted for more than half the revenues of the majors; the largest four local carriers represented a similar proportion in their class. Occasionally, a secondary carrier would join the ranks of the trunks, as Allegheny Airlines did when it acquired several lesser companies and became USAir, but major carriers never fell to the status of second-tier firms.

Federal regulation resulted in uniform pricing of passenger fares among carriers and exclusive access to routes by individual companies. This effectively blocked the entry of new firms into the industry. Like other oligopolists, trunk airlines developed various nonprice forms of competition, the most important of which was the aircraft fleet. Plane design and engineering determine flying speed and passenger payload, the major determinants of total passenger revenue. Between 1936 and 1970 four rounds of technology advanced commercial aircraft from the DC-3 to the 747 and from speeds of less than 200 to more than 600 miles per hour. Travel range increased by a factor of three and the number of passengers per plane by 20. This made long-distance and transcontinental flights the most efficient and profitable, so trunk lines competed most vigorously for passengers on those routes.

Another form of nonprice competition was personal services. Airlines provided new and imaginative services as a way of luring passengers from rival carriers. Trunk carriers followed United's lead in developing "hub and spoke" facilities in which core cities interconnected the various destinations serviced by the carrier. Hub systems enabled individual carriers to route large numbers of through-fare passengers exclusively on their flights.

Air transport was a rapidly growing industry during the three decades following World War II. Passenger miles more than tripled in the first decade, tripled once more during the second, and grew by nearly that much again in the third. During that time, industry employment also more than tripled, to more than 300,000 in 1977. Growth rates differed among specific crafts and classifications, however. Industry emphasis on nonprice competition partly explains these differences. The number of office employees in the airline labor force declined by nearly half, and that of operating flight personnel including mechanics declined slightly; meanwhile, the number of flight attendants and other passenger service employees more than doubled.

Airline revenues and profits always fluctuate in the short run. Operating revenues depend on the state of the economy and the price of airline tickets. Consumer demand for air travel is sensitive to changes in expendable consumer income and price. If income falls or fares increase, potential air travelers make other plans. Industry profit performance is therefore erratic. Rates of return on capital investment in airlines ranged from 1.24 to 11.8 percent during 1955–68. During the recession of 1970, the ratio fell back to 1.2 percent, rose and fell again in the mid-1970s, and later bounced back with the next recovery.

Industry productivity gains have been impressive. At an annual rate of 12.3 percent during 1947–78, they led all other industries listed in Table 5. Productivity in airlines is measured by changes in the ratio of revenue ton-miles (RTM) to total employees. Average annual increases in RTMs per employee were considerably above the national productivity average for the 1960s because of the replacement of the DC-6 fleet with 707s and 727s. The figure dropped to 4.1 percent during 1968–76, but was still above average.

Major airlines had the ability to pay higher labor costs. Except during economic recessions, the effects of rate regulation, barriers to entry by new firms, and high productivity increases enabled them to pass on negotiated increases in higher fares—subject only to competition from alternative modes of transportation—and to recoup labor costs through productivity.

Airline Unions. Airlines are unionized along craft and occupation lines on a company-by-company basis. The Railway Labor Act which covers the industry specifies that bargaining units be structured along craft or job classification lines. Ratios of unionization generally are highest on the trunks. In the largest four carriers, approximately six of every 10 employees were union members in 1978. Flight crews and ground support workers were organized more thoroughly than were ground passenger service and office employees. The Air Line Pilots Association (ALPA) represented pilots on all major trunks except American and on most local carriers. The International Association of Machinists (IAM) had mechanics under contract on all major carriers except American and Pan Am, where the Transport Workers Union (TWU) was certified. Other crafts and classifications were less effectively organized. Several unions, including independent organizations, represented flight attendants and office employees. This fragmentation by craft and carrier resulted in occasional jurisdictional raiding among unions and decertification elections. The Teamsters, for example, displaced an independent union at Pan Am and Braniff and the IAM at Western and tried unsuccessfully to replace unions at Northwest and National.

Airline unions have not normally cooperated with one another. Their independent bargaining power made cooperation unnecessary, and law and contract prohibitions made it illegal to conduct sympathetic job actions in support of other airline unions.

These factors were noticeable during the 1981 air traffic controllers strike, which was illegal under federal law. ALPA was willing to undermine another craft with which it had organizational differences over the control of flight operations and whose predicament was not directly and immediately hurting the pilots. When the mechanics had struck Northwest earlier that year, the pilots continued working and their union claimed to be "neutral" in the dispute. The machinists, by contrast, aided striking traffic controllers in ways short of sympathetic walkouts, which would have put the union in violation of Railway Labor Act provisions and made it liable for employer damage suits under its contracts with the airlines. This is not the only industry where unions have no history of close cooperation. Printing and construction are two others.

Relative Economic Bargaining Power. Bargaining units in airlines are also fragmented. Each carrier negotiates separately with individual unions for each craft or classification. As Table 10 shows, at the beginning of the 1980s, contract expiration dates were staggered by company, union, and craft. Clear industry patterns do not emerge.

In 1977, the 20 major trunk and local airlines had a total of 134 separate union contracts in effect. In the 1980–81 bargaining round, only the machinists negotiated several common expiration dates among their contracts. The IAM also came closest to establishing comparable settlements.

Prior to airline deregulation, outside observers had endorsed common expiration dates and pattern settlements in the industry to stabilize labor relations and discourage union "whipsawing" of carriers.

Structural conditions made individual carriers vulnerable to strikes and strike threats. They could not maintain operations, legally or practically, if any of the key crafts struck; other carriers got windfall passengers and revenues if one of them was shut down; fixed costs of staying in business remained high during strikes, and

Table 10. Airline Industry Contract Expirations By Unions and Major Airlines, 1980–81

Union	Month and year of expiration	Airline	Craft or classification	Number of workers covered
Machinists	10/81	U.S. Air	Mechanics and others	1,500
	10/81	TWA	Mechanics and others	12,500
	11/81	National (Pan Am)	Mechanics and others	1,500
	11/81	Northwest	Mechanics and others	3,130
	11/81	United	Mechanics and others	18,600
	12/81	Eastern	Mechanics and others	11,500
Airline Pilots Association	7/80	Northwest	Pilots	1,500
	11/80	U.S. Air	Pilots	1,100
	1/81	United	Pilots	6,200
	7/81	Delta	Pilots	3,000
	9/81	TWA	Pilots	4,000
	12/81	Braniff	Pilots	2,000
Allied Pilots Association (Ind)	10/81	American	Pilots	4,000
Transport Workers Union	2/80	American	Mechanics and others	10,300
	7/80	Pan Am	Mechanics and others	6,000
	1/81	National (Pan Am)	Flight Attendants & others	1,400
Teamsters	12/81	Pan Am	Clerical, office, service	7,000
Airline Employees Association (ALPA)	6/80	National (Pan Am)	Clerical, office, service	3,200
	6/80	Republic	Clerical, office, service	1,700
Association of Flight Attendants	4/80	United	Flight Attendants	8,000
Independent Union of Flight Attendants	4/81	Pan Am	Flight Attendants	4,500
Association of Professional Flight Attendants	8/81	American	Flight Attendants	5,400
Flight Attendants (ALPA)	10/81	Republic	Flight Attendants	600

Source: BNA, *Collective Bargaining: Negotiations and Contracts,* "Calendar of Negotiations," 1980 and 1981 (Washington: 1982).

revenues did not recover immediately to their prestrike levels; air travel cannot be stockpiled in anticipation of labor stoppages, as can steel or coal supplies. With fragmented bargaining units, individual unions could impose successively higher settlements upon the single carrier. Airline unions therefore rejected repeated carrier attempts to consolidate industry bargaining structures.[1]

Six of the trunk carriers responded to union power in 1958 with a Mutual Aid Pact (MAP) to discourage strikes. Payments were made into a strike fund by participating lines that were not being struck based on their estimated revenue increases as a result of the dispute plus a share of normal industry sales. The struck carrier was reimbursed for revenue losses out of this fund. By 1969, MAP was reimbursing trunk and local airlines for 35 to 50 percent of normal operating losses during strikes, the actual amount depending on the length of the stoppage. Government approval of MAP and the benefit formula was obtained over union protest. The strike fund was abolished in 1978, however, as part of a political compromise involving passage of airline deregulation legislation.

A study of individual carrier receipts from and payments into MAP during 1958–78 reveals considerable disparity among carriers. Northwest and National, the two most frequently struck companies, netted $188 and $120 million in receipts. National collected $54 million in a single stoppage, a 127-day flight attendants' strike. United and American, on the other hand, contributed a net $173 million. Of the local carriers, Texas International was the leading beneficiary, collecting $9 million during a 124-day strike by its office and service employees. Changes in the frequency and duration of strikes during the two decades of MAP suggest that airline strike insurance made carriers less inclined to settle and instead to take longer strikes than would have been the case otherwise.

Industry strike benefits also may have enabled the largest recipients to hold down their labor costs compared to those of the major contributors by fighting their unions with subsidized strikes. According to industry sources, labor costs as a ratio of revenues for the two leading beneficiaries, Northwest and National, were 27 percent and 37 percent in 1974, while those for United, American, and Eastern, the three largest contributors, averaged 42 percent.[2] As for

---

[1]One explanation for structural fragmentation of airline bargaining is the preference for specific craft and carrier units of the National Railway Labor Act, which was extended to cover air transportation in 1936.

[2]William Carley, "United Airlines Strike Reflects Industry Drive to Curb Labor Costs," *The Wall Street Journal*, May 11, 1979, p. 1.

Texas International, under deregulation it was reorganized as the parent holding company of the leading nonunion carrier based in the North.

Collective Bargaining Outcomes Prior to Deregulation. Data on industry wages and compensation costs are not readily available. Unpublished Labor Department data show that airline employee earnings for comparable job skills are equal or above those in high-wage basic manufacturing and transportation industries. In the course of justifying its Mutual Aid Plan, the industry claimed that from 1967 to 1973, average employee compensation rose by 75 percent in airlines, compared to about 50 percent in all industries. Finally, earnings data based on 1969 population census results show that the average yearly earnings of nonsupervisory airline employees are somewhat higher than those holding comparable job classifications in manufacturing industries. Airline mechanics and typists, for example, made about one-tenth more than the same occupations in all manufacturing. Such comparisons are imprecise, however, and often based on small samples of wage earners.

Bargaining outcomes in airlines typically follow the pattern established by one craft and a key carrier. It becomes the minimum terms of settlement at other companies. "Major substantive changes have invariably been conceded by one of the carriers," says Mark Kahn, "after which the union involved finds it relatively easy to obtain the same concession from others."[3] There is also evidence of "pattern-plus" bargaining by strong airline unions, in which union demands exceed the recently negotiated gains at other lines and become the new pattern for subsequent economic settlements.

Multiunion representation, fractured bargaining structures with undefined pattern trends, and wide variations in carrier performance encourage lengthy bargaining processes as the parties often wait for a clarification of industry trends. Mandatory mediation efforts under the Railway Labor Act also can delay the process. Expired contracts frequently are extended for months or years before final settlement. A relatively low level of strike activity occurred in airlines during the 1960s, with a total of 12 work stoppages involving 38,000 employees. In the 1970s, there were 17 strikes, nine lasting 75 days or longer. The increase reflected a rise in strike inci-

---

[3]Mark Kahn, "Collective Bargaining on the Airline Flight Deck," in *Collective Bargaining and Technological Change in American Transportation*, ed. Harold Levinson, Charles Rehmus, Joseph Goldberg, and Mark Kahn (Evanston, Ill.: Transportation Center at Northwestern University, 1971).

dence nationally, but also responded to increasing airline resistance to union demands during a period of economic recession and rapid inflation, the industry's strike insurance fund, and the effects of rival unionism in some crafts and classifications.

Industry Deregulation and Depression, 1979–83

Airlines are a dramatic example of how established union bargaining power can be undermined by government deregulation. Direct price competition in product markets and the entry of new, low-cost carriers have pressured traditional companies to lower operating costs. Lead firms no longer have the ability to pass on higher labor costs or to absorb them through productivity gains from expanding output levels. The impact of deregulation on airline labor relations was compounded by simultaneous depression in the industry. Whether the unions have been permanently crippled remains to be seen, and will depend on their future success in organizing the relevant airline work force, which is rapidly changing, and their willingness to cooperate more closely with one another than in the past.

Deregulation. The infant domestic airlines industry was brought under federal regulation in the 1930s. Congress established the Civil Aeronautics Board (CAB) to control the number of carriers, where they flew, and how much they charged for their services. Unions and labor relations fell within the Railway Labor Act, a law that is similar in many respects to the National Labor Relations Act, but which encourages craft more than industrial unionism and tends to prolong contract bargaining in order to avoid stoppages.

By the mid-1970s, there was considerable agitation for airline deregulation. Economists argued that carriers no longer needed protection from competition and had grown inefficient and unresponsive behind their regulatory wall. Deregulation, they predicted, would result in lower fares, more jobs, higher profits, and better service. In addition, econometric studies of airline bargaining outcomes suggested that labor relations would be unaffected by the change. On the basis of one set of calculations, it was predicted that deregulation would increase rather than erode union bargaining power. Industry structure would be relatively unaffected and major carriers would have greater ability to pay. "In other words," the authors concluded, "airline collective bargaining should continue to reflect the continuing impact of the former regulatory environment."[4] Opponents of deregulation claimed it would lead to bankruptcies, elimination of service to small and intermediate cities, fewer jobs and chaotic labor relations, higher fares, and, eventually to increased industry concentration through consolidations. Most airlines and all of the major unions opposed deregulation.

Support continued to build for some sort of legislation, however. Groups that normally hold opposing views, such as the Conservative Union and Ralph Nader's consumer coalition, were united in favor of deregulation. Both the Ford and Carter Administrations urged it, and by 1978, so did a majority in Congress. The Airline Deregulation Act which was passed that year phased out the CAB and gradually opened all domestic routes to competitive pricing and new carrier entry. Some safeguards were specified, including continued service to small cities and compensation for workers displaced by the effects of deregulation.

The new law changed industry structure and behavior. Structurally, the industry composition changed from noncompetitive major and feeder carriers to competitive major carriers, expanded local and regional airlines, and low-cost, nonunion entrants. Behaviorally, direct price and route competition, with an emphasis on reducing operating costs, supplanted passenger services as the dominant forms of intercarrier competition for increased market shares.

Several mergers and acquisitions took place, as carriers maneuvered for position in the altered environment. Pan American, an international airline, acquired National, a domestic carrier. North Central, a regional company, acquired two other airlines and reorganized itself as Republic, a major carrier. Continental tried to merge with rival Western Airlines in order to establish its control over certain routes and expand into others, but the government intervened on antimonopoly grounds.

Some local carriers broadened their operations to challenge the majors. Air Florida failed to acquire other regional companies but then expanded routes along the East Coast and to Europe in competition with Eastern and Trans World Airlines (TWA). Southwest Airlines entered lucrative long-haul routes against industry giant United. The new competitors undercut prevailing passenger fares. They could do so because they were only partially unionized or negotiated contracts with independent unions below industry stan-

---

[4]Wallace Hendricks, Peter Feuille, and Carol Szerszen, "Regulation, Deregulation, and Collective Bargaining in Airlines," *Industrial and Labor Relations Review* (October 1980), p. 71.

dards. They also had greater operating flexibility than the established trunk carriers, purchased second-hand, fuel-efficient aircraft at bargain prices, and expanded their flight services with short-service, low-cost employees.

While regional carriers expanded into routes and hub cities previously dominated by the majors, dozens of new firms entered the industry. Before deregulation, there were 33 domestic passenger airlines; by 1982, there were 70. An estimated 14 of the new firms were nonunion, including New York Air, People Express, Midway, and Muse. These companies have the same operating advantages over major carriers as the regional companies, but they also pay lower wages and fringe benefits than anyone else and offer travelers "no frills" flights to most large and medium-sized cities. The new entrants took markets from major and regional carriers alike. New York Air and People Express originated in the heavily-traveled Northeast corridor, Midway operated out of Chicago, and Muse did business in the West.

Low labor-cost regional carriers were willing to depress fares below the majors' break-even revenue levels. Nonunion carriers then sometimes drove them down even more. An internal TWA survey estimated that it cost People Express and Southwest 5¢–6¢ per-seat-mile to operate compared to TWA's 10¢–13¢. Two-thirds of the passengers flying during the summers of 1980 and 1981, normally the most profitable season for airlines, did so under reduced fares. By late 1981, the majors had lost sizable market shares to the new rivals.

Industry Depression, 1981–83. In August 1981, as the industry was emerging from a brief downturn, some 13,000 air traffic controllers employed by the federal government and represented by the Professional Air Traffic Controllers Organization (PATCO), struck against the government's final contract offer and in violation of a prohibition against strikes by federal workers. The Reagan Administration fired the 12,000 strikers who refused to return to work within 48 hours and eventually had PATCO decertified as the bargaining agent. The immediate effect on air traffic was to cut in half the number of flights nationwide. The government then restricted airline activity at the nation's busiest airports while new controllers were recruited and trained.

Initial forecasts and comments from the industry on the impact of the curtailment were optimistic. Many saw the constraints as an opportunity for individual carriers to drop unprofitable short-haul flights, ground inefficient aircraft, and raise prices on heavily travelled hub routes. There was such a precedent. When the OPEC oil embargo reduced air traffic in 1974, the industry scaled down operations, raised prices, and reported record profits. No one expected the same thing to happen this time, but the outlook was for long-term benefits for the carriers.

Instead there was a deep recession. The number of airline passengers, which had dropped sharply after the strike and forced cutbacks, remained depressed as the nation headed into a severe economic downturn. By the end of 1981 four of every 10 airline seats were flying unfilled and the trunks alone had laid off 20,000 workers. That year the majors lost $672 million, whereas in 1978, their profits were $1.2 billion. The industry was damaged further by the government's high interest rate policies. Long-term industry debt more than doubled.

Most fare-cutting involved long-haul flights, especially transcontinental runs. The majors were particularly vulnerable because their fares were overpriced. They had used these lucrative routes to subsidize more costly short-haul flights. As rival firms captured increasing shares of the long-haul market, the majors withdrew services from small and intermediate cities. Smaller carriers came in to fill the void, but without competition from other companies, and in the absence of price regulation, they hiked fares considerably. By the end of 1981, average air travel ticket prices had risen 71 percent since 1978, almost twice the rate of increase in consumer prices generally during that time.

Trunk carrier performance during the industry restructuring and depression depended more on good management than on unionization. Delta Air Lines and USAir maintained profitable operations in both 1980 and 1981. Each company is estimated to be at least 20 percent more efficient than the other trunk carriers. Neither carrier overexpanded its capacity or incurred onerous debts. Both maintained and even improved effective hub-and-spoke systems, and undertook "controlled growth" programs prior to the crisis. Both offered reduced but profitable fares for the duration, and both have had high levels of labor productivity.

USAir is unionized whereas Delta is not except for its pilots. But USAir has never experienced a serious labor strike, and through the years it has carefully avoided negotiating restrictive work rules. It refused, for example, to use three-member cockpit crews in new aircraft, as most other trunks agreed to do. Delta reportedly pays competitive or slightly superior salaries and wages and provides generous economic security benefits. It has escaped extended unionization by getting workers to identify with the company rather than with a particular craft or classification. Delta does not lay off permanent employees during recessions or reorganizations and maintains an elaborate internal employee communications and grievance process.

Industry Responses. Major carriers had to respond to this changing environment. They tried initially to stabilize fares at profitable levels. Eastern took the early lead in this attempt by raising its prices after the 1980–81 fare wars. The other trunks followed, but each time the effect was overwhelmed by external events and ended in failure. Soon Eastern was locked into rate wars in its New York-to-Florida routes and metropolitan shuttle flights. Under increasing financial constraint, Eastern abandoned the lead role.

American Airlines stepped into the breach. In early 1982, it tried to stop mutually damaging price competition between itself and Braniff in the Dallas hub. America's president suggested over the phone that Braniff's president raise his ticket prices 20 percent. "I'll raise mine the next morning," he promised. "You'll make more money and I will too."[5] Government prosecutors obtained evidence of the conversation and charged illegal "collusive monopolization." A federal court dismissed the charge on grounds the suggestion was merely a "solicitation" and not an attempt to fix prices. The following year American offered nonprice incentives, including bonus flights to its regular travelers, and announced a new fare formula. United and other majors followed with similar promotional programs. Their fares were set according to route mileage, with higher prices for short-haul and lower ones for long-haul flights, resulting in an overall increase.

A simultaneous strategy by trunk carriers was to meet the price competition of low-cost carriers and to cut back any of their own operations that were in jeopardy, but also to expand new hub locations based on market surveys. With their superior financial reserves, the big carriers could outlast the small ones in competitive fare wars. After several encounters of this sort, a few of the low-cost operators asked for a revival of government regulation in order to protect them against the aggressive practices of the more powerful trunks. Aggressive marketing and price competition by United, American, and Northwest pushed previously profitable and rapidly growing Midway Airlines into the red ink by early 1983, forcing the

---

[5]"U.S's American Airlines Suit Barred," *The New York Times*, September 14, 1983, p. D-9.

nonunion carrier to reverse its low-cost, "no frills" strategy and become a high-priced, luxury operator catering to business travelers. Air Florida was forced into bankruptcy. Finally, in the scramble for passengers, the majors also infringed on each other's markets. Development of hub activities by American in Dallas, United in Denver, and Delta in Atlanta infringed upon the revenues of established companies such as Eastern and Continental.

Nevertheless, by 1982 almost all the airlines were curtailing operations and laying off workers. Between 1981 and mid-1983, the industry displaced nearly 30,000 persons, about 8 percent of its total labor force.

Despite these and other efforts, the industry could not be stabilized. No sooner would the majors rally around the initiatives of one company than another would find itself in difficulty and resort to fare cuts and discounts. American's rate formula eventually fell victim to Continental's declaration of bankruptcy in August 1983 and subsequent resumption of operations at greatly reduced fares. This response triggered another round of price wars. Unable to resume normal operations and achieve previous profit margins in the face of deregulation and depression, the carriers looked increasingly to their unions for economic concessions and work rule changes.

Concession Bargaining

Airline labor was a logical place to make cost reductions. Operating costs in the industry are divided about evenly among labor, fuel, and equipment. Unable to control the latter two, management demanded concessions from its unions, initially on the grounds that they were necessary to offset fare cuts by low-cost operators, but later because the industry needed them to get through the depression.

Union concessions are not new to airlines collective bargaining. Early in the 1970s, ALPA accepted cost-saving changes in its Eastern and TWA contracts to avert threatened lay-offs. A few years later, during the 1974–75 recession, ALPA and other unions agreed to pay freezes and reductions at Eastern and Pan Am in return for future reimbursement and wage increases based on profitable operations.

More recently, the fragmented structures and staggered contract expirations shown in Table 10 have been transformed into a pattern of concession settlements. Many of the contracts were extended during 1981–83 until identifiable trends emerged in the concession movement. No single settlement established the pattern because union structures, relative bargaining power, cost problems, and preferred contract solutions differed among the carriers. Some imitation of concession terms occurred within crafts and classifications and among carriers which settled with their unions at the same time.

Table 11 traces major bargaining settlements in selected carriers during 1981–83. The 1981 round started with Braniff and its four unions. Braniff, which was suffering financially from managerial error, had asked for pay cuts. Three unions agreed, but a Teamster rejection stymied the plan. Shortly afterward, Braniff's flight attendants won a 25 percent wage increase and improved fringes over two years. Within weeks, however, the company reported record operating losses and again asked for reductions. This time the unions agreed, including the flight attendants. Later that year ALPA accepted a second round of cuts and work rule changes. The following year Braniff went into bankruptcy proceedings.

A key concession in 1981 was between United and ALPA. It featured work rules rather than pay reductions, because those were more important to the company. Under the existing contract, United had to use three-member cockpit crews where other companies used two. The union agreed to the two-member crew and more flying time in exchange for a pay increase and job guarantee for all regular pilots. United also promised ALPA it would not start a double-breasted, nonunion carrier, nor would it phase down its airline and diversify into unrelated fields. These givebacks by a strong craft to the industry's largest firm reinforced the concession trend.

Over the next several months unions accepted 10 percent pay cuts and work rule modifications at Continental, Pan Am, Republic (except the Machinists), and Western. Pan Am won concessions from all of its unions in return for employee stock ownership and a seat on Pan Am's board of directors. Eastern and TWA failed to negotiate pay freezes and rule changes even though their pilots had agreed earlier to a one-year freeze. Union acceptance depended on whether employees believed in the need for cost-saving. At American, unions refused 5 percent pay reductions because the carrier was operating profitably. On the other hand, unions sometimes reversed themselves when members became convinced reversals were necessary. Western Airlines workers turned down a wage freeze, but several months later accepted pay cuts when Western announced operating losses due to fare cuts by rival carriers.

In the next round of concessions, the carriers focused on work

Table 11.   Concession Bargaining in Selected Airlines, 1981–83

Carrier	Year, unions, and concession terms		
	1981	1982	1983
Braniff	10 percent pay reduction for all crafts; ALPA later makes additional pay and rules concessions	Company declares bankruptcy	—
United	ALPA trades rules changes for job guarantees	IAM settles for modest rule changes and discontinued COLA	—
Continental	10 percent pay reduction for most workers	ALPA accepts pay freeze and further rule changes	Company declares bankruptcy and nullifies contracts
Pan Am	10 percent pay reduction and freeze for all crafts; employee ownership plan in return	All crafts extend pay cuts; some discontinue COLA and accept rule changes	All crafts extend pay cuts; some discontinue COLA and accept rule changes
Republic	10 percent pay reduction for all crafts except IAM	Pilots and flight attendants accept additional pay cuts; IAM refuses	Temporary 15 percent pay cuts; reduced fringe benefits
Western	ALPA accepts one-year pay freeze, other crafts resist; all crafts later accept 10 percent pay reduction	All crafts agree to extend 10 percent pay reduction	All crafts accept 15 percent pay cut for nine months in return for 25 percent employee ownership in the company
American	Crafts reject 5 percent pay reduction	ALPA accepts rule changes	All crafts accept work rule changes and a two-tiered pay structure
Eastern	ALPA accepts one-year pay freeze	—	IAM rejects pay freeze. Later all crafts agree to one-year pay cuts and freeze based on evidence of financial need; 25 percent ownership in return
TWA	—	ALPA accepts pay freeze and rule changes	ALPA agrees to 10 percent pay cut and reduced vacation benefits
Northeast	—	IAM strikes over requested rule changes; compromise settlement on rules; discontinued COLA	

Sources: USDL, BLS, "Current Wage Developments"; The Bureau of National Affairs, Inc. *Daily Labor Report;* reports in the commercial and business press.

rule changes for greater flexibility in job assignments and on more hours worked for the same pay. Cost savings were needed, they said, to offset losses from fare cutting, to finance capital debt payments, and to compensate for poor profit ratios. American Airlines cited its ongoing price war with Braniff as justification for a pay cut to last "as long as the ill-advised fares remain in effect." The Machinists signed a two-year pact with United that called for pay raises and minor rules changes, but struck Northwest for nearly a month over work rules. ALPA negotiated a pay freeze and rule changes at TWA, work rule modifications at American, and second rounds of concessions at Republic and Continental. It and other unions extended for an additional year the previously negotiated pay cuts at Pan Am and also agreed to accept cost-saving rule changes.

An important settlement in 1983 involved American's mechanics and ground support employees. The Transport Workers Union made substantial work rule concessions. Under the threat of being replaced by strikebreakers and having the carrier withdraw its wage package, rank-and-file members voted against the recommendation of their negotiating committee and approved the offer. The settlement allowed American to use part-time workers, assign jobs out of classification, subcontract bargaining unit work, and pay new hires one-third less than current levels. The company estimated that these and some economic changes would reduce labor costs by 30 percent, making American's level "comparable to the lowest-cost operator out there."[6] Later that year American negotiated substantial concessions from its pilots and flight attendants, including work rule changes and greatly reduced pay levels for new employees, in return for pay hikes and job guarantees.

Also in 1983, Eastern demanded concessions from the Machinists in a contract that had expired in late 1981. Although Eastern's other unions already had made givebacks, the IAM was holding firm. It claimed that Eastern chairman Frank Borman had overextended the company's long-term debt structure by purchasing unnecessary aircraft, and that he now wanted the unions to make up the difference with wage concessions. Borman weakened his bargaining position prior to the actual negotiations by announcing for the benefit of Eastern's creditors that the carrier would earn $130 million that year. This prediction discredited the plea for concessions. A strike deadline was set and negotiations went down to the wire, with both sides threatening a lengthy stoppage if no agreement

---

[6]"What Labor Gave American Airlines," *Business Week*, March 21, 1983, p. 34.

was reached, before Borman settled for sizable wage and benefit increases.

Still, the Eastern settlement did not reverse the concession momentum. Western, Republic, and TWA came back to their unions for additional labor cost reductions, and in each instance received most of their demands. At Western, the concessions were made in return for a minority ownership share in the company. Republic had obtained $73 million in temporary wage concessions the year before, but came back now that the pay freeze had expired and asked for $100 million more over nine months. TWA made its demands under the threat that Trans World Corporation, the parent owner, might sell the airline. Even Delta asked for and got from its pilots a minimal pay increase and work rule modifications. Thus, by late 1983 every airlines union except for the machinists had negotiated at least one round of contract concessions with every major carrier.

Texas Air Corporation

Texas Air Corporation was organized as the parent holding company of Texas International Airlines, a small regional carrier. Under president Frank Lorenzo, Texas Air established New York Air in 1980 as a nonunion subsidiary doing business in the Northeast corridor. In 1982 Texas International acquired the much larger Continental Airlines, a trunk carrier. New York Air and Continental later became embroiled in bitter labor disputes.

New York Air. New York Air began as a nonunion competitor with major carriers in shuttle flights between large metropolitan locations. It flew older planes and paid pilots about half as much as unionized rivals. It avoided the machinists union by contracting out its aircraft maintenance. It has since expanded operations to other parts of the country, following a low-fare, "no frills" strategy.

From the outset, airline unions labeled New York Air a runaway shop, a means of increasing Texas Air's range of operations without having to deal with organized labor. Texas International pilots and flight attendants were represented by ALPA and one of its affiliated unions. ALPA vowed to defeat New York Air in order to prevent erosion of its Texas International units and to discourage similar "double breasting" ventures by other union carriers. To do so, it pledged a $1 million effort. Joined by representatives of other craft organizations, ALPA staged informational picketing at airports and challenged New York Air's operating status under federal law. It also initiated a "corporate campaign" to boycott the carrier's operations and publicize its nonunion policies and to pressure banks and other businesses to sever their ties with the company. The campaign had no apparent adverse effect on New York Air.

Continental Airlines. In 1981, Texas Air acquired the larger carrier Continental Airlines despite resistance by Continental management and unions. The following year it merged Continental, the nation's eighth largest trunk carrier, with Texas International Airlines. By August 1983, the IAM had rejected heavy contract concessions and prepared to strike Continental, the only airline which had yet to settle with the union in the 1980–81 round of bargaining shown in Table 11. The pilots already had given up $100 million in concessions to Continental and the flight attendants were negotiating amid rumors the carrier was planning to train replacements for them in the event of a walkout. Altogether, the company wanted $150 million in additional employee givebacks.

As the deadline approached, Continental negotiators withdrew the concession package and said that economic conditions had continued to deterioriate and it now needed greater givebacks than originally estimated. Management wanted work rule changes and a wage settlement below IAM contracts at other carriers; it also planned to eliminate several hundred service jobs through subcontracting. Claiming that Continental had wanted a confrontation from the beginning, some 2,000 machinists and service workers struck.

Immediately Continental fired the service workers whose jobs it had planned to subcontract out, began hiring replacements for striking machinists, and threatened to fire those who failed to report to work. With hub terminals in Houston and Denver, Continental claimed it was operating 85 percent of its flights despite the walkout. ALPA declared neutrality. The machinists did not ask flight attendants to honor the picket lines for fear they too would be replaced. Such a confrontation had not occurred in airlines in years. When asked why Continental was acting this way, a company spokesman explained that "it has long been our corporate goal to reduce labor costs." Continental's president called union standards "a vestige of the history of a regulated environment."[7] From 1980

---

[7]"Continental Airlines To Fire Employees Who Stay on Strike," *The Wall Street Journal*, August 15, 1983, p. 6; "Continental's Turnaround Bid," *The New York Times*, August 22, 1983, p. 29.

through 1982, the company had declared losses of $142 million, but outside analysts had attributed them more to operating difficulties than to labor costs.

The union traced the change in labor relations at Continental to its takeover by Texas Air. "With Lorenzo, you're just a pawn in his money-making game," complained a veteran Continental pilot. Union experiences with Texas International and New York Air had caused apprehension even before the IAM strike. "We were afraid he would try busting unions, and he is proving us right," said a negotiator for the flight attendant's union. Even in industry circles Lorenzo was known for his hard attitude toward labor. "At Texas Air, well, let's just say employees rank second to Mr. Lorenzo's goal of achieving profits," observed an airlines industry consultant.[8]

More than one month into the strike, Continental made another unprecedented move in airline negotiations. It filed bankruptcy under Chapter 11 of the Federal Bankruptcy Code, which permits a firm in financial difficulty to seek court protection against creditors while it reorganizes operations in order to pay debts and become profitable. Continental did not claim it was insolvent, but said high labor costs were making it unprofitable.

The company had offered pilots and flight attendants a stock ownership plan after the machinists struck, in exchange for $100 million in concessions. Both groups rejected the proposal. Continental blamed their action for its decision to declare bankruptcy. If its pay scales had been comparable to those at two of the company's small competitors, company officials claimed, Continental would have made $71 million in 1982 instead of losing nearly twice that amount. Chapter 11 bankruptcy normally allows an employer to rescind existing labor agreements; therefore Continental canceled its contracts with the machinists, pilots, and flight attendants; within a few days it had laid off two-thirds of its workers and resumed operations as a low-fare, nonunion carrier. Both the pilots and the flight attendants joined the IAM strike. The unions also challenged Continental's bankruptcy petition in federal court.

The pilots' strike was effective. Continental had not made arrangements for replacement pilots because the company did not believe ALPA would become involved. Not only did the union strike, it promised to pay striking Continental pilots the same money they would get by working at the reduced pay rate being offered by the

---

[8]Kevin P. Helliker, "Two Years After Buying Continental Air, Texas Air's Chief Still Facing Resentment," *The Wall Street Journal*, September 8, 1983, p. 33.

company to strikebreakers. "If Continental is successful in impos-
ing its wages and working conditions, that's going to be a role model
for other carriers to follow," explained ALPA's president. "We are
going to make Chapter 11 so difficult and so expensive that no company can use it to slide out of its labor contracts easily."[9]

There was reason for unions to be concerned. A week after
Continental's bankruptcy petition, Eastern Airlines, the industry's
second-largest firm, gave its workers an ultimatum that unless they
accepted 15 percent pay cuts, Chapter 11 bankruptcy was an option
Eastern would have to consider. In this instance a concession settlement was worked out without incident. But as long as the industry
environment was unsettled carriers could resort to such an extreme
measure.

In early 1985, nearly two years after Continental's declared
bankruptcy, the machinists and attendants called off their strikes.
Significant numbers of their members already had returned to
work. ALPA continued the walkout.

Frontier Airlines. A union concern is that troubled union carriers might organize nonunion subsidiaries as a way of operating outside their labor contracts, much like union construction companies
set up "double breasted" subsidiaries. The experience at Frontier
Airlines illustrates the process in air transportation. Frontier, a
unionized regional carrier, did a profitable business in the Denver
area until United and Continental established hub operations there
and nonunion companies also began taking market shares.

Frontier's parent company, Frontier Holdings, announced
plans to organize another operating subsidiary. Frontier Horizon
would be a nonunion carrier, said the company, and would fly between Denver and major coastal cities. It also intended to pay employees 30 percent less than competitive carriers did.

The unions at Frontier feared that Frontier Horizon would
take business from their carrier and eventually force it out of business. Although dozens of Frontier pilots were on layoff at the time,
the parent company said the new subsidiary would not recruit new
employees from Frontier's seniority rosters. This position was ironic
in view of earlier concessions by ALPA. Frontier's pilots were the
first in ALPA to accept two-member cockpit crews on 737s, and in
1982 they had taken pay cuts. Frontier's machinists also were vulnerable to displacement as a result of the reorganization. Frontier
Holdings owned and operated a nonunion aircraft service firm,

---

[9]"Lorenzo Battles To Keep His Airline Aloft," *Business Week*, October 17, 1983, p. 42.

which presumably could perform maintenance work for the new operating subsidiary.

Frontier's five unions formed an employee coalition to oppose the reorganization and its possible impact on their bargaining units. Calling Frontier Horizon a "runaway shop," the coalition promised to do what was necessary to stem the open shop move in their company. It threatened court or Railway Labor Act challenges to the legality of the new enterprise, and implied the possibility of union disruption of Frontier Horizon's operations if the company meshed the services of two carriers as the parent company's public announcements had suggested it would.

Ozark Air Lines. Frontier's decision to operate nonunion was the opposite of a decision made by Ozark Air Lines to seek labor peace in response to the new environment. Ozark, a St. Louis-based regional airline, had a reputation for being hostile to unions and taking a hard-line approach to collective bargaining. Flight engineers struck for nearly two months in 1979 and mechanics for almost a month the following year in stoppages which halted two years of route expansion under deregulation. The setback prompted management to make peace with its unions. "Both sides made the obvious effort to improve relationships," Ozark's president said. "I think we've become more open, more accessible and more involved with the employees."[10] Local union representatives welcomed the change in labor relations and adopted a more cooperative posture than in the past. Ozark's profits in 1981 exceeded previous levels.

Employee Stock Ownership. In a period of concession bargaining, one possible compromise is for union workers to give up future earnings in exchange for certain rights and guarantees in an employee stock ownership plan. The airlines probably have gone farther in that direction than employees in any other industry. Several of the largest carriers have negotiated employee ownership plans as bargaining tradeoffs with their unions.

From management's perspective, an agreement that trades deferred wages for shares of company stock is a convenient and relatively painless way to generate badly needed cash in a financial crisis. To the workers, such a plan promises job security and eventually perhaps a slice of the profit pie in return for a specified loss of earnings. More important, perhaps, is the opportunity it offers workers and unions to participate directly in the corporate investment and operating decisions that largely determine future job security and economic settlements.

---

[10]Sheila Teft, "Ozark Sprucing Up Image," *Chicago Tribune*, February 3, 1982, p. 3.

Employee ownership as a bargaining tradeoff for troubled firms gained national attention in 1981 with the Chrysler financial bailout. As a condition of providing more than $1 billion in federal loan guarantees to keep the company in business, Congress insisted that the UAW agree to substantial wage and benefit concessions. In return, Chrysler gave unionized production workers the chance to participate in a stock ownership plan that previously had been reserved for white-collar employees. In an earlier round of concessions, the corporation had given a seat on its board of directors to UAW president Douglas Fraser and had agreed to union participation in future employee fund investment decisions.

Also in 1981, Pan American negotiated an employee ownership plan with its five unions. Top executives met with union heads, provided them with internal financial information showing the company to be in critical operating condition, and asked for a pay cut and freeze. Union officials agreed to consider the request but indicated there would have to be a reciprocal guarantee of "employee input into the decision-making process."[11] A few months later, members of all the unions voted to accept a temporary wage cut and freeze. The stock ownership plan they received in lieu of wages also gave their unions a seat on Pan American's board of directors. The chief negotiator from ALPA was chosen to fill the position.

By voting their shares as a block, union members presumably could influence board decisions. By the end of 1982, they owned an estimated 13 percent of the company's outstanding shares, making them collectively the largest stockholder. It seemed to make them more solicitous over Pan American's operating difficulties than they had been in the past. The chairman of the five-union labor council reflected this sentiment: "As Pan Am's largest shareholder, we are all dedicated to doing whatever is necessary to return Pan Am to profitability in 1983."[12] This included extending the wage freeze for another year and modifying union work rules to get an additional 12 to 15 percent of work for the same pay. In the case of the pilots, at least, the trade was said to be worthwhile. "I've got a good job and a good way of life," said a senior Pan Am pilot after the second round of concessions. "I would like to keep it," he added, explaining why he had voted for the givebacks.[13]

---

[11]"Four Unions At Pan Am, Chairman to Discuss Employee Aid for Firm," *The Wall Street Journal*, July 7, 1981, p. 42.

[12]"Pan Am Reaches Pacts on Wage Concessions With 3 More Unions," *The Wall Street Journal*, December 23, 1982, p. 10.

[13]Agis Salpukas, "Givebacks Cost a Pan Am Captain Little, But Mean a Lot to Airline," *The New York Times*, January 30, 1983, p. 6-F.

The employee ownership plan at Pan American was followed by others at Western Airlines, Republic, and Eastern Airlines. The last exhibits one of the most extensive systems of union participation in corporate decisions.

Labor relations at Eastern had been confrontational in the past. Management blamed union workers for part of the carrier's increasingly desperate financial situation, accusing them of exploiting negotiated work rules and neglecting passenger service. The unions attributed Eastern's poor performance to unwise investment strategies and alleged insensitivity and unresponsiveness in labor relations.

After several years of continuous financial losses, Eastern insisted on economic concessions and work rule changes from the unions. These demands were rejected, in part because Eastern had tried unsuccessfully to bluff the machinists into making concessions earlier in the year. Then the company offered to have an outside auditor examine the books and make recommendations based on its assessment of Eastern's financial position. The unions agreed to this.

Negotiations resumed based on the auditor's report and the parties soon worked out an employee ownership plan in return for wage concessions. Union workers would give up 18 to 22 percent of their earnings during 1984, a total of $360 million in temporary wage losses. They also agreed to cooperate with management efforts to improve productivity by 5 percent, provided existing work rules were not violated. For this, the workers would receive stock shares amounting to 25 percent of total ownership of the company by the end of the year. The three unions would also elect four persons to Eastern's 21-member board of directors. (Nonunion employees, who had accepted similar earnings reductions, also got one place on the board.) Finally, an agreement with the machinists similar to the others specified 12 types of permanent union participation in Eastern's decision-making process. They included:

(1) ongoing reviews of business plans and the union right to protest unacceptable plans to the board of directors
(2) unlimited access to company financial data
(3) job security guarantees and a reduction in subcontracting out of bargaining unit work
(4) joint review of overall labor-management relations
(5) joint review of supervisors' roles and functions
(6) implementation of an employee involvement program
(7) joint trusteeship of the employee pension plan

(8) joint review of how employee benefit plans are administered

(9) full company disclosure of all consultants it hires.[14]

These provisions for union participation in previously exclusive and nonnegotiable areas of decision making are unprecedented among major union contracts. They could usher in a new relationship between labor and management at Eastern and serve as a model for imitative negotiations elsewhere. If successful, the employee ownership experiments in air transportation would establish the industry as a leader in this new direction in economic bargaining.

Summary

Union bargaining power in airlines depended mainly on the ability of individual crafts to stop production and the ability of carriers to pay negotiated labor costs as a result of government regulation and the oligopolistic control of fewer than a dozen trunk carriers. Regulation and consolidation provided the spatial limitation within which craft unions effectively organized and bargained. They organized along narrow craft lines and job classifications and bargained separately with individual carriers. A union could thus use its or another union's settlement at one carrier as the basis for negotiations at another. Individual carriers might be whipsawed against each other and made separately vulnerable to union demands. Economic recessions weakened union power, however, because airlines suffered disproportionately.

In order to offset labor's bargaining edge, trunk carriers established a strike insurance system. Under the arrangement, operating carriers subsidized struck lines in order to minimize pattern-breaking settlements made by weak carriers. The results were not entirely satisfactory to the companies and, in any event, the plan was made inoperable by the Airlines Deregulation Act of 1978.

Government deregulation together with industry depression shifted the bargaining environment against labor. Deregulation permitted entry of new firms, some of which are nonunion, and generally destabilized the old trunk-feeder industry structure upon which the unions had based previous organizing and bargaining success. Depression lowered the operating levels of most carriers

---

[14]"Unions Accept Plan to Assist Eastern, Swap Big Pay Cut For Quarter Ownership," *Daily Labor Report*, December 8, 1983, No. 237, pp. A9–A10.

and forced some to curtail routes. New competition and decreased consumer demand pushed the industry into successive fare wars. Lower fares brought down total revenues and prompted airlines to take unusually tough bargaining positions, including demands for steep economic and work rule concessions.

To reassert themselves at the bargaining table, airline unions would have to organize the industry's new relevant work force and modify traditional bargaining structures to accommodate the new situation. They also would have to cooperate and coordinate their activities more than in the past. It is likely that future organizing efforts among nonunion carriers will be jointly planned and executed. Contract bargaining may become synchronized in order for unions to standardize conditions at the expense of the old pattern-plus negotiations.

Another possibility is for negotiated employee ownership plans—in exchange for union participation in previously exclusive managerial decisions—to establish a new direction in airlines labor relations. Although there is little in American labor relations history to suggest participatory unionism of this sort, changing institutions have forced movement along those lines. The results could be instructive for negotiations in other changing environments.

Key Words and Phrases

concentrated and regulated industries	"whipsaw" bargaining
trunk airlines	"pattern-plus" bargaining
Mutual Aid Pact	two-tiered wage structure
revenue, ton-miles	price elastic demand for air travel
nonprice competition	employee stock ownership

Review and Discussion Questions

1. Describe union bargaining power in the airline industry before deregulation. After deregulation.

2. Explain how companies can use "double-breasted" operations to circumvent union contracts.

3. The Eastern Airlines-Machinists agreement, involving concessions from both union and company, has been hailed as a model. Describe its main provisions.

Chapter Resources and Suggested Further Reading

Sources used to describe the airline industry before deregulation are H. M. Gray, "The Air Transport Industry," in *The Structure of American Industry*, rev. ed., edited by Walter Adams (1954); Mark Kahn, "The Airline Industry," in *Collective Bargaining and Technological Change in American Transportation*, ed. Harold Levinson, Charles Rehmus, Joseph Goldberg, and Mark Kahn (1971).

Collective bargaining in airlines before and after deregulation is discussed in U.S. Department of Labor Bureau of Labor Statistics, *Collective Bargaining in the Airline Industry* (1979); Mark L. Kahn, "Airlines," in *Collective Bargaining: Contemporary American Experience*, ed. Gerald G. Somers (1980); "The Demands Airlines are Pressing on Labor," *Business Week*, December 7, 1981; S. Herbert Unterberger and Edward Koziara, "The Demise of Airline Strike Insurance," *Industrial and Labor Relations Review* (October 1980); Wallace Hendricks, Peter Feuille, and Carol Szerszen, "Regulation, Deregulation, and Collective Bargaining in Airlines," *Industrial and Labor Relations Review* (October 1980); Herbert R. Northrup, "The New Employee-Relations Climate in Airlines," *Industrial and Labor Relations Review* (January 1983).

Articles in the business and national press were used in the discussion of low-cost, nonunion carriers, the various rounds of concession bargaining, and union responses to industry changes following deregulation. These include Michael Hoyt, "Hard Times Hit the Pilots' Union—and Its Lofty Self-Image," *In These Times*, November 4-10, 1981; "Airlines in Turmoil," *Business Week*, March 21, 1983; Margaret Loeb and Thomas E. Ricks, "Future of Eastern Airlines Hinging on Chief's Credibility With Unions," *The Wall Street Journal*, September 29, 1983; Stratford P. Sherman, "Eastern Air Lines On the Brink," *Fortune*, October 17, 1983.

6

Industrial Bargaining

The bargaining power of an industrial union depends on a combination of product market and production characteristics of the industry and upon success in organizing the work force. When industry ownership is concentrated in the hands of a few large producers with production processes involving intensive use of machines and equipment, employers are likely to be able to pay higher labor costs. They can pass on the costs to buyers of their products and services, and also can recover some or all of the increase through productivity gains. Industrial union bargaining power therefore is a derived power, depending upon the employer's market power and technological capability.

It is necessary for the union to organize the relevant work force and to keep it organized, no matter what changes occur in the method and location of production. The union also should seek to avoid competitive bargaining situations with other unions in the same industry, and to negotiate master agreements covering all the production facilities of individual employers or perhaps of the entire industry. Industrial unions thus have a stake in industrial stability and continuity, once the industry or national employer has been organized and brought under an appropriately centralized bargaining structure. Industrial change is the natural enemy of entrenched union bargaining power. Strong industrial unions have a vested interest in the corporate structures, market boundaries, and production technologies that prevailed when they organized the industry and which they took into account when they designed their own organizational and bargaining structures. The overriding concern of industrial unions today therefore is that, like the crafts discussed previously, they do not control the forces of structural and technological change in industry. Instead, they try to redress the adverse effects of these changes through economic bargaining.

140

To understand industrial bargaining, one needs to know the origins and evolution of the organizational context within which it occurs. The market factors that lead to concentrations of industrial ownership and the circumstances under which industrial workers unionize have to be considered. Earlier chapters make reference to historical instances of market structure and the development of industrial bargaining. This chapter begins with a description of industrial concentration and then examines three cases of economic bargaining by industrial unions.

The first case concerns the brewing industry, which is dominated by a few firms; the second involves men's clothing, a nonconcentrated industry organized by the Amalgamated Clothing and Textile Workers Union. A local bargaining case study follows; it concerns crisis bargaining at an outboard motor manufacturing plant in Wisconsin.

Industrial Concentration

The history of American industry suggests a customary evolution from competition to concentration in product markets. Rapid expansion of output in a new industry usually involves an increasing number of firms and widening profit margins among the most enterprising of them. This leads to stagnating output and fluctuating profits—markets become saturated and the leading firms compete vigorously for larger shares in order to absorb excess production capacity. Eventually the problem is solved through consolidation, when a wave of mergers and acquisitions engulfs the industry.

Three Merger Waves. Consolidation of basic manufacturing in America did not occur because a few firms made better products and sold them at lower prices and therefore grew internally. In most instances it was because they bought up or eliminated competitive rivals and established controlling market shares. There have been three great merger waves in American industry. The first consisted mainly of horizontal combinations and occurred during 1897–1905. (Horizontal consolidation brings under common ownership and management firms that previously competed as sellers in the same product market.) A number of companies, among them U.S. Steel, General Electric, Swift, Borden, Eastman-Kodak, Dupont, and International Paper, represented generally successful merger efforts by leading firms to monopolize growing industries. Other markets were shared by two firms whose mergers and acquisitions had given them duopoly control, including International Harvester and Allis-

Chalmers, Anaconda and American Smelting (ASARCO), and American Tobacco and R. J. Reynolds. By 1904, the corporations that had been formed in the first merger wave owned 40 percent of American manufacturing capital.

The second merger movement started after World War I and lasted until the Great Depression. A greater number of combinations took place than in the first instance, but they were generally smaller in size and more often vertical rather than horizontal in structure. (Vertical integration, it will be recalled, combines firms which previously had buyer-seller relationships, such as auto assembly and auto parts companies.) Diversified mergers also made an appearance. General Motors, for example, made horizontal and vertical acquisitions in autos, including Chevrolet and Fisher Body, but also in unrelated industries, such as the electrical products manufacturer Frigidaire. Elsewhere, copper companies vertically integrated forward by acquiring brass fabricators; tire companies integrated backward by purchasing cotton-cord producers. General Foods became a huge diversified food processor and distributor through dozens of acquisitions. Even local product markets were caught up in the movement. National Dairy Products (Sealtest and Kraft) consolidated more than 360 independent ice cream and fluid milk producers and, as a result, substantially increased its market share in more than a dozen big states. The second merger wave further consolidated American industry. Between 1925 and 1931, the share of total manufacturing assets owned by the 100 largest corporations rose from 36 to 44 percent.

The third merger wave spans much of the post-World War II period. It became noticeable during the 1950s, peaked, then paused in the late 1960s before being resumed vigorously in the next decade. In 1981, at least 2,395 mergers took place for a total transaction value of $83 billion. Twelve mergers each were valued at more than $1 billion, led by the $7.5 billion acquisition of Conoco by Dupont, the largest U.S. corporate takeover to date. The third merger wave is characterized by (1) acquisition of small and medium-sized firms by large companies, (2) a dramatic rise of conglomerate corporations, and (3) expensive mergers by rich oil companies.

In earlier merger waves, traditionally competitive industries such as clothing and food processing were largely untouched, but this time they were taken up in conglomerate acquisitions. At least 3,322 corporate buyouts occurred during 1959–62, directly affecting 819,700 workers, a majority of whom were employed by small firms. These workers together represented 5.3 percent of the manufacturing work force. Blair pointed out that if the 1959–62 rate of corporate acquisitions continued, by 1978 one in every five employees in manufacturing would be working in acquired firms.

Since the 1950s, major oil companies have undertaken massive consolidations. Armed with annual cash flows that sometimes equaled the entire assets of more than half of all U.S. manufacturing companies, the 20 largest domestic petroleum firms acquired at least 226 separate firms during 1956–68. Of these, 29 were oil and alternative energy producers (horizontal consolidation), 52 were crude oil producers (vertical backward), 117 were petroleum-related manufacturers and distributors (vertical forward), and 28 were unrelated firms (conglomerate). The acquisitions gave them important ownership positions in coal, chemicals, fertilizer, copper and other industries.

The Development of Industrial Bargaining

Table 12 lists selected industries according to their product type and organizational structure. Each is organized by industrial

Table 12. Selected Private Sector Industries Characterized by Industrial Unionization, According to Type of Industry and Organizational Structure

	Industry type	
Organizational structure	Manufacturing	Nonmanufacturing
Concentrated	Steel Auto Telephone equipment Tire Oil refining Aluminum Meat packing Paper Flat glass Chemical	Telephone service Operating railway
Nonconcentrated*	Garment Textile Baking Furniture	Retail grocery Power utility Department stores Mass transit Lodging Eating and drinking places

*Regional concentration is frequent among these industries, as in the case of bakeries and retail grocery.

unions. Of the four categories in the matrix, union success has been highest among the manufacturing industries, with the exception of chemicals.

None of several international unions has been able to organize chemical workers extensively and exclusively. The companies often are paternalistic and antiunion. They pay reasonably high wages and benefit levels, resist organization drives vigorously, and, where they are organized, fragment their bargaining structures on a plant-by-plant basis. Independent unions also frequently represent single plants in the industry.

Industrial unions have had less success in nonconcentrated industries. Textiles, sportswear, and furniture, for example, have not been effectively unionized since the southern migration of firms following World War II. Nor are unions consistently strong in the nonconcentrated, nonmanufacturing industries. Of the six industries listed in Table 12, mass transit is heavily unionized and retail grocery and utilities are nearly so, but the other three are probably less than 25 percent organized. These are national averages, however, and therefore conceal specific areas of union strength. In some metropolitan areas, hotels, restaurants, and department stores have been under union contracts for years. Important segments of these industries, however, such as fast-food and discount retail chains, successfully resist unionization.

CIO national committees organized most of the concentrated sectors in the 1930s and 1940s. Some were fledgling AFL unions that had defected to the CIO. In the tire industry, the AFL's United Rubber Workers of America (URW) withdrew from the Federation and joined the CIO in 1936. AFL leaders had insisted the skilled trades and maintenance workers in tire plants be represented by their respective craft organizations rather than by a single industrial union. Companywide contracts were negotiated by URW with each of the industry's Big Four producers by the late 1940s; in economic bargaining, Goodyear, the lead firm, normally acted as the pattern-setter. Breakaway movements from the AFL also occurred in autos and West Coast longshoring, as a CIO committee meanwhile won bargaining rights in the largest plants of the four leading meatpackers.

Events in the furniture industry illustrate union problems in nonconcentrated manufacturing. Rivalry between two unions stunted union growth in the past and contributed to the industry's present low level of unionization and fragmented bargaining structure. The largest eight firms account for less than a fourth of industry sales; fewer than half the industry's production workers are in bargaining units and most of the negotiated contracts cover single plants. When the AFL and CIO merged in 1955, the two unions began coordinating their activities, but their organizing successes were in the north at a time when furniture manufacturing was relocating. By the end of the 1970s, an estimated 60 percent of the industry was located in Southern states, yet only about 25 percent of the members of the larger union lived in the South. The union moved its headquarters to Nashville, Tennessee, and initiated new organizing campaigns.

After years of competitive craft and industrial unionism, the retail grocery and retail department store industries now have industrial unions that bargain with area employer associations or individual chain operations in the area. This is partly due to union mergers. The Retail Clerks International Association (RCIA) abandoned its craft-based tradition after World War II, and as a result greatly expanded its membership. The other major union, the Meat Cutters, organized grocery chain butchers and meat counter employees. In 1979 the two organizations merged, with the clerks as the dominant partner, to form the United Food and Commercial Workers.

Industrial unionism in retail department stores began in 1940 when the Retail, Wholesale and Department Store Union was formed by breakaway RCIA locals in New York City. Internal political fighting and disaffiliation partially offset its earlier organizing gains, but the union continued to grow with the industry. The Service Employees International Union, a large, diversified service-sector organization, also represents retail store employees along industrial union lines.

The Beer Industry

Industrial unionism has existed in domestic brewing for nearly a century. No single union dominated the industry historically, but unionization levels were high and negotiated wages were above industry averages. Recent structural and environmental changes have moved the industry toward a double-tiered system—large modern breweries owned by major producers and aged frostbelt plants operated by regional or lesser national firms.

The Industry. Brewing is dominated by two firms, Anheuser-Busch (*Budweiser*) and Philip Morris (*Miller*). Together they account for more than half of the industry's sales. As Table 13 shows,

Table 13. Output and Market Shares of the Largest Eight Domestic Brewers, 1981

Brewer	Output (millions of barrels)	1981 Market share (%)	1980–81 Increase in output (%)	1970 Market share (%)
Anheuser-Busch	54.3	29.8	8.2	17.7
Miller	40.3	22.1	8.0	4.1
Schlitz	14.2	7.8	– 5.3	12.1
Heileman	14.0	7.7	5.3	—
Pabst	13.5	7.4	– 10.6	8.4
Coors	13.0	7.1	– 5.8	5.8
Stroh	9.8	5.4	0	2.6
Olympia	5.8	3.2	– 4.9	2.7
Largest eight	164.9	90.5		
Rest of industry	17.6	9.5		
Industry	182.5	100.0		

Source: Industry analyst Sanford C. Bernstein & Company, reported in *Chicago Tribune*, December 15, 1981.

in 1981 Busch had 30 percent of the market and Miller had 22 percent, compared to Busch's 18 percent and Miller's 4 percent in 1970. While the eight largest firms controlled 91 percent of industry sales, third-ranked Schlitz had only 8 percent. An indicator of the fundamental change occurring in the industry, Schlitz was losing markets rapidly and later would be acquired by another firm.

Busch and Miller expanded their markets through internal rather than external growth. Barred by antitrust law from acquiring rival brewers, Busch promoted sales of its own brands aggressively. It undertook expensive advertising campaigns, used price-cutting tactics to capture local and regional markets from smaller brands, and established exclusive marketing arrangements with distributors and taverns.

Miller rose from tenth to second place in the industry within five years of its acquisition by Philip Morris in 1972. The parent company promoted Miller *Lite* beer through saturation advertising to differentiate its brand from the others. By 1977, Miller had 17 percent of the industry but was not yet making a profit for Philip Morris because of the huge promotional budget. Miller's strategy— combined with Busch's emphasis on similar kinds of sales efforts— firmly established mass marketing as the primary means of survival and growth in the beer industry.

The effect was to weed out competitors and concentrate the industry. During 1950–80, the market shares of the top five and 10 producers increased from 19 to 75 percent and 28 to 94 percent, respectively. Beer production more than doubled, but only one-tenth as many firms remained at the end of the period.

Expansion by Busch and Miller came at the expense of local and regional brewers and most of the other top 10 companies. In 1947 there were 404 domestic producers; 20 years later more than two-thirds of them had disappeared and only 41 companies were in business. Local brands had been driven from the industry, but established national firms such as Schlitz and Pabst also were left with excess production capacity and eventually were acquired by other brewers. While some of the regional brands dropped out of the industry or changed owners, two of them, Heileman and Stroh, made brand and plant acquisitions that enabled them to move into the industry's top five ranking.

Industry consolidation, construction of large automated breweries, and increases in the ratio of supervisory employees combined to reduce the number of brewery production workers. Hourly employment fell from a post-World War II high of 65,000 in 1953 to 40,000 in 1968. During the decade after 1972, it dropped to 30,000. In the mid-1970s, the capacity of regional breweries typically ranged up to 1.5 million barrels per year, well within the area of peak efficiency at that time. The big companies then built automated breweries having capacities of several million barrels. A few of them had plants of even eight to 10 million barrels capacity. Whereas a regional brewery might produce a million barrels of beer a year using about 250 regular hourly employees, an automated Busch or Miller plant could make eight times as much product with two or three times as many production workers.

The Union. Organizing and strike activity occurred in brewing well before the turn of the century. Skilled German brewers unionized as early as 1850; unskilled workers struck the New York brewers over unsafe working conditions and shorter hours. A second effort resulted in a negotiated contract and grievance procedure. This success triggered union efforts elsewhere and prompted the formation of an opposing employer organization, the National Association of Brewers (NAB).

The United Brewery Workers (UBW) was the AFL's first industrial union. Chartered in 1887, it took in all brewery workers regardless of skill or occupation. The reasons for this approach were rivalry from the Knights of Labor, the relatively small number of craft workers employed by breweries, the UBW's early socialist philosophy, and the relative ease with which employers could break craft strikes by replacing the few skilled workers involved.

The union had considerable organizing success around the turn of the century. By 1908, it claimed 95 percent of the nation's brewery workers. A number of conditions favored unionization. The labor force was heavily laced with German immigrants having union traditions. Improved transportation, mechanical refrigeration, and pasteurization of beer fostered the rise of national brands and large plants. Some 1,700 domestic breweries produced 22 times as much beer in 1908 as 2,000 of them had in 1870. Average annual output per brewery had multiplied 20 times. Like the early commercial printing centers, these beer "factories" in metropolitan areas made inviting targets for unionization.

The union also had bargaining power. Beer was a working class beverage, so union boycotts against area brewers were effective. Selected strike activity and strong brewery worker identification with the union also gave the UBW power. NAB countered with a mutual aid pact under which Association members agreed not to sell beer to the wholesale customers of struck breweries; in practice it did not offset the union's bargaining leverage. Nevertheless large brewers sometimes won lengthy strikes by replacing union workers and riding out product boycotts. In any event, however, wages and working conditions in brewing were among the best in American manufacturing.

Labor-management strife in organized plants was discouraged by the common threat of prohibition in America. Legal prohibition of alcoholic beverages was bad for both labor and industry. A cooperative effort therefore developed around the issue, which carried over into labor relations and paved the way for amicable resolution of issues.

The Brewery Workers had more problems with another union than with most employers. Its industrial union philosophy brought the UBW into jurisdictional conflict with the Teamsters. The fierce and sometimes violent competition between them debilitated the UBW and led to its expulsion from the AFL and subsequent affiliation with the CIO. Finally, after continued defeats in key locations, UBW agreed in 1972 to be absorbed by the IBT as a separate department. Some UBW locals, notably Local 9 in Milwaukee, stayed out of the merger and affiliated directly with the AFL–CIO.

Bargaining Structures and Outcomes. Changing corporate organization, historic union rivalry, and shifting geographic production patterns resulted in segmented bargaining structures among three unions: the dominant Teamsters (IBT), the remaining UBW locals, and the machinists (IAM), which originally entered the industry as a craft organization. The IBT has had master agreements covering 11 Busch plants and all but one of Schlitz's several breweries, but has had separate contracts in three of Miller's five plants. UBW Local 9 negotiates separately with Miller in Milwaukee as do the machinists in Fulton, New York. Local 9 negotiations with Miller in Milwaukee once included the Schlitz and Pabst plants there.

The rest of the industry bargains single-unit contracts. All of Heileman's agreements reportedly cover individual plants. A UBW local was decertified at the Coors plant in Golden, Colorado, following an 18-month strike over a company attempt to revoke the union shop clause. The AFL–CIO responded with a nationwide boycott of Coors, an effort supported by environmental and other nonunion groups opposed to the Coors family's conservative political activities. Most other breweries are unionized, even those located in southern and rural areas.

Brewery workers earn comparatively high wages. During 1972–83 average hourly earnings in brewing increased 138 percent compared to 107 percent in the total private economy and 122 percent in other nondurable goods industries. But by the end of the 1970s a two-tiered wage and benefit structure was emerging. The distinction involved small breweries and the large but aging facilities of national brewers on the one hand and the big, automated plants of major brands on the other. At a 1982 IAM conference, for example, "delegates from the larger breweries reported recent contracts have produced major wage and benefit increases, while delegates from the smaller breweries reported that many of the breweries are calling for 'give-backs.'"[1] Heileman demanded union concessions before agreeing to keep open newly acquired breweries; independent brewers wanted concessions on grounds they were necessary for small brewers to survive in the rapidly changing industry.

Concession Bargaining in Milwaukee. The situation facing previously strong local unions at major breweries was illustrated by events at the aging Schlitz, Miller, and Pabst plants in Milwaukee. UBW Local 9 got into a strike with Schlitz in 1981, when the company was experiencing a serious slump in sales and operating its breweries at less than 60 percent of their combined capacity. The

---

[1]"Brewery/Construction Workers Hear Mixed Industry Report," *The Machinist* (June 1982), p. 6.

century-old Milwaukee facility accounted for about one-quarter of Schlitz's production capability. Schlitz had prepared for a showdown with the union over company demands for a wage and benefit freeze and work rule givebacks by withdrawing from the citywide bargaining association and negotiating separately. The UBW settled with Pabst and Miller for modest contract gains but called a strike and boycott against Schlitz. "The union's almost doing them a favor," observed one industry analyst, noting that Schlitz did not need the plant's production.[2] The year before it had sold two of its eight breweries in order to reduce excess capacity.

As the strike entered its second month, Schlitz announced it was closing the brewery, stunning the community and the more than 700 strikers. This was one week after the company had disclosed plans to merge with Heileman. Heileman officials claimed no involvement in the shutdown decision, but it was clear the combined firm would not need the Milwaukee production. Schlitz's major consumer market was in the south, where its newest, most efficient breweries were located.

The Heileman merger was called off after the government raised antitrust objections. Stroh, a fast-growing Detroit regional brewer, later acquired Schlitz in an unfriendly takeover. The Milwaukee plant was not reopened.

Two years later UBW Local 9 struck Miller. This time the dispute involved employer demands for greater control over work processes and the right to displace large numbers of production jobs. Miller kept the plant open by transferring supervisors from its other breweries. The strike lasted two months and ended with the elimination of about one-fifth of the union work force in exchange for wage and fringe benefit improvements. It was expected that most of the job displacement would be offset by the early retirement of eligible members. The union also resisted a management proposal to allow subcontracting out of bargaining unit jobs.

In 1983 the local made similar job concessions at the Pabst plant. Roughly 10 percent of the jobs were lost by ending beer deliveries from the factory to area retail establishments and transferring the function instead to regular distributors. Additional jobs would be displaced gradually through production reorganizations and employment reassignments made possible under the agreement. In return, average wages in the plant were brought up to industry standards.

---

[2]"Schlitz's Milwaukee Brewery Is Struck; Move May Help Ease Firm's Overcapacity," *The Wall Street Journal*, June 2, 1981, p. 10.

Plant Closings. Steadily increasing output by fewer firms has reduced the number of breweries, especially in the northeast and midwest. The industry reported 465 separate plants in 1947, 154 in 1967, and 82 in 1980.

Actual and threatened plant closings disarm unions at the bargaining table. Striking workers in three local unions at the Iron City beer plant voted to return to work after the company announced the brewery would be closed. They then accepted the same concession offer they had rejected overwhelmingly two days before. The new agreement tied future wage increases to the company's profit performance rather than to comparability, cost-of-living, and productivity. This was in 1981. Later that year the company's chief executive officer became president of Pabst. Within months Pabst had gotten contract concessions from unions at its New Jersey and Illinois breweries.[3]

Pabst later closed the Illinois plant on grounds that declining sales in the midwest necessitated a shutdown either there or in Milwaukee, the company's two oldest facilities. Pabst chose to get additional union concessions in Milwaukee and to close its Peoria facility. Machines were transferred from Peoria to the Milwaukee brewery, which became the sole Pabst plant in the midwest.[4]

In sum, brewing is a highly unionized but rapidly changing industry. Bargaining outcomes differ depending on the structure and performance of firms. Unions that represent workers in aging plants of marginal producers have difficulty negotiating economic settlements that maintain the historic high wage and benefit standards of the brewing industry. They bargain under the threat of declining sales markets and for workers who are in technologically obsolete and poorly located plants. Unions that have multiplant contracts with the leading firms or separate agreements with brewers in modern plants and secure product markets do much better at the bargaining table. They take advantage of their capital-intensive, low cost-per-unit production environments to negotiate

---

[3]Thomas Petzinger, Jr., "New Pabst Chief Uses Ploys From Success in Pittsburgh to Prepare for 'Guerilla War,' " *The Wall Street Journal*, December 18, 1981, p. 23. The Milwaukee local, in response to its declining position, affiliated with the Auto Workers union in 1984; by that time its membership at Pabst and Miller was down to 2,500. BNA, *Daily Labor Report*, March 27, 1984, p. 3.

[4]The IBT accused Pabst of violating its labor contract in closing the plant. An arbitrator ruled in favor of the union but allowed the company to keep the plant closed if it could negotiate a termination agreement with the union. The matter finally was settled by a second arbitration award giving the displaced Peoria workers severance pay, extended insurance coverage, and a fully funded pension plan. "Pabst Must Pay More to Former Employees, *Chicago Tribune*, July 8, 1982, sec. 4, p. 9.

satisfactory economic settlements; the other brewery unions are pressed to make contract concessions in order to keep their plants open.

Men's Clothing

Men's clothing is a nonconcentrated industry in which the union has the institutional power to make employers pay but competition in product markets prevents them from doing so. The industry is fragmented, competitive, seasonal, and labor-intensive. In response, the union, which is the largest organization in the industry, must assume major responsibility for stabilizing business and protecting established employers. It assists employers in product markets instead of exacting unrealistic demands from them in labor markets.

The reasons for union dominance are the historically high level of unionization among industry workers, the absence of competitive union bargaining, and the industrywide bargaining structure. The sources of industry inability to pay are weakness in product markets, due to foreign imports of clothing and nonunion domestic suppliers, and low productivity gains because of labor-intensive production methods. Table 8 shows a lower annual rate of increase in hourly earnings for the clothing industry during 1953–76 than for all other industries.

The leading four firms in men's and boys' suits and coats, the major portion of the domestic tailored clothing industry, in 1972 accounted for 19 percent of sales, while the largest eight represented 30 percent. However, there has been a gradual concentration trend as a result of mergers and acquisitions by established garment manufacturers and outside conglomerates. Profits for individual firms can be high, but they are also erratic. Frequent bankruptcy is an industry characteristic. The failure rate for apparel manufacturers in the 1970s was nearly twice the average for all employers.

Technology in the clothing industry remains largely unchanged—sewing, cutting, and pressing machines being used in 1900 have not been significantly modified. Laser cutting, ultrasonic sewing, and computer processing are available, but they do not radically alter labor skill requirements. In addition, these techniques are too expensive for small producers and inappropriate for nonstandard garment production. Productivity figures in clothing are not reliable. However, between 1960 and 1974, total production increased four times faster than the number of production hours worked. Payroll costs as a percentage of revenue declined considerably. This happened despite relatively smaller capital investments in clothing production than in industry generally. For the entire apparel industry, of which men's clothing is one segment, the level of plant and equipment per worker was the lowest among 29 manufacturing industries surveyed.

Production jobs in men's suits and coats have declined steadily, for a decrease of 40 percent between 1969 and 1980. This drop is due mainly to foreign imports. Workers also put in fewer average hours and earn lower wages than do those in manufacturing generally. In 1950, wages in men's clothing were 7 percent less than in all manufacturing, but in 1960 they were 18 percent less. During the 1960s, a period of general economic expansion, when low income groups normally improve their earnings relative to those of higher-paid workers, the differential narrowed to 13 percent.

The structure of the industry discourages the union from pressing for more. Contracting and subcontracting of production work from large to small shops forces employers to reduce labor costs. Domestic firms are encouraged to look for cheap labor here or abroad. Overseas garment shops pay production workers as little as 20 cents an hour. At home, increasing numbers of Latin and Asian immigrants locate in the metropolitan centers and become a ready supply of exploitable labor for transient sweatshops. This occurs now more often in women's than in men's clothing, but the potential is vast and in neither instance have the relevant workers been unionized effectively.

Another employment option is homework, which again is a more frequent practice in women's garments. Homework refers to the performance or completion of clothing production by workers in their homes. It resembles the cottage industry methods that were common in America before the Civil War.

The Amalgamated Clothing Workers of America (ACWA) was formed in 1914 as a breakaway industrial union from the craft-dominated United Garment Workers. The ACWA, which eventually displaced the UGW, spoke for the immigrant metropolitan garment workers, who by 1910 accounted for 70 percent of the industry work force. From the 1930s on, it represented 80 percent or more of the workers. Revival of a nationwide manufacturers' association enabled the ACWA to establish industrywide bargaining in 1937 in place of local and regional contracts.

A cooperative spirit resulting from the industry's precarious economic situation governs the bargaining relationship. The

ACWA makes wage and other concessions when the industry falls on hard times, offers strategic financial loans to established employers, and provides technical assistance to firms in production and marketing methods. If the parties let the union-nonunion wage differential widen for the industry, the market attracts nonunion products. In the 1950s, negotiated wages were estimated to be about the same as those in nonunion firms. The advantages for union workers were their negotiated fringe benefits and economic security.

Formal labor disputes are rare. The only industrywide strike occurred in 1974, 53 years after the industry locked out ACWA members in 1921. At issue was employer refusal to pay both deferred wage increases and COLA adjustments at a time when foreign-made clothing was pouring into domestic markets and employment was falling. After a 10-day walkout which would have jeopardized production of new fashions if continued, the union settled for fringe benefit improvements, significant wage increases over three years, and a COLA clause to compensate for inflation rates greater than the deferred wage increases. About 110,000 workers struck some 750 firms—a ratio of about 150 workers per employer, evidence of the industry's fragmented structure.[5]

Industrywide benefit plans can jeopardize earnings when employers are small and therefore vulnerable to outside forces. This was evident after the 1974 settlement. ACWA had to delay temporarily its largest deferred wage increase in order to divert the money to the union's health insurance program, which was dangerously underfunded. Employer contributions into the fund depended on the number of production hours worked, and industry employment had fallen by 30,000 jobs.

The 1980 industrywide contract increased wages 14 percent over 18 months. The industry average hourly rate at the time was $5.00, compared to an all-manufacturing average of $7.27. The short duration of the contract, which covered about 30,000 fewer workers and 50 fewer companies than in 1974, was in response to high inflation rates and depressed industry sales. ACWA claimed in 1976 that 60,000 industry jobs had been lost to imports since 1969, 45,000 of them in men's suits and coats and 10,000 in shirts.

---

[5]In 1977, ACWA merged with the Textile Workers Union to form the Amalgamated Clothing and Textile Workers Union. The combined organization had as its initial objective the unionization of J. P. Stevens to give momentum to a wider campaign in southern textiles and clothing.

Local Union Industrial Bargaining: A Case Study

Background to Bargaining. The case concerns the negotiations between a Steelworkers local and the Milwaukee plant of Evinrude Motor, a manufacturer of outboard motors and a subsidiary of Outboard Marine Corporation (OMC). OMC was formed in 1956 through the merger of Johnson Motor, another outboard motor producer, and Outboard Motors Corporation, which in 1929 had acquired Evinrude and two more outboard motor manufacturers. It had about half the outboard motors market in the world. OMC's strong market position gave it above-average profits in the industry and for all U.S. manufacturing firms. Earnings were used to make diversified acquisitions in snowmobiles (Cushman), chainsaws (Pioneer), and rotary mowers (Lawn-Boy).

The local has represented production workers at Evinrude's Milwaukee plant since the end of World War II. Wages and fringe benefits there in the late 1970s were the highest among OMC plants and matched those of other leading employers in the Milwaukee area. About 1,800 hourly workers were in the bargaining unit. OMC's other outboard motor plant was located in Waukegan, Illinois, and organized by an independent union.

Contract negotiations at the Evinrude plant in 1978 were directly affected by an economic problem facing the parent company. For years, OMC and Mercury had dominated outboard motor sales at home and overseas. OMC was the stronger company because it marketed two well-known brands compared to Mercury's single brand. Although they competed for larger market shares, OMC and Mercury avoided direct price competition and instead vied with one another on the basis of advertising, new product features, and improved distribution methods. Their labor costs were comparable.

By 1978, however, Japanese producers had moved aggressively into the field. Three Japanese-based conglomerates entered the industry in the 1970s, and quickly captured much of OMC's Pacific and Far East markets. The most immediate threat to OMC, however, came from a cooperative venture between Mercury and Yamaha, one of the Japanese companies. Mercury marketed Yamaha motors in this country under the Mariner brand and at prices 5 to 10 percent below comparable domestic models. Yamaha in turn sold Mercury motors in the Orient. The effect was to sandwich OMC's two brands, which are similar in size and price, between the higher-priced Mercury and the lower-priced Mariner. Mercury's share of the market jumped.

The foreign competition drove OMC's profits below industry levels. This occurred despite an increase in OMC's total sales revenues. The outlook was pessimistic and the price of OMC's stock fell by two-thirds between 1972 and 1978.

Management's Decision to Cut Labor Costs

OMC managers made organizational and operating changes in response to the deteriorating outboard motor market. They increased investment in new plants and equipment by one-third, much of it to build an automated parts depot and to purchase bigger, faster manufacturing machines. The firm discontinued production in three unprofitable unrelated divisions and closed yet another. It cut product prices in overseas markets threatened by the Japanese and initiated direct factory distribution to overseas retailers in order to reduce marketing costs.

In addition, OMC made plans to trim labor costs at the Evinrude plant. Prior to the 1978 negotiations, OMC's president visited Milwaukee and met with the union bargaining committee. He described the company's market losses and tests made on rival Japanese motors; they were of good quality, he said, and though not equal to Evinrude and Johnson performance standards, low prices made them a consumer bargain. The company was resisting, he told the union, but to be successful it needed labor's cooperation. While he did not elaborate then, it soon became clear that Evinrude management wanted to scrap the production incentive system.

The local union interpreted the president's visit as a friendly gesture prior to contract negotiations, but the limited information he provided about the firm's operating position did not help the union to prepare its bargaining demands. "Having access to the financial reports did not provide enough information," Robert Glaser, USW international representative and chief union negotiator, said later. "We realized that some money had been lost. But we could not ascertain the cause."

Contract negotiations in the outboard motor division involved patterns between the Evinrude and Johnson plants. Evinrude customarily negotiated first and established the economic pattern for the union in Illinois. The Steelworkers was stronger than the independent organization because it was larger and the Milwaukee plant was OMC's only machine shop—it made parts and components for both the Evinrude and Johnson lines and for other OMC divisions. When OMC curtailed output in operations unrelated to

Evinrude, some 45 Milwaukee workers were permanently laid off; when strikes occurred at two other locations prior to the Evinrude negotiations, about 500 Milwaukee workers were laid off for weeks.

The usual sequence of negotiations was reversed in 1978 because of a prior change in Johnson's contract expiration date. For that reason, and because of OMC's financial troubles, the Evinrude union adopted two major bargaining objectives: to maintain existing jobs and to match the Johnson plant's economic settlement. A long strike at the Johnson plant convinced the Evinrude local that 1978 was not the year for an innovative contract. They also knew management would make its own demands regarding incentives.

Union negotiators acknowledged that the existing wage incentive system was obsolete in view of new product lines and machine-controlled jobs. Privately they conceded that inequities resulted: some workers could not make a fair rate under the system while others made a day's production quota in less than eight hours. Outdated incentive systems can be a vexing issue in metal manufacturing negotiations. Change is difficult because of divisions inside bargaining units over whether the system should be retained, modified, or eliminated. Vested interests in existing systems develop among workers who benefit most from them; political blocs form to resist what are seen as union concessions. If a majority of the workers approve of things as they are, the political opposition against negotiating changes can be decisive.

Responsible union negotiators then have to persuade the membership that change is inevitable and that resistance will diminish long-run earnings and job security. Workers have legitimate doubts that this is true; even if they are convinced it is, they question whether they should trade future for present benefits.

Rank-and-file sentiments at Evinrude were decidedly against a change in the incentive system. Several newly elected negotiating committee members were chosen for their public opposition to such change. They were a sizable minority on the committee. But both Glaser and the local president, who was also a member of the committee, believed fundamental change was inevitable. To them, it was better to negotiate a new or revised incentive system while the local still had enough bargaining leverage to do so effectively. Due to aggressive rank-and-file opposition, however, the official local union position was that a new system was unacceptable and the old one should be "patched up."

Glaser and the local president devised an appropriate bargaining strategy. As the most experienced local negotiators, they assumed leadership roles. They would center the early negotiating sessions on minor changes in contract language and do so as long as possible to avoid raising prematurely the disruptive incentive issue. Final settlement on economic items also would be postponed. Then, when management made its incentive proposal, they would reiterate the official union bargaining position in opposition and take Evinrude's proposal to the membership, but without recommending that it be accepted.

Meanwhile, they wanted to convey to company negotiators that the manner in which the incentive issue was presented to the members would probably determine whether they accepted it. If it was modified to include union language proposals and presented together with a sizable economic package, a "fair presentation" of management's plan to the members by the bargaining committee might win membership approval and avert a lengthy strike. They wanted to inform management of this just before the contract expired. This tactic, they believed, would require the company both to negotiate union proposals on incentive language and to make a generous economic package. "That is where our real power was," Glaser recalled. "If the company wanted a new incentive plan, their final offer would be a good one; if they didn't, then we were prepared to accept the consequences."

Fringe benefit improvements rather than wage increases were the union's chief economic objective. Sickness and accident insurance benefits at Evinrude were below those at Johnson following the recent strike settlement in Waukegan, so the local would use that as its target pattern. Evinrude's pension benefit formula was inferior to those in some of Milwaukee's other metal manufacturing firms, so the local intended to use area standards as the basis of comparison on that issue. Union figures to justify insurance and pension improvements centered upon the 19 percent rise in the cost of living over the life of the expiring contract. Union demands thus reflected local objectives and tactics, patterns negotiated inside OMC and in the Milwaukee area, and the economy.

An additional local bargaining concern was administration of the insurance plan. Unsatisfactory experiences with claims adjustments caused the union to look for an alternative carrier. Another company was approached and prepared an estimate of the cost at which it would offer the same coverage. Union negotiators planned to use that estimate to support their demand. They knew the company opposed a change and believed their demand might encourage improved administration of the existing plan and also could be traded for something else late in the negotiations.

Union bargainers were willing to accept the negotiated wage increase at Johnson—5 percent in the first year of the contract. Evinrude workers already had high earnings. A clause in their contract required the company to pay prevailing area wages and on that basis the union had requested and won a number of wage adjustments a year earlier. (It obtained a copy of a confidential area wage survey prepared by Milwaukee employers and found some differentials in favor of workers in other firms.) In addition, deferred wage increases and cost-of-living adjustments under the current contract had given the average Evinrude bargaining unit member a 6.5 percent increase in earnings.[6]

It was important that local negotiators familiarize themselves with bargaining outcomes in OMC's non-Evinrude divisions earlier that year. Evinrude bargaining committee members traveled to Waukegan to talk to union officials there. They saw Johnson's last offer during the strike. This gave them an indication of what to expect in their talks. They also communicated with USW local officials at an OMC plant in Ontario, Canada. Differences in Canadian labor law and national wage policy nevertheless minimized the relevance of the Canadian experience for Evinrude.

Bargaining Over the New Incentive System

Negotiations began at Evinrude six weeks prior to contract expiration. Early sessions were used mainly to let everyone at the table discuss their priorities and general concerns, especially those on the

---

[6]Local union negotiators made these computations. Prior to negotiation of the 1975 contract the average hourly wage was $6.46. The contract increased wages by 4.5 percent in 1975, 1976, and 1977; it also delivered $0.74 per hour in cost-of-living adjustments during this time. In April 1975, the effective date of the agreement, the CPI stood at 158.6 (1967 = 100); in February, 1978, it was 188.3, for a 29.7 point increase, or an 18.7 percent rise (188.3 − 158.6 = 29.7; 29.7/158.6 = .187, or 18.7 percent). The average yearly salary in the Evinrude bargaining unit prior to the contract was $13,436.80 ($6.46 × 2,080 hours per year: 52 weeks × 40 hours); in February, 1978, it was $16,993.60 ($8.17 × 2,080).

Using 1967 = 100 as the base period, real average annual earnings before negotiation of the contract in 1975 (using 1967 as the base year) were $8,472.13 ($13,436.80/1.586) and in February, 1978, were $9,024.75 ($16,993.60/1.883). The increase in real annual earnings, expressed in constant dollars, was $552.62 ($9,024.75 − $8,472.13). In other words, the purchasing power of the annual earnings of the average Evinrude bargaining unit member had increased during the life of the 1975 agreement by $552.62, or by 6.5 percent ($552.62/$8,472.13).

Evinrude workers did about twice as well as did workers generally during this period in keeping up with inflation. Average weekly take home pay for workers nationally in February, 1978, expressed in 1967 dollars, was $92.04, compared with $87.11 in February, 1975, for a gain of $4.93 per week—$256.36 more a year. They had more than kept up with rising prices as a result of combined deferred wage increases and cost-of-living adjustments provided for in their contract and of the wage adjustments made in 1977 on the basis of area inequities.

union committee who would not be taking an active part in the actual negotiations. This was to allow them to "air their feelings," as one official described the process. Agreement was reached by the parties on some minor contract language changes.

In order to postpone serious bargaining over the controversial incentive issue, the union restricted discussions to items it knew management would stubbornly resist, but which it planned to trade away later anyway. These "bargaining items," as Glaser called them, were to change insurance carriers and to create a new job classification at the top of the existing incentive system that would pay more than the current maximum rate.

When contract expiration was two weeks away the bargaining committee had to present management's last offer to a membership meeting under the local bylaws. Union negotiators knew there was no chance for the offer to be ratified, nor did they intend it to be, but they wanted to judge membership sentiment at the meeting in order to assess relative bargaining priorities and willingness to strike.

Apprehension and uncertainty over the incentive system clearly dominated rank-and-file attitudes at the meeting. Committee members informed the gathering of management's proposal to introduce a new incentive system, but they indicated the union had been firm in its opposition. The local president then reminded the members that he had warned them this would happen when the existing incentive system became indefensible. He also discussed an option available to management in the event the union refused to accept a change. The company could begin to enforce strictly the rules governing the system, a situation that he said would become "unbearable" for the union. The meeting ended with indications that the members wished to avert a strike.

During the next several bargaining sessions most remaining language changes were agreed to by the parties. Neither the money item nor the incentive issue was resolved. Further progress was not possible without addressing the incentive problem. As planned, the union responded to the proposal to replace the incentive system with a counterdemand that the existing system be "patched up." Specific suggestions were made by union negotiators on how that might be accomplished. But management's subsequent counter offer, as union leaders anticipated, involved rigid enforcement of incentive rules and standards. Some members of the committee feared it would be worse for the union than the new system.

"The real bargaining was now taking place within our own

committee," Glaser explained. "Committee members agreed the old system was gone, but they did not want to begin a new system." He and the local president persuaded a majority of the committee that, like it or not, management's final offer would include a new incentive plan, that management would take a long strike over the issue, and that eventually the members would have to accept a new incentive system. Therefore, they argued, it was in the members' interest for the union to bargain over management's incentive proposal while it could still get protective contract language on production standards.

But the union did not want to shift the talks away from management's incentive proposal too early. Therefore it asked management to videotape some actual plant operations and then set standards on them as if they were under the incentive system. This request moved the negotiations closer to the contract expiration date without an agreement having been reached. Union negotiators wanted to bargain over the incentive issue and unresolved economic demands in a crisis atmosphere. Their assumption was that people accept fundamental change most easily during crises.

Three days before the contract expired and five before the membership was scheduled to vote to ratify or reject the company's offer, the union proposed retaining the old incentive system. Management insisted this was unacceptable and said it would take a strike. OMC preferred even a lengthy strike which would decide the matter to constant worker disruptions in response to strict enforcement of the present system. The union indicated it was prepared to negotiate.

Before they could accept a new incentive system, committee members told management, extensive protective language would have to be included. Even if such language were negotiated, they could not advise the members to accept the changes after having repeatedly spoken against them. But they would give the proposal "fair representation." Management properly interpreted these remarks to mean that if the negotiated economic package was satisfactory then a modified incentive system might be approved without a strike.

Negotiations progressed rapidly. Management agreed to all the union's incentive language proposals. It also improved its economic offer. The union reciprocated by dropping its demands over insurance carriers and the additional incentive classification. After several hours of bargaining, union negotiators, convinced there was still additional "money on the table," indicated that improvements in existing dental and pension benefits might be enough to get the new incentive system ratified by the members even without a favorable committee recommendation. Management negotiators recessed to discuss the matter. When they came back to the table they agreed to the improvements and a settlement was reached.

The membership met three days later. In previous ratification sessions, Glaser and the local officers had alternated their presentations. This time, Glaser made the entire presentation following an opening statement by the local president. When he finished, a motion from the floor asked for a poll of bargaining committee members to see whether they favored ratification. Three said they recommended rejection of the incentive plan but acceptance of other provisions. Five members made no recommendation in the incentive matter but noted that management agreed to the union's language changes and was prepared to take a long strike over the matter. They added that even if the local won the strike and preserved the old system, the company could initiate a strict enforcement policy. The bargaining unit would have gained nothing. Protracted battles would be fought from a position of weakness.

Glaser responded to questions and criticisms from the floor for some time until a motion to ratify the agreement was put to a vote. The members ratified the settlement by a three-to-one margin.[7]

Summary

American industry continuously evolves from decentralized to centralized corporate structures. Industrial organization economists and historians identify three periods of great merger activity, first at the turn of the century and twice more in the 1920s and after World War II. The pattern of acquisition has changed from mainly horizontal and vertical integration to diversification. Economic concentration forced American labor to adapt its structure accordingly, from craft to industrial unionism during the 1930s and from distinctive to consolidated organizations recently.

Industrial unions have had their greatest bargaining power in concentrated industries. Oligopolistic organization and adminis-

---

[7]OMC sales and earnings fell sharply in 1980 and the company laid off about one-third of its employees and consolidated the marine engine operations in the Wisconsin plant. Despite a rebound in 1981, OMC officials indicated they were seeking to diversify the firm in order to be less dependent on outboard motors in the future. Mark Potts, "Outboard Marine Pilot Knew Seas Would Be Choppy," *Chicago Tribune*, February 10, 1982.

tered price practices in basic manufacturing gave employers the ability to pay, as did the steady productivity gains experienced in most of these industries during the postwar era. Recently, however, foreign competition and declining investment in domestic plants eroded their ability to pay and put them in conflict with the industrial unions over negotiated labor cost increases. Basic steel is discussed in the next chapter as a case study of events in concentrated manufacturing industries.

The results of industrial bargaining in nonconcentrated industries are uneven. Product market competition discourages large economic settlements in one segment of the industry but not elsewhere. Unions therefore try to establish association bargaining which includes all or most of the employers. Centralized negotiations in labor markets can offset the effects of nonconcentrated product markets on the terms and conditions of employment.

The three case studies in this chapter illustrate diverse trends in industrial bargaining. In brewing we see what happens to historic union bargaining power when the industry becomes concentrated and polarized structurally between first and second-tier firms. Unions having multiunit contracts with lead companies which produce in modern breweries have the greatest negotiating success in the industry. Consolidated bargaining structures, secure product markets for the employers, and capital-intensive breweries result in both ability to pay and ability to make pay. Unions with single-plant contracts in marginal firms and production facilities cannot use whatever bargaining leverage they might have because employers claim financial weakness and threaten to close unprofitable operations if they strike.

Men's clothing also demonstrates the trouble industrial unions have in negotiating economic standards when conditions otherwise favor union ability to make employers pay. Unionized garment manufacturers do not have the ability to pay because of foreign and domestic competition and frequent low productivity in their plants. Changes in the composition of the work forces in these industries may also undermine historic union ability to make employers pay.

Negotiation of a new production incentive system at the Milwaukee, Wisconsin plant of Evinrude-Outboard Motor Corporation illustrates the dynamics of local bargaining in a concentrated industry experiencing unaccustomed competition in its product markets. Japanese entry into world markets for outboard motors brought pressure on plant managers and union negotiators to adjust to new cost imperatives by replacing the existing incentive system with another. The prospect of fundamental change in working conditions generated deep-seated opposition from the rank-and-file membership. Skillful bargaining by union representatives and timely tradeoffs by management enabled the parties to negotiate a settlement package that was acceptable to the membership and which might have averted a costly conflict.

Key Words and Phrases

relevant work force	vertical integration
industrial concentration	conglomerate corporations
horizontal consolidation	

Review and Discussion Questions

1. What does it mean to say that "industrial union bargaining power . . . is a derived power . . .?"

2. Describe the factors that determine bargaining outcomes in the brewing industry.

3. In the men's clothing industry, the union "assists employers in product markets instead of exacting unrealistic demands from them in labor markets." Explain.

4. What was the single most important factor forcing a revision of the incentive plan at Evinrude?

Chapter Resources and Suggested Further Reading

The introduction to this chapter is based on Alfred D. Chandler, Jr., *The Managerial Revolution in American Business* (1977); John Blair, *Economic Concentration: Structure, Behavior and Public Policy* (1972); Walter Galenson, *The CIO Challenge to the AFL: A History of the American Labor Movement, 1935–1941* (1960).

The section on industrial unionism in brewing is taken from Kenneth G. Elzinga, "The Beer Industry," in *The Structure of American Industry*, 6th ed., ed. Walter Adams (1982); U.S. Congress, Senate hearings, *Mergers and Industrial Concentration*, statement and testimony of Willard Mueller, 95th Congress, 2nd Sess., 1978; Nuala McGann Drescher, "Brewery, Flour, Cereal, Soft Drink and Distillery Workers of America," in *Labor Unions*, ed. Gary M. Fink (1977); Hermann Schlutter, *The Brewing Industry and the Brewery Workers' Movements in America* (1910);

Sidney A. Wolff, Arbitration award, *In the Matter of Pabst Brewing Company and Brewery Workers Union, Local 770, IBT*, April 13, 1982.

The discussion of economic bargaining in the men's clothing industry draws from, U.S. Department of Labor, Bureau of Labor Statistics, *Technological Change and Its Labor Impact in Five Industries*, Bulletin 1961 (1977); Elton Rayack, "The Impact of Unionism on Wages in the Men's Clothing Industry, 1911–1956," *Labor Law Journal* (September 1958); "Clothing Workers Renew Drive To Curb Job-Destroying Imports," *AFL–CIO News*, February 14, 1976; David Berliner, "Men's Wear Workers on Strike," *The Washington Post*, June 4, 1974; William Serrin, "Combating Garment Sweatshops Is An Almost Futile Task," *The New York Times*, October 13, 1983.

Sources used in the Evinrude Motors–United Steelworkers Union case study include unpublished documents made available to the author by Robert Glaser, International Representative, United Steelworkers of America, and, from the business press, "Sputter, Sputter," *Forbes*, March 20, 1978.

7

Industrial Bargaining in Basic Steel

Basic auto and steel manufacturing exemplify economic bargaining along industrial lines. Negotiated settlements in these industries become the bases for outcomes in other metal manufacturing industries and sectors of the economy. Industrial union leadership from 1940 until the AFL-CIO merger in 1955 came out of the Steelworkers and Auto Workers unions. Steel and auto production workers were two of the highest-paid groups of industrial workers after World War II. They enjoyed some of the best fringe benefits and strongest economic security protections found in American industry. But when industrial unions were called upon to make contract concessions during the early 1980s, auto and steel were in the forefront.

Economic bargaining in steel had come full circle between 1946 and 1983. From initial animosity between the union and the industry after World War II, the relationship became increasingly amicable and cooperative during the middle years. Beginning in the late 1970s, however, with the shutdown of numerous furnaces and mills and a growing number of unresolved disputes in local workplaces, amity gave way to strife. Local union leaders vacillated between compromise with the industry and resistance, while the international union expressed a rising sense of betrayal at Big Steel's structural reorganization and operating reductions. Steel managers began blaming the union and economic bargaining for industry's operating difficulties, something they had not done since the 1950s.

The Industry. Formation of U.S. Steel in 1901 brought the industry under control of financiers like J. P. Morgan. Previously it had been run by daring and imaginative entrepreneurs, men who were emotionally competitive. The bankers, by contrast, were instinctively cautious and collusive, concerned mainly with secure properties and investments, and with stable markets and safe profits. Innovative steel production and distribution was of little interest to them. Steel simply happened to be the commodity in which they traded.

This pecuniary outlook shaped the corporate structure and behavior of U.S. Steel. Because it reigned as industry leader, product price rigidity and target profit pricing emerged as the industry standards. Steel prices were set by U.S. Steel and announced by its president, Judge Elbert Gary, at the famous dinners he hosted for top industry executives. Prices were fixed to lend stability and predictability to what had been a competitive, chaotic industry during the years prior to the formation of U.S. Steel. The success of these efforts was remarkable. Bessemer rails, an industry staple at that time, which had fluctuated wildly in price before 1901, sold at $28 per ton throughout 1901–16, rose erratically in price during World War I, and then held steady at $43 during 1922–32, after which the depth of the Great Depression made administered pricing in steel impracticable.

The after-tax target rate of profit in steel has been 8 percent of net worth. During most of its history, U.S. Steel averaged profit levels at or near the target. From 1917 to 1938, its average annual rate of return was 7.3 percent; from 1953 through 1968 it was 8.6 percent, ranging from a low of 4.9 percent in 1962 to a high of 14.8 percent in 1955.[1]

U.S. Steel coordinated prices and production levels to realize its target rate of return at about 80 percent of operating capacity. In other words, if the company ran its mills at an 80 percent rate of utilization, it would make an 8 percent rate of return at the determined prices. Either a price decrease or a reduction in operations would result in profits below the target rate, but price cuts would also undermine future profit margins. The company chose therefore to restrict production and maintain or increase prices during economic recessions. For this strategy to work, U.S. Steel had to know that rival producers would not undercut its prices. During prosperous years they seldom did, but in severe business cycles they might. With the next recovery, however, the industry once again would fall in line behind the price leadership of U.S. Steel and rates of return would rise for everyone.

U.S. Steel lost much of its monopoly position in the industry

---

[1] Walter Adams, "The Steel Industry," in *The Structure of American Industry*, 5th ed., ed. Walter Adams (New York: Macmillan, 1977), pp. 106–16.

during the decades after 1901. Other integrated companies grew up and challenged its markets until domestic steel production was dominated not by one but by several giant firms. In 1904, U.S. Steel accounted for 61 percent of the market, while the top eight producers had 84 percent; by 1947 U.S. Steel had 34 percent but the top eight still controlled 80 percent of the market. This pattern has continued. In 1980 U.S. Steel's share was one-fifth and the largest eight companies had three-quarters. U.S. Steel nevertheless maintained its leadership position.

Under U.S. Steel leadership, price and output levels were raised periodically by steel executives in response to corporate objectives rather than changed by economic markets in response to natural supply and demand conditions. Industrial organization economists find that oligopolized industries such as steel were characterized in the postwar period by excessive prices, inferior product quality and innovation, and lagging technology. This was generally the case in steel, and to that extent the industry's later operating difficulties were self-inflicted.

Loss of Leadership. The domestic steel industry came out of World War II still the undisputed world leader. Since 1920, it had produced more than half the world's steel supply and was a net exporter of steel products. In 1950, Japanese steel accounted for less than 3 percent of world production and had a negligible trade surplus. By 1980, the domestic industry had fallen to 14 percent of world output and had an 11-million-ton export deficit, compared to Japan's 16 percent of global steel supply and a 35-million-ton export surplus. As Table 14 shows, in 1983 the United States was the world's third largest steel producer, behind the Soviet Union and Japan; several industrialized countries, including the United States, provided less steel in 1983 than they had in 1973.

The emergence of Third World steel producers has intensified international competition. Subsidized and protected by their governments and able to take advantage of low domestic labor costs, Brazilian, South Korean, and other developing-nation producers, increased output and export levels while the rest of world steel languished. During 1970–82 the newcomers expanded their share of global markets from 7 to 17 percent. While United States, European Common Market, and Japanese raw steel production dropped from 457 to 329 million tons during that time, Third World output nearly doubled, from 42 to 81 million tons. By 1982, imports were taking 40 percent of the West German market—more than twice the import ratio as in the United States—and Japanese steelmakers were protesting alleged dumping by South Korean steel producers.

Table 14. Steel Production in Developed and Developing Nations, 1973 and 1983

Nation	Millions of tons of raw steel 1973	1983	Percentage change 1973–1983
USSR	145	168	16
Japan	129	107	−17
US	151	85	−44
China	28	44	60
W. Germany	55	39	−28
Italy	23	24	3
France	28	19	−30
Poland	15	18	17
Czechoslovakia	15	17	15
Britain	30	17	−44
Brazil	8	16	105
Rumania	9	15	63
Belgium-Luxembourg	24	15	−37
Spain	12	14	18
Canada	15	14	−5
S. Korea	1	13	930

Source: American Iron & Steel Institute, *Annual Statistical Report*, 1973, 1983.

Imports became a problem for domestic steel during the late 1950s. Imports had represented no more than 2 percent of the U.S. market. The ratio rose steadily to 17 percent in 1968 and averaged 15 percent during the 1970s. A major contributor to this rise was the difference in prices charged by United States and foreign producers. Between 1960 and 1975, domestic steel prices, which were already much higher than import prices, rose 104 percent, compared to 60 percent for Japanese and 78 percent for European steel. Domestic prices increased in stair-step fashion, while steel output was restricted in order for U.S. firms to maintain prices; import prices, by contrast, fluctuated up and down while steel output expanded steadily. In other words, foreign steel producers adjusted price to constantly expanding steel output (and jobs) while American companies adjusted steel output to constantly rising prices.

International cost comparisons are difficult to make with confidence, but it is generally estimated that by the late 1970s the Japanese were producing raw steel at least $100 cheaper per ton than were U.S. firms. Precise figures for various studies range from $100 to $160 per ton, most of the difference being attributed to higher U.S. labor costs. Domestic industry sources put the major blame for their cost disadvantage in high hourly wages and restrictive union work practices. The Steelworkers union concedes the wage gap but claims that inferior plants and equipment are the principal causes.

Both sides blame foreign government subsidies for much of the production cost differential.

While government subsidies are a factor in steel production and export patterns, they do not explain the long-term decline of the domestic industry. More important are the relative efficiency with which different nations use productive factors to make steel and the relative prices that they pay for these factors. Looked at this way, domestic steel's problems can be attributed to high hourly labor costs, high raw material prices, obsolete equipment and inefficient plant layout, and higher profit margins than foreign producers.

The three major inputs in steel production are labor, coke, and iron ore. In 1980, the combined price of these factors per ton of steel produced was $303 in the U.S., $240 in the European Community, and $187 in Japan. While the hourly cost of steel labor was higher in this country than in Japan, the relative cost had been changing in favor of U.S. producers. In 1960, U.S. companies paid eight times as much for an hour of labor than did the Japanese, but in 1980 only twice as much. This shift was due to a rapid increase in Japanese wage benefit levels toward the end of the 20-year period and a devaluation of the U.S. dollar relative to the Japanese yen near the beginning.

Comparative prices of raw materials also turned against U.S. steelmakers during this time. American firms paid 39 percent less for coke in 1960 than did the Japanese but only slightly less in 1980; they paid nearly one-fifth less for iron ore in 1960 and one-third more in 1980.

Despite the favorable trend for U.S. companies in changes in hourly labor cost, they did not improve labor productivity relative to the Japanese. Per unit costs of production labor in Japan rose by only 1 percent during 1960–80 compared to costs in this country. By contrast, Japanese producers capitalized on the comparative price advantages they experienced in coke and ore. Their unit production costs decreased by 2 percent for coke and by fully one-third for ore relative to those in this country.[2]

────────

[2]Hans Mueller and Kiyoshi Kawahito, *Steel Industry Economics: A Comparative Analysis of Structure, Conduct and Performance* (New York: International Public Relations Co., Ltd., 1978), pp. 16–22. Another study shows that the ratio of labor cost per ton between U.S. and Japanese steelmakers fell from 3.5:1 to 3:1 during 1970–76; total cost per ton had widened 15 percent in favor of the Japanese during 1960–70, due mainly to increases in raw material costs to U.S. producers. Robert W. Crandall, *The U.S. Steel Industry in Recurrent Crisis: Options in a Competitive World* (Washington, D.C.: Brookings Institution, 1981), p. 48.

Direct comparisons of labor productivity figures are hazardous because of differences in work customs and product mixes among nations. But Japanese steel producers clearly have been more efficient users of labor than the Americans in the 1960s and 1970s. At the beginning of that period they used as much as one and one-half times the hours of labor per ton of steel produced as did the domestic industry. By the late 1970s, however, the Japanese probably used less labor to make a ton of steel than the Americans.[3]

Steel Technology. The U.S. industry is aged and outmoded. An industry in one country is more or less efficient than that in another depending on the extent to which its steel production process is mechanized and automated. That factor will be determined by the type of equipment and the plant layout. In today's steel market, this means using oxygen and electric rather than open hearth furnaces in basic steelmaking, continuous casting rather than ingot pouring and slab rolling, and robotic rather than mechanical systems in finishing mills.

In all but one of these areas, the U.S. fell behind its major overseas rivals. American steel companies invested in millions of tons of obsolete, open hearth ovens during the 1950s, when their competitors were putting in oxygen and electric ovens. It was not until the 1970s that basic oxygen furnaces were used significantly in domestic output, but in the next decade the ratio leveled at below 60 percent, compared to 75 to 80 percent in Europe and Japan. Roughly 20 percent of U.S. mills use continuous casting, but the ratio is twice that in Europe and close to 70 percent in Japan. Moreover, when domestic firms do install casters, they usually get the machinery and expertise from abroad.

Nearly one-third of American steel capacity is electric furnace, which makes this country a world leader in that category. Most of this is used by "minimills"—small, typically independent plants that use scrap metal rather than iron ore to produce steel. In 1981, 45 such facilities reportedly operated in this country. They accounted for around one-tenth of total domestic production but were the fastest expanding part of the industry. Often nonunion operations, the minimills are low-cost producers of wire rod, bars, and other light products.[4]

Even with the introduction of new technology, U.S. steel plants

---

[3]David Hecker and Mill Lieberthal, "Wage Costs and Prices in Basic Steel Products," *Labor Studies Journal* (Winter 1981), p. 264.

[4]Dan Swinney, David Bensman and Jack Metzgar, "The Crisis in Steel: Jobs, Profits, Communities," *Labor Research Review* (Winter 1983), pp. 7-11.

often could not be brought up to competitive levels of productivity. They are aged, too small, and badly designed to accommodate advanced production techniques. Optimal plant size in steelmaking is thought to be around four million tons per year. Three-fourths of the basic mills operating in the United States in 1980 were smaller than that. Those and many more plants also are poorly located geographically for world production and distribution, have inefficient work flow systems, and combine modern and obsolete equipment and work processes.

An additional source of low productivity in American steel is the industry's historic practice of cutting back output in order to shore up steel prices during recessions. If industry production is curtailed from 80 to 60 percent of capacity, for example, labor productivity immediately falls. Workers are not used efficiently during downturns. Blair correlated percentage changes in labor productivity and steel output for 24 of the post-World War II years before 1972. In 13 of those years, both productivity and output changes were positive and in seven they were negative; in only four of the 24 years did productivity and output move in opposite directions (but in three of those years a decline in steel output was accompanied by a very small increase in productivity).

High steel prices charged by domestic producers resulted in higher profits for them than for other major steel industries despite their greater cost of production. According to a Federal Trade Commission study, U.S. steel companies had higher profits as a percentage of sales during 1961–71 than either the Japanese or European Community industries. When profits were measured as a percentage of corporate equity, the U.S. rates were the same as in Japan but higher than in Europe. A more recent report by the federal Office of Technology Assessment shows that domestic companies had higher net earnings as a percentage of assets than four other leading steel industries during 1969–77.[5]

Industry Responses. While the domestic industry's profit performance compares favorably with those of overseas industries, industrial profits generally are higher in this country than abroad. U.S. steelmakers therefore assess their earnings ratios with those of alternative domestic industries. Since they are not committed to steel production as such, the temptation is to disinvest from steel

---

[5]John Blair, "Market Power and Inflation: A Short-Run Target Return Model," *Journal of Economic Issues* (June 1974). The domestic and foreign profit ratios were: United States, 6.7 percent; Japan, 1.7 percent; West Germany, 2.9 percent; United Kingdom, 5.3 percent; and France, 8.3 percent.

into other more promising fields. Corporate diversification thus is an important industry response to the new competition. As a result of several large acquisitions, less than half of U.S. Steel's revenues were in steel by the early 1980s. Armco Steel, after diversifying heavily into nonsteel industries including energy, changed its corporate title to Armco Inc. National Steel, the third largest domestic producer, reorganized itself as the steel subsidiary of a new parent company named National Intergroup. When asked why National chose to acquire a leading savings and loan institution instead of investing in steel modernization, the firm's chief executive officer explained that the operating problems present in steel, "such as capital and labor intensity, import vulnerability and extensive environmental controls, do not, in the main, exist in the fields of financial services."[6]

The overall impact of steel diversification on the structure of this historic basic manufacturing industry has been remarkable. By 1981, nonsteel businesses accounted for 38 percent of industry assets, 27 percent of sales revenues, and 34 percent of operating profits. Nonsteel assets as a share of total steel company assets increased by 9 percent just between 1979 and 1981.

A second industry response is to idle permanently a significant portion of its total steel capacity. Between 1977 and 1981, the industry reduced domestic steel production capability by nearly seven million tons. Four major plants were closed in 1977, totaling 5.4 million tons. Over the next two years, U.S. Steel and Jones & Laughlin shut down an additional 3.1 million tons of capacity. Paradoxically, domestic steel consumption increased sharply during this period and the industry had to operate at its highest level in years and even to purchase raw steel from foreign suppliers.

The economic depression that began soon afterward drove down the steel utilization rate to 73 percent of capacity in 1980 and led to a resumption of mill closings. By the end of 1981, U.S. Steel had closed 13 mills and displaced 13,000 workers. Then, in 1983, the company announced plans to close one-third of its remaining basic steel capacity plus additional finishing and fabricating mills. New top management claimed the firm's goal was to restructure operations in order to break even financially at half of its operating capacity.

---

[6]Agis Salpukas, "National Steel to Acquire United Financial Corp.," *New York Times*, March 7, 1979, p. D-1. In 1984, National Intergroup offered to sell its steel division to U.S. Steel, but the deal was called off when the government raised antitrust objections.

The objective of the industry was to produce less steel—perhaps one-third less over time—but at much lower costs and higher prices. "Even in recessions, there should be a relatively comfortable balance of supply and demand," *Iron Age*, the industry's trade journal, editorialized in 1981. It noted that "most major mills have lowered their break-even points," and "the profit curve above the break-even point is now very steep." In fact, it reported, "U.S. Steel made money on steel even though raw metal output was the lowest since 1947." But the company was not going to increase total capacity. "Do you think you're going to go out and build new coke ovens, new blast furnaces, new steel shops?", U.S. Steel chairman David Roderick asked. "I don't think anybody's going to do that."[7]

The third industry response to the competitive threat was trade protection. Efforts by the steel industry to restrain foreign imports reveal a desire to return the U.S. steel market to the pre-1960 period in which buyers were dependent on domestic suppliers. The federal government has responded sympathetically to requests for import restraints. During 1969–75 the government and the industry negotiated agreements with foreign nations and producers in which the latter voluntarily restricted the quantity of carbon steel products they exported into this country. In 1974, Congress passed a trade law which established procedures for domestic manufacturers to seek legal restrictions on imported goods under certain conditions. On the basis of these provisions, import quotas were imposed on European exporters of specialty steel products in the late 1970s, after the Japanese had accepted voluntary quotas. Also under the 1974 Act, a Trigger Price Mechanism (TPM) was adopted in 1978 to apply to steel imports. It was then temporarily suspended and reinstated. Trigger prices were set by the federal government as a floor under which foreign steel could not be sold in this country. In practice, the trigger price becomes the minimum price for domestic firms. Because they are set at levels close to domestic steel list prices, the result is that the federal government protects the industry's price system and assists its target profit performance. An 8 percent rate of return was included in TPM calculations.

Experiences with import quotas and the trigger price have not been encouraging. They were undertaken ostensibly to give domestic steel the necessary funds and time to modernize and become more competitive. Yet the industry did not close the production cost

---

[7]George J. McManus, "Steel Scales Down to Drive Its Profits Up," *Iron Age*, May 25, 1981, pp. 27–8.

gap during that time. Instead, protection led to higher domestic and imported steel prices. It is estimated that the TPM alone cost U.S. consumers about $1 billion a year.[8]

The industry's other response to instability was aimed at steel labor. Big Steel insisted on economic and work rule concessions from the union. To the workers, it seemed that the companies wanted back the gains made in nearly four decades of bargaining.

The Steelworkers Union. Before the turn of the century the iron and steel industry was effectively organized by the Amalgamated Association, a militant craft organization that laid down unilateral pay and work standards and then shut those mills in which their demands were not met. The Amalgamated was defeated in 1901 by the newly formed U.S. Steel Corporation after the union had struck unsuccessfully for companywide bargaining rights in response to the consolidation of steel production and fabricating. After that, the Amalgamated came under cautious and somnolent leadership. It entered into tacit understandings with iron manufacturers and small steel companies, assuring them strike-free operations and protection against more militant unions and disgruntled workers in return for exclusive recognition rights. With the failure of the violent steel strike of 1919, in which the Amalgamated played a minor role, the union was no longer a relevant factor in the industry.[9]

Throughout the 1920s, Big Steel remained nonunion. Unorganized wage markets coupled with administered price practices created an interesting contrast. Wages fluctuated with changing supply and demand conditions, but steel prices remained constant for long periods. During 1904-34, steel wage scales were changed 20 times, from a low of 15 cents in average hourly earnings in 1905 to a high of 46 cents in 1921.

When economic depression and federal labor legislation threatened the steel industry with collective bargaining in the early 1930s, the employers established company unions. These organizations were challenged not by the Amalgamated, whose leaders wished to be, in their words, "associates rather than antagonists," but by the Steel Workers Organizing Committee, a CIO organization. SWOC sympathizers split the company unions internally by making more militant demands than they did and by recruiting

[8]Crandall, *op. cit.*, pp. 129-39.
[9]H. W. Hoagland, "Trade Unionism in the Iron Industry: A Decadent Organization," *Quarterly Journal of Economics* (May 1917).

company union officers into SWOC. Faced with a determined and growing organizing effort, U.S. Steel, in an astonishing reversal of its historic militancy against unions, voluntarily recognized the CIO, thereby avoiding the confrontation and violence that afflicted other basic industries.

U.S. Steel chairman Myron Taylor made the decision to recognize the union. He was persuaded that the company's longrun interests coincided with recognition of an independent industrial union. The depression was eroding U.S. Steel's ability to maintain price and wage stability, the source of its leadership position. Declining sales put downward pressure on prices, despite cutbacks in steel production of up to 80 percent, and encouraged other producers to lower their wages in order to get a competitive advantage.

Taylor wanted to standardize industry labor costs, even if that meant trade unionism and centralized collective bargaining. Hourly labor costs at that time took one-third of industry revenues, so wage stabilization not only would eliminate labor competition, but would also contribute to price stability. Peaceful labor relations moreover increased the likelihood that U.S. Steel's recent heavy investments in new productive capacity would be profitable. Taylor hoped the new capital would restore U.S. Steel's corporate leadership after years of technical lag and obsolete product lines. "If (CIO President) John Lewis could furnish the industry with a floor under wages, could one be certain that his demand for recognition was the knock of doom and not of opportunity?," Lloyd Ulman asked in his analysis of Taylor's action.[10]

SWOC was reorganized as the United Steelworkers of America (USW) in 1942. It became one of the nation's largest labor organizations, boasting 1.24 million members in 1980. It is also one of the most diversified, as a result of mergers with other unions and of organizing campaigns outside its traditional steel base. In addition to steel, USW negotiates national master agreements in metal mining, containers, and aluminum, and it holds major contracts in metal manufacturing, chemicals, foundries, and shipbuilding. Altogether it has national union bargaining councils in 19 industries. So diversified has the union become that steel workers presently account for less than half the membership.

Collective Bargaining. Modern steel bargaining can be divided into three stages. The first, from 1945 through 1960, was marked by

---

[10]Lloyd Ulman, "Influence of the Economic Environment on the Structure of the Steel Workers' Union," Industrial Relations Research Association, *Proceedings* (1961), p. 6.

industry strikes in five of the 10 national negotiating rounds and above-average economic settlements. The second occurred during 1961–79 and spanned the period when domestic steel lost its market dominance at home and abroad; this phase was characterized by strike-free settlements but more modest wage and benefit gains. The current stage began with the industry downturn and mill closings of the early 1980s and has been characterized by alternating union-management cooperation and hostility and by concession bargaining.

U.S. Steel's first signed contract with SWOC was in 1937. One month later, the U.S. Supreme Court upheld a National Labor Relations Board order requiring Jones & Laughlin Steel to recognize and bargain with the union. Dozens of other companies also began dealing with SWOC after the decision, although most of "Little Steel" continued to resist the union. Subsequent CIO election and strike victories and pressure from the federal government brought the rest of the industry under unionization before and during World War II.

Conflict Bargaining, 1945–59. Postwar steel settlements were an important part of the 1945–49 rounds of industrial bargaining described in Chapter 3. Industry prosperity and union ability to strike effectively prompted substantial wage and benefit packages and solidifed organized labor's position.

Union bargaining leadership became centralized in the hands of the international president and executive board. USW members do not vote on basic steel settlements negotiated by the leaders; instead a council consisting of the elected presidents of all steel locals votes to accept or reject proposals submitted by the officers. Top union officers are elected by membership referendum, but they seldom faced organized opposition during this period. Instead, leadership succession was orderly and predictable.

Bargaining structures also became consolidated until, in 1959, an industrywide settlement was negotiated to cover all of Big Steel. It then became the pattern settlement for smaller steel producers and fabricators. In industrywide negotiations, international union officials met in Pittsburgh with a team of management representatives headed by U.S. Steel's chief negotiator.

During 1947–62 annual hourly wage increases in steel averaged 5.6 percent compared with 4.8 in motor vehicles and 4.6 in all industries. In 1962, gross hourly earnings (including negotiated incentive payments) exceeded those in autos by 26 cents and in all manufacturing by 86 cents. North-South wage differentials were eliminated by the mid-1950s and cost-of-living clauses and supplemental unemployment benefits were incorporated into basic steel agreements.

Big Steel had the ability to pay higher labor costs throughout this period but it was not offsetting them through productivity gains. Nor were the higher wages explained by above-average profits and output growth. Annual productivity increases in steel averaged 2.2 percent for 1947–62, compared to 5.2 in motor vehicles and 2.8 in all manufacturing. Profits as a ratio of net worth averaged 10 percent in steel, 16 percent in autos, and 11.5 percent in all manufacturing. Between 1947 and 1964, hourly steel worker productivity rose 52 percent, output 46 percent, and prices 89 percent. Wage and fringe benefits levels increased 138 percent, while the number of production jobs fell 9 percent.[11]

Steelworker wages and benefits rose sharply during this period of conflict bargaining, much faster than those for all industries. The price the workers paid for these gains was to get blamed for steel price increases. Further, in the mid-1950s U.S. Steel made a successful effort to raise the target profit rate from the historic 8 percent mark. The company increased steel prices greatly in three successive rounds of across-the-board raises.

The company put responsibility for a $6 per ton raise in 1957 on the new union contract, which U.S. Steel claimed would increase labor costs $3.50–$4 per ton. A Congressional committee then investigating steel industry pricing practices conducted its own investigation of the increase and reported that the company's figure included the earnings increases it had also given to nonunion employees—who were paid one-third more than union workers— and that it vastly overestimated the expected costs of negotiated fringe benefits. The committee arrived at an anticipated labor cost increase per ton of between $2.50 and $3.[12]

Cooperative Bargaining, 1960–79. The postwar strike era in steel ended in 1960, when Big Steel and USW signed an agreement settling the industry's longest walkout. In a 116-day stoppage, the union had forced steel to back down from its stated attempt to weaken work rule clauses in basic contracts. These rules restricted unilateral industry elimination of crew sizes as a way of reducing labor costs. During the strike many independent steel users had

---

[11]Jack Stieber, "Steel," in *Collective Bargaining: Contemporary American Experience*, ed. Gerald Somers (Madison, Wis.: IRRA, 1980) pp. 196–97; Frank Pierson, *Unions in Postwar America: An Economic Assessment, op. cit.*, pp. 62–75.

[12]John Blair, *Economic Concentration, op. cit.*, p. 634.

turned to foreign producers for raw steel supplies, a practice often continued after the settlement.

Weakened domestic demand for steel resulted in relatively slower economic gains for steelworkers during the 1960s than in preceding years. It also shifted attention from increases in direct earnings to improvements in fringe benefits and economic security for workers laid off or permanently displaced as a result of industrial dislocation. Cost-of-living clauses were dropped from Big Steel's master agreements, but supplemental unemployment benefits were nearly doubled. Early retirement benefits were negotiated, as well as the 13-week "sabbatical" vacation for long-service employees, in order to create more bargaining unit jobs. This change in emphasis increased the ratio of fringe benefit costs to base hourly earnings from 5 to 21 percent during 1949–68.

National economic policies aimed at curbing inflation also affected steel union bargaining objectives. The Kennedy Administration's wage-price guidelines were taken seriously by USW president David McDonald. In an act of labor statesmanship, McDonald accepted a national steel settlement that was within the government's guidelines but well below those negotiated by other major unions. For this and other shortcomings in the eyes of the membership, McDonald was defeated in the union's 1965 presidential election by another international officer.

Steel imports and layoffs escalated sharply in the later 1960s, alarming both union and industry and prompting them to devise cooperative strategies. In their 1971 contract language, the parties agreed it was in their mutual interest to minimize future work stoppages and to link future earnings to "the long-term prosperity and efficiency of the steel industry." They also pledged themselves to obtain protective legislation against further steel imports and to increase industry productivity. Nothing was said, however, about steel's pricing practices or its diversification and capital investment policies.[13]

Despite such cost-saving declarations, the 1971 agreement greatly increased steel labor earnings. The open-end escalator clause was restored and costly pay incentives were spread throughout the industry. Still, these increases did not widen the average la-

---

[13]*Agreement Between United States Steel Corporation and the United Steelworkers of America, Production and Maintenance Employees, Eastern Steel Operations, Western Steel Operations.* August 1, 1971, Pittsburgh, Pennsylvania, Section 1, "Purpose and Intent of the Parties," pp. 3–5.

bor cost differential between domestic steel and its chief international competitor, Japan.

In fact, Hecker and Lieberthal claim that negotiated labor cost increases during this time accounted for only a small part of total steel price increases. They base their conclusion on calculations of annual changes in prices and labor costs. Using steel industry figures, they measure the "composite price per ton of steel" and the "wage employee cost per ton of steel." Composite price is the average price per ton of all basic steel products produced and shipped in a particular year, assuming a constant mix of products, even though in practice the mix changes over time. Wage employee cost per unit is the mathematical product of the cost per hour of production labor—which includes direct wages and both negotiated and government-mandated fringe benefits—times the estimated number of hours of production labor required to make a composite ton of steel products. Hecker and Lieberthal estimate the number of production labor hours by dividing total annual hours (number of hourly workers × average hours worked per week × 52 weeks) by total steel shipments.

Their figures show that labor cost increases were responsible for only a fraction of the increases in steel prices during 1960–80. While hourly wages and benefits rose considerably, the number of wage labor hours required to make a composite ton of steel fell, by their calculations, from 11.7 in 1960 to 6.4 in 1980. During this time, labor costs per ton increased 165 percent and steel prices increased 250 percent. In 1960, wage labor costs represented 36 percent of the price of a composite ton of steel, in 1970 they were 31 percent, and in 1980, only 27 percent.

Increases in steel wage labor costs per ton were much lower than increases in price per ton. The difference is illustrated in Diagram 2. During 1960–67, a period of relative wage and price stability, the increase in wage labor costs was 26 percent of the rise in price per ton; from 1968 through 1973, when wage and price increases accelerated, the ratio of labor cost to price increases per ton declined to 16 percent; and during 1974–80, which was the period of fastest increase in both labor costs and prices, it climbed again to 26 percent. In other words, throughout the years 1960–80, per unit increases in hourly labor costs explained no more than one-fourth of the price increases per ton of steel. Moreover, Hecker and Lieberthal found no consistent relationship between steel wage and price increases after allowing a year's time lag for labor cost increases to influence prices.

Diagram 2. Wage Labor Costs and Composite Steel Prices, 1960–80

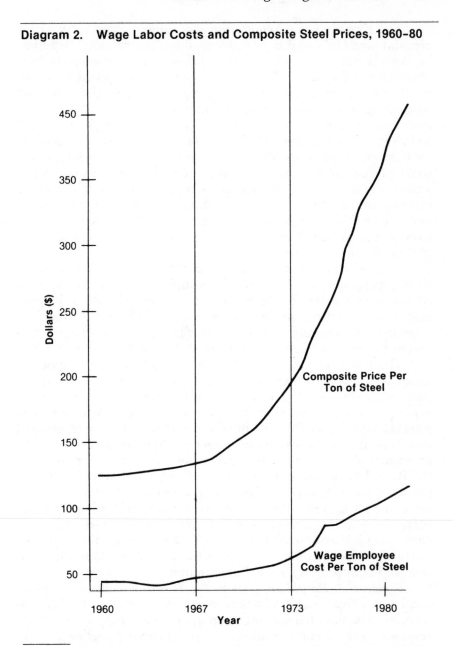

Source: David Hecker and Mil Lieberthal, "Wage Costs and Prices in Basic Steel Products," *Labor Studies Journal* (Winter 1982), p. 265. Figures are based on data published by the American Iron and Steel Institute.

The Experimental Negotiating Agreement. Prior to the 1974 negotiations, USW and Big Steel signed an Experimental Negotiating Agreement (ENA) under which they sought to staunch the flow of steel imports and discourage users from building prestrike inventories. ENA publicly committed the parties to settle their contract bargaining differences without production stoppages. If an agreement could not be reached voluntarily, the outstanding issues would be submitted to binding outside arbitration. Workers were guaranteed annual wage hikes of 3 percent or more in return for the no-strike pledge. They were also assured financial bonuses and preservation of their right to strike over local issues, subject to international union authorization. Minimum wage increases and an improved COLA formula were incorporated in the initial ENA bargaining round, but hefty economic packages were negotiated in each of the next three rounds.

The 1977 talks featured union demands for a "lifetime security" program. Individual workers would be assured income and economic guarantees in the event of a long-term layoff or job displacement. In return, the industry wanted greater control over work assignments. Despite rumors of a stalemate, the negotiators reached agreement well within the time limit specified under ENA.

The three-year pact called for wage and benefit increases of about 30 percent, which compared favorably with the economic packages being negotiated in other industries. It contained an income protection plan which guaranteed early retirement for most workers with at least 20 years of service if their jobs were threatened and "suitable" work was not available for them. Improvements and extensions also were made in supplemental unemployment benefits (SUB) and in health and insurance benefits. The industry did not get the work rule concessions it had asked for. Nevertheless, because the settlement failed to address satisfactorily the problems of plant closings, subcontracting of union work, and unilateral changes in job assignments, the union's basic steel conference narrowly rejected the contract on the initial vote. After some deliberation, it was approved on the second ballot.

Concession Bargaining, 1980–83. The 1980 contract negotiations took place against a backdrop of mill closings and rising joblessness. The national steel agreement also was being undercut. In response to threatened shutdown and bankruptcy, steel locals were making contract concessions that created a two-tiered system of wages and conditions within the industry.

In 1979, U.S. Steel got the international union to hold elections among workers at its three Ambridge fabricating plants to decide whether they would take pay cuts and escalator clause restrictions to keep the plants open. The aging mills were noncompetitive, according to the company, because wages were several dollars per hour more than those in the independently-owned fabricating mills that were not under the basic steel contract. (Bureau of Labor Statistics industry wage data show approximately a $4 per hour difference between basic steel and steel fabricating in 1979.) Over the years, Ambridge had phased down from 15,000 employees in 21 mills to 3,000 in the three plants, 2,000 of whom were USW members. Following a leadership recommendation to accept, the concessions were approved in balloting at two locations, but were rejected by workers in Gary, Indiana. The Indiana plant was closed and the other two were kept open.

Later that year, Wheeling-Pittsburgh, which claimed financial distress, asked workers at its Pittsburgh-area tube and sheet mill to accept reductions in incentive earnings because, the company said, they were much above industry averages. The workers agreed, and a year later Wheeling asked for concessions at all of its mills, including additional givebacks at Pittsburgh. It wanted hourly workers to pass up two scheduled COLA increases and forego a negotiated pay bonus. Again the workers agreed, this time at the urging of both international and local officers.

Shortly afterward, Big Steel's collective bargaining association notified the union that Wheeling-Pittsburgh had withdrawn from the group, thereby removing the company from the direct impact of future settlements. Wheeling then asked for a second round of companywide concessions. This time, the union agreed to exchange scheduled wage and benefit increases—valued annually at $3,500 per worker—for a stock ownership plan. Wheeling used the savings from these two rounds of concessions to purchase continuous casters from Japan.

Major USW demands in the 1980 contract talks included advance notice of plant closings, restrictions on contracting out of union work, "substantial" wage hikes, and improved income protection and economic security provisions, especially in pensions. Industry bargaining initiatives again focused on improving productivity. Employers generally wanted greater flexibility in using labor and more cooperation from the union in shop floor discipline. They also insisted that captive fabricating mills be severed from the basic steel agreement to make them cost competitive with independent producers. Industrywide negotiations now covered fewer than 300,000 workers in nine companies.

A three-year contract was agreed upon and ratified without incident. It provided a 35 percent economic package, but diverted some of the scheduled wage increases to finance the workers' pension fund, which was being heavily drawn down by thousands of displaced workers entitled to the income protection benefits negotiated in 1977. Employed steelworkers were thus paying for part of the income security benefits of former steelworkers by foregoing wage increases. The contract also signaled a move toward formal union-management cooperation at the plant level. Subject to local union approval, joint participation teams would be established in separate mills to improve productivity through direct labor involvement in the production process.

Between the 1980 and 1983 bargaining rounds, the number of production jobs in steel dropped sharply. During the 1960s, production employment had fluctuated between 400,000 and 450,000, but in the 1970s it fell steadily to about 340,000. When the upturn in steel occurred during 1978–79, hourly employment nevertheless remained constant. It rose somewhat over the next 18 months, but again in 1982, the number of jobs plunged by more than half to the lowest level in fifty years.

Analysts attributed steel's crisis to a failure to modernize the mills and a stubborn adherence to increasingly obsolete price and output practices. But industry officials insisted the problems were misguided government policies and overpaid workers. In April 1982, U.S. Steel presented the union with an internal study of steel production costs which, in effect, put the burden of saving hourly jobs on the union. The report concluded that "the ability to control unit employment costs is now essential to the continued existence of the steel industry."[14] On that basis, the industry asked union leaders to reopen the contract, which was due to expire in 1983, and to negotiate concessions.

USW leaders agreed, and at subsequent bargaining sessions the industry said it wanted $6 billion in labor cost savings, mainly from wage freezes and cost-of-living deferments. The industry promised in return to finance its dwindling supplemental unemployment fund. As if to punctuate these demands with a concrete warning, U.S. Steel announced it would be closing the Fairfield works near Birmingham, Alabama. The local union had turned down company plans to cut crew sizes through job combinations and subcontracting of production work, changes which would have reduced production workers by one-fifth.

---

[14]"Steel's Self-Portrait Is Grim Indeed," *Industry Week*, July 12, 1982, p. 19.

However, it was not a propitious time to ask steel workers for concessions. U.S. Steel was acquiring Marathon Oil for $6.3 billion. Workers had been told that reductions in their living standards and more onerous working conditions would result in modernized steel mills and greater job security, but now they saw the lead firm rapidly disinvesting from the industry. Moreover, unilateral employer changes in work rules were generating hostility in the mills. Union leaders talked of a growing "credibility gap" between the industry and its work force.

USW's basic steel conference nevertheless authorized the international to enter into concession talks. In response to steel's $6 billion figure, USW offered $2 billion in givebacks by freezing wages for three years and tying future cost-of-living payments to productivity gains. Industry negotiators rejected this counteroffer, so the leadership submitted the $6 billion package to a ratification vote but with a recommendation to reject, which the workers did—overwhelmingly.

Within a few months, however, the union agreed to a resumption of talks. This time, the parties agreed on a concession package much below the industry's initial figure. It would have cut direct labor costs 11 percent by reducing hourly rates an average of $1.50 and eliminating two COLA payments. It also would remove some 90 nonsteel subsidiaries from the master agreement. This offer too was defeated by the union council, despite leadership support. It was beaten because continued mill shutdowns had convinced enough local union officials that worker concessions did not buy jobs. Local members at Bethlehem's huge Lackawanna, New York, complex subsequently turned down work rule concessions there because they had gotten no assurance from management that the cost savings would be reinvested in Lackawanna. Bethlehem eventually closed most of the works, displacing some 6,000 jobs. Labor cost reductions were put off until 1983 contract negotiations.

When new contract talks began early that year, USW negotiators made it clear that the price of concessions was job security. They were under internal pressure to do something to save steel jobs. Total USW membership had declined by 500,000 since 1981, bringing the figure down to about 700,000. In basic steel, only seven companies still participated in industry bargaining after a recent withdrawal by Allegheny Ludlum. (In 1985 the bargaining committee would be abolished altogether.)

A 42-month contract was negotiated and ratified sooner than might have been expected in the tense atmosphere surrounding the talks. The agreement cut average steel wages for the first time, by $1.25 an hour, and eliminated some cost-of-living payments. But it did not deflect scheduled wage increases into the SUB fund, as earlier concession demands would have done, nor did it remove the escalator clause, as the industry also wanted. In addition, the international union was unable to win its major language objective. No restrictions were placed on subcontracting and plant shutdowns. Finally, the ENA was abandoned at the industry's insistence.

It later was estimated that the three-and-one-half-year concession package was worth $3 billion. As a percentage of worker earnings, the givebacks probably were greater than those made by the UAW in autos, but no more than some of those in meatpacking, tires, airlines, and trucking. Nor did the steel concessions introduce a two-tiered wage structure between new and existing workers, as happened often in other concession bargains.

USW did agree to labor-management negotiations over work rules at the plant level. This change represented a major union retreat from the principle of industrywide standards. In practice, it enables employers to whipsaw individual mills, under the threat of shutdowns and phasedowns, unless workers agree to job combination and elimination. It could mean the demise of entire crafts and production crews, as firms consolidate operations to reduce capacity and introduce new technology to cut production costs. Big Steel thus got the work rule flexibility it had failed to negotiate in 1977 and 1980.

As it turned out, however, the 1983 concessions did nothing to save jobs. Additional layoffs and shutdowns occurred soon after. "We're being hit with at least one plant closing or bankruptcy a day," lamented a USW headquarters staff employee. "The feeling around here is that we're in a state of siege."[15] Several months later the union received additional plant-level concession demands and shutdown threats.

In late 1983, U.S. Steel sent a letter to some 4,700 union members at five plants; it warned them that their jobs were in jeopardy if they did not accept further sacrifices. In two locations they were asked to accept extensive job combinations, reduced crew sizes, and virtually unlimited management rights to subcontract work; in three others they were expected to take a 25 percent cut in wages

---

[15]Carol Hymowitz, "Once-Powerful Steelworkers Union Is a Casualty of Shakedown in Industry," *The Wall Street Journal*, October 12, 1983, p. 31.

and benefits. Company officials also hinted darkly to the press that workers at many more plants might have to make further concessions in order to save their jobs.

This renewed effort drew an angry response from the union. Acting USW president Lynn Williams called an emergency meeting of the international executive board. (Williams had been elected by the executive board temporarily to succeed Lloyd McBride, a strong supporter of tactical union concessions, who had died weeks earlier.) The board drafted a policy statement that rejected all future local concessions that would impinge upon the master agreement. Accusing U.S. Steel of overstepping its right to negotiate separate plant concessions, the statement said that unless the international intervened its locals "would be whipsawed by threats of plant closing, diversion of orders from one plant to another, false promises, and many other pressure tactics." This approach "would soon result," it predicted "in our collective bargaining policy being determined by weakness and division—not by strength and unity."[16] Union cooperation with the industry to save jobs through contract concessions thus, for all practical purposes, had ceased.

U.S. Steel made no immediate response to this shift in union policy. But two weeks later the corporation made a stunning announcement. Not only did it plan to close four of the five plants in which it had asked workers to make further concessions— meanwhile promising to reopen and possibly expand the closed Fairfield works, where local members now were ready to accept management work rule demands—but also to close or phase down more than a dozen others. Altogether, the jobs of about 15,000 production workers were at stake. The planned reductions would trim U.S. Steel capacity by 5 million tons, nearly one-sixth of its total amount, mostly affecting bar, rod, and wire production, which was vulnerable to both import and minimill competition. The "reconfiguration," as U.S. Steel's chairman called it, would leave the company as primarily a sheet, plate, and pipe producer and also would reduce its break-even point of production from 70 to 60 percent of operating capacity—the company's long-run goal, he said, was to bring the ratio down to 50 percent.[17]

---

[16]BNA, *Daily Labor Report*, No. 240, December 13, 1983, pp. A5–A6.
[17]Steven Greenhouse, "U.S. Steel Closings Expected," *The New York Times*, December 27, 1983, p. A1.

Summary

Recent bargaining experiences in the steel industry illustrate what happens to earnings, benefits, and jobs when a previously secure industrial oligopoly comes under direct price competition from foreign and domestic producers. Once an industrial union wins recognition rights from a powerful industry like steel, which successfully resisted unionization and collective bargaining for more than three decades, it can turn the industry's oligopolistic structure and administered price system to its own bargaining advantage. In the absence of foreign or domestic price competition, the major steel producers could pass on higher labor costs in the form of successive price hikes without fear of being undercut. In fact, the evidence suggests that they could raise prices by more than enough to compensate for negotiated labor cost increases and still put the onus on the union. Industrial union strength in these situations rested on a demonstrated ability to shut down production during national strikes. Steelworkers, as a measure of their union's success in this regard, eventually became the highest paid hourly workers in the country.

A period of frequent national stoppages and strained labor-management relationships in steel was ended during the early 1960s. The parties renounced hostilities and began to cooperate in efforts to protect the industry's dominant market position. There were no strikes and for a time USW leaders moderated their demands at the bargaining table. But the industry failed to take advantage of the new era in labor relations to upgrade its plant and equipment and meet the growing import threat. Instead it sought federal trade protection against the competition while diversifying its assets into nonsteel activities.

The steel industry also phased down plant capacity. By threatening to close additional plants, it extracted concessions from the workers, both in local and national bargaining. USW policy was to make strategic contract concessions in the hope of delaying or avoiding shutdowns, and meanwhile to help the industry obtain government trade protection. Big Steel continued to phase down operations, despite the vague commitments it had made to the contrary following earlier union concessions. With the death of USW president Lloyd McBride, who had been the driving force behind the union's concession policy, the international executive board formally rejected givebacks as a jobs-saving policy. U.S. Steel later announced it was closing or phasing down about one-sixth of its steel capacity.

The union was in no position to prevent the action or to retaliate against it. USW's post-World War II bargaining power had derived from the industry's product market dominance and its own ability to strike effectively nationwide. Now the industry had lost discretionary control over steel markets and also had no reason to expect or fear widespread strikes from its demoralized work force and debilitated union. The prognosis is for a scaled-down domestic steel industry, one that produces far less raw steel and fewer finished products but which does so in more efficient mills; one which employs union workers, but not nearly as many of them as in the past, and at competitive wages and benefits but without strong contract language and union work rules.

Key Words and Phrases

price leadership
target-profit pricing
unit labor costs
utilization rate

experimental negotiating
agreement (ENA)
break-even point

Review and Discussion Questions

1. Speaking of financiers who gained control of the steel industry, the author says: "Steel simply happened to be the commodity in which they traded." What is the import of this statement?

2. Describe the historical "target-profit pricing" standard of U.S. Steel.

3. What factors explain the long-term decline of the domestic steel industry?

4. What have been the industry's responses to its economic difficulties?

5. What is the outlook for employment, wages, and benefits in the steel industry?

Chapter Resources and Suggested Further Reading

Description of steel industry structure, behavior, and performance is based mainly on these sources: Walter Adams, "The Steel Industry," in *The Structure of American Industry*, 5th and 6th eds., ed. Walter Adams (1982); Walter Adams and J. B. Dirlam, "Steel Imports and Vertical Oligopoly Power," *American Economic Review* (September 1964); Leonard W. Weiss, *Case Studies in American Industry*, 2nd ed. (1971); Robert Crandell, *The U.S. Steel Industry in Recurring Crisis: Policy Options In a Competitive World* (1981); Hans Mueller and Kiyoshi Kawahito, *Steel Industry Economics: A Comparative Analysis of Structure, Conduct and Performance* (1978); and reports for various years of the American Iron and Steel Institute, *Annual Statistical Report*.

Major sources used in the section on steel unions and collective bargaining are H. W. Hoagland, "Trade Unionism in the Iron Industry: A Decadent Organization," *Quarterly Journal of Economics* (May 1917); Lloyd Ulman, "Influence of the Economic Environment on the Structure of the Steel Workers' Union," Industrial Relations Research Association, *Proceedings* (1961); Jack Stieber, "Steel," in *Collective Bargaining: Contemporary American Experience*, ed. Gerald Somers (1980); Frank C. Pierson, *Unions in Postwar America: An Economic Assessment* (1967); Dan Swinney, David Bensman, and Jack Metzgar, "The Crisis in Steel: Jobs, Profits, Communities," *Labor Research Review* (Winter 1983); Richard Kalwa, "Collective Bargaining in the Basic Steel Industry, 1977–1983," (1983).

Sources from the business and commercial press include George J. McManus, "Steel Scales Down to Drive Its Profits Up," *Iron Age*, May 25, 1981; Agis Salpukas, "National Steel to Acquire United Financial Corp.," *The New York Times*, March 7, 1979; James M. Perry, "Idle Mills, a Dearth of Hope Are Features Of Ohio's Steel Towns," *The Wall Street Journal*, January 20, 1983; "U.S. Steelmakers Slim Down for Survival," *Business Week*, May 31, 1982; Carol Hymowitz, "USW Warns U.S. Steel, Other Producers That It Will Reject Further Concessions," *The Wall Street Journal*, December 14, 1983; Steven Greenhouse, "U.S. Steel Closings Expected," *The New York Times*, December 27, 1983, and "U.S. Steel Plans Closings, Cuts Of 15,430 Jobs," *The New York Times*, December 28, 1983.

8

Conflict Bargaining

Labor relations in a number of industries and firms are characterized by conflict. Contracts rarely are negotiated without a struggle. Frequently the attempt is to undermine or oust the union as bargaining agent. Conflict bargaining often occurs in industries experiencing structural transition, especially where the change heightens competition in product markets. New technology and shifts in government policy also produce conflict bargaining.

Part of the new conflict can be traced to changing managerial attitudes. Unlike the view that dominated management thinking in the 1950s and 1960s, managers began to believe in the 1970s that unions and collective bargaining are not inevitable institutions. Management often went on the offensive to resist unionization in new facilities, transfer work from bargaining units to supervisory personnel or outside contractors, relocate operations in traditionally nonunion parts of the country or overseas, and adopt a more militant position in economic bargaining.

This chapter describes conflict bargaining in a variety of settings. It begins with labor confrontation in the intercity bus industry. Unions successfully organized and bargained nationwide with Greyhound, but had to struggle with Trailways over tactical bargaining structures. A highly publicized strike occurred at Greyhound in 1983, in which the company tried to lower labor costs substantially and to gain more control over the workers.

Also considered is the impact of large conglomerate, multinational enterprises. Their new structures undermine established labor relations by introducing different corporate goals and philosophies and giving management unprecedented mobility and resources with which to challenge unions. The chapter discusses labor relations in the subsidiaries of one such firm, Litton Industries. This is followed by brief discussions of domestic labor practices of

191

foreign-based multinational firms in several industries. Finally, a case study describes negotiations between unions and Litton Industries over the transfer abroad of production operations at two typewriter plants.

Intercity Bus

During a November 1974 strike by Greyhound bus drivers, the company's president attributed the dispute to labor cost differentials between Greyhound and Trailways, the two dominant firms in the intercity bus industry. Greyhound drivers, he pointed out, are "already the highest paid in the country" but "for some reason we don't pretend to understand," he said, the striking union, the Amalgamated Transit Union (ATU), negotiates contracts covering Trailways drivers "that permit much lower wages and benefits."[1] Within a week, however, the strike was settled along the lines of the union's demands, presumably because Greyhound wished to avoid a nationwide shutdown during the holiday season.

Earlier that year the president of Trailways explained why a two-year strike against a single operating division of his company was having no effect on Trailways operations. If the union shut down only one of the more than 20 Trailways bus divisions, it would not impede systemwide profits, he explained: "We just make 'em up from the other subsidiaries."[2]

Labor cost differentials between Greyhound and Trailways were large. A 1969 comparison showed Greyhound paying its drivers a standard 15-1/2 cents per mile and Trailways paying from 8-1/2 cents to 11-1/3 cents. Fringe benefits and noneconomic provisions also favored the ATU at Greyhound.

These disparities were due to differences in bargaining structure. Greyhound negotiated a single contract for a systemwide bargaining unit; Trailways negotiated 17 separate contracts in its unionized divisions and operated a few others nonunion. Strikes or strike threats at Greyhound were nationwide, but those at Trailways were local or regional. Trailways strikes therefore could be circumvented by strategic managerial rerouting and rescheduling of buses from other divisions or by use of strikebreakers in the struck unit, something Greyhound could not do on a national scale. Long, unsuccessful strikes and legal processes occurred frequently in individual Trailways divisions.

---

[1]*The Wall St. Journal*, November 19, 1974, p. 2.
[2]*The Washington Post*, February 11, 1974, p. C-7.

Both Greyhound and Trailways were subsidiaries of conglomerate holding companies. Greyhound's parent, Greyhound Corporation, owned and operated an insurance company, a food service system, a money order business, and Armour Meatpacking. Trailways' parent, TCO Industries, had been acquired by Holiday Inns, the diversified innkeeper. Both holding companies consolidated their regulated transportation operations in a corporate group apart from the other businesses. But while Greyhound Corporation combined its bus lines, most of which had been acquired from railroads, into a single corporate entity called Greyhound Lines, TCO Industries preserved the separate identities of its acquired bus carriers.

Centralized labor relations among Greyhound bus divisions began in the early 1950s. After years of regional pattern bargaining, by 1974 ATU and Greyhound negotiated a single systemwide agreement and direct labor cost differentials among divisions were eliminated. Representation rights for drivers at Trailways, by contrast, were divided between ATU and the Brotherhood of Railway Trainmen (BRT). The two organizations were competitors. Not only did they refuse to coordinate contract negotiations but they also raided each other's units following unsuccessful strikes. Each tried more than once to establish a consolidated bargaining structure at Trailways, but was unable to do so despite lengthy strikes. Neither could negotiate contracts approaching those at Greyhound.

In 1969, ATU and BRT finally set aside their differences long enough to petition the NLRB for an employee election covering all Trailways units to determine if the workers wanted a single, consolidated bargaining unit. They proposed that such a unit would be represented by the two unions jointly; if the workers voted down the single unit, they agreed, there would be no union representation at all. In a three-to-two decision, the Board rejected the proposal on grounds that Trailways bus divisions shared neither common labor relations policies nor common working conditions and economic standards and also had a long history of separate bargaining structures which should not be disturbed without the company's consent.

The Safeway Trails Strike

Analysis of one of several strikes by Trailways drivers demonstrates the consequences for unions of fragmented bargaining structures in a hostile environment. In 1964 Trailways acquired Safeway Trails, a Washington, D.C. to New York City carrier which at that time paid the highest wages and fringes in the Trailways system.

From the beginning BRT alleged that normal Safeway passenger business was being diverted by TCO to other Trailways divisions which had lower labor costs than Safeway. Earlier, Safeway had supported another Trailways division in its effort to enter Safeway's lucrative commuter passenger market between Philadelphia and New York. It is unlikely that an independent carrier would support such efforts by a rival company. In addition, Safeway's revenues from charter bus runs, which can be diverted by the parent company's travel service subsidiary to other Trailways carriers regardless of regular schedules, had declined while those of the Trailways divisions that interconnected with Safeway had increased by up to one-half.

A bargaining impasse over this and other contract issues led to a strike by Safeway's 300 regular drivers. The stoppage developed into a bitter struggle that lasted nearly three years during 1972–75. Safeway suspended operations for 10 months but then resumed services using supervisors in place of the striking drivers. Next it hired permanent replacements, in addition to about 50 strikers who returned to work.

Despite the length of the strike, revenues and earnings of Holiday Inns' travel and transportation group did not suffer. Revenues did decline in the first year of the strike, but reached a new high in the second; gross profits also declined and then rose.

The local was decertified two years later, without having negotiated a strike settlement but after calling off the walkout unconditionally. Several unfair labor practice charges brought by the union during the early months of the strike were also decided about that time. Following instructions from a federal appeals court, the NLRB found that Safeway had illegally tried to have the business manager removed as chief union negotiator. This action converted the economic strike into an unfair labor practice strike for which the company was responsible. The Board nullified its previous decertification of the local and ordered Safeway to resume contract bargaining with the union and either reinstate the strikers or give them back pay. A new contract between Safeway and the union was eventually negotiated.[3]

In 1979, Holiday Inns sold its Trailways division to a privately held investment group. Officials of the holding company explained the sale as a move to get out of the transportation business and reinvest the money in hotels, casinos, and restaurants. Since 1977,

---

[3]The relevant NLRB cases are: *UTU Local 1699 v. NLRB*, 546 F.2d 1038, 94 LRRM 2028 (CA DC, 1976); *Safeway Trails, Inc.*, 233 NLRB 1075, 96 LRRM 1128 (1977).

Trailways had failed to capture a larger share of interstate bus revenues from Greyhound and to cut its operating costs.

A change in company policy regarding consolidated bargaining structures occurred in 1983. ATU negotiated the first nationwide agreement with Trailways, covering some 4,000 workers and consolidating 11 area agreements that previously were negotiated separately. Wage increases were agreed upon and some fringe benefits were standardized throughout the system. In return, the union accepted changes in work rules and other modifications designed to reduce labor costs. These concessions might have been made in exchange for the national contract.

The Greyhound Strike

ATU waged a bitter, violent strike against Greyhound in November 1983. It did so in response to company demands for extraordinary union concessions with nothing in return. The strike ended with a substantial rollback in wages and benefits. Only their stubborn refusal to return to work earlier, despite repeated Greyhound threats that they would lose their jobs permanently if they did not, saved members from having to take even greater cuts.

Under new leadership and federal deregulation of the intercity bus industry, Greyhound Corporation adopted an uncharacteristically aggressive posture in both its product and labor market. Greyhound Lines, its bus subsidiary, began positioning itself for eventual deregulation of routes and fares by dropping unprofitable local runs and petitioning the Interstate Commerce Commission for additional long-distance routes which would bring it into competition with smaller carriers. Greyhound, which had 62 percent of the nation's scheduled routes, disaffiliated from the American Bus Association, the industry's trade group. ABA then came out against further expansion by the industry giant.

Greyhound had initiated the 1983 round of bargaining with a list of contract concessions. These included a 9.5 wage cut and extended freeze, a 5 percent wage contribution to the previously noncontributory pension fund, increased employee payments for health and welfare coverage, reductions in several fringe benefits, and a two-tiered pay structure in which new employees would receive 20 to 25 percent below the current rates. Greyhound also wanted work rule changes, including unlimited use of lower-paid, part-time employees in place of regular union workers. The company estimated the overall savings at 17 percent; the union said it was more like 23 percent, and accused the carrier of "trying to cut the substance out of what took us 35 years to get."[4]

In its defense, Greyhound cited 30 to 50 percent higher labor cost differentials with Trailways, the entry of low-cost carriers under deregulation, and the effects of low-price airlines on intercity bus travel. People Express airline had taken 45 percent of Greyhound's New York-Buffalo passengers with no-frills fares, according to the company. Despite current profits, Greyhound claimed large 1982 losses in the bus division and insisted that without labor cost reductions it would not be a future competitor.

When Greyhound refused to modify its demands the ATU struck. Some 12,700 members walked off their jobs, including 7,000 drivers. Immediately Greyhound announced it would begin recruiting replacements for the strikers and that it planned to resume limited bus service. Thousands of applicants lined up at company terminals across the country—the long-term unemployed, new labor force entrants, displaced manufacturing workers, and the part-time employed. By the time the strike ended the company claimed to have received 57,000 replacement applications. New hires started at wages proposed by Greyhound prior to the strike.[5]

Greyhound officials estimated publicly that a six-month strike—the length of time needed to get back to full-scale operations—would cost the company $20 to $40 million, but also said that it was worth that much to reduce labor costs permanently. Greyhound Corporation's increasingly diversified structure made it possible for the parent company to risk a costly strike to achieve its objective. The transportation division represented only 20 percent of its 1982 revenues. During the strike, Greyhound's new chairman and chief executive officer disclosed that he was considering selling or franchising Greyhound Lines to nonunion operators. This was not an empty threat, for he recently had sold Greyhound's Armour Foods division after the union had made contract concessions.

Greyhound resumed limited operations after two weeks of the strike. Since Greyhound earned 75 percent of its profits on 25 percent of its routes, it could become profitable again by Christmas. To attract needed passengers, the company announced half-price fares nationwide, a reduction Trailways quickly matched.

Resumption of services resulted in mass union picketing, per-

[4]BNA, "Greyhound Struck By Transit Union Over Proposal to Reduce Pay in New Contract," *White Collar Report*, November 9, 1983, p. 414.

[5]BNA, "Transit Union Members Voting On Greyhound Lines Proposal," *White Collar Report*, November 23, 1983, p. 468.

sonal harrassment of strikebreakers, vandalism of buses, and an estimated 200 arrests nationwide. It was the country's most violent labor dispute in years. Greyhound claimed it was employing 1,300 strikebreakers.

A week after it had resumed operations Greyhound made a second offer to the union. Like the first proposal, this one was said to be a "final offer." Other than reducing the desired wage cut from 9.5 to 7.8 percent, however, the proposed terms remaind the same. The union's Greyhound Council voted against the package but put it to the membership for ratification. It was rejected by 96 percent of those voting. This prompted a militant speech by Greyhound's chairman the following day, in which he expressed "absolutely no optimism that a settlement will be reached." Strikebreakers were now considered as "permanent replacements," he stressed, and Greyhound "will go forward full bore." The company had no plans to return to the bargaining table, he added.[6]

The ATU received support from large numbers of unions at the local and national levels. Organized labor viewed the Greyhound strike as symbolic of the new management aggressiveness and part of a larger struggle to preserve established terms and conditions of employment. AFL–CIO affiliates endorsed a boycott of Greyhound and two unaffiliated unions, the Teamsters and the Miners, supported the effort. Thousands of rank-and-file union members joined ATU pickets at bus terminals across the country. Members of more than 50 unions appeared with pickets outside Greyhound's corporate headquarters.

At a rally outside Boston, the Massachusetts AFL-CIO president told Greyhound strikers and members from other unions, "There's a lot more at stake here than just your local or the ATU. It's a trade union movement."[7] As if to demonstrate it, an estimated 3,000 unionists rallied in California in support of the strikes at Greyhound, Continental Airlines, and McDonnell Douglas, where several UAW locals had been out since October.

Negotiations resumed a few days after the strikers rejected Greyhound's second offer. The ATU Greyhound Council had conveyed through a federal mediator that it was prepared to make further concessions. Once the negotiations began, a settlement was

---

[6]Henry Weinstein, "Greyhound Set for Long Haul," *Los Angeles Times*, November 30, 1983, pp. 1, 21; "Greyhound to Attempt Full Service With Replacements for Strikers," *The New York Times*, November 30, 1983, p. A-24.

[7]Wendy Fox, "Unions Rally to Support Bus Strike," *Boston Globe*, November 17, 1983, p. 42.

reached and ratified by the membership nearly three-to-one. Greyhound resumed normal operations a few days before Christmas, ending the 45-day walkout.

The three-year settlement contained wage and fringe benefit cuts but excluded most of the company's noneconomic demands. Wages were cut 7.8 percent and COLA payments were suspended until May 1986. Workers had to contribute 5 percent of their pay into the pension fund, give up two paid holidays, and take reduced vacation time and meal allowances. They also had to assume a large share of their health and welfare plan costs. New employees would be paid 20 to 25 percent below the rates in the old contract and would work under a reduced pension benefit formula, but Greyhound agreed not to hire new people until regular employees had been returned to work.

A union gain in the settlement was preservation of existing seniority rights during the post-strike recall of workers. Strikebreakers, who had been led to believe that their jobs would be permanent regardless of the strike outcome, instead were put at the bottom of the seniority list and therefore did not keep their jobs. In addition, Greyhound dropped its demands for the right to hire part-time employees to do bargaining unit work at lower pay and no fringe benefits, to modify future pension benefits for current retirees, and to work some terminal employees on split shifts. It also agreed to a successorship provision in which the union contract would remain in force in the event the bus operations were sold or leased.

Under the settlement Greyhound would reduce labor costs significantly and gain a competitive edge over Trailways. Despite its lower hourly wage rates, Trailways had been paying about 3¢ more in labor costs than Greyhound for every dollar of sales revenue received. Total union labor costs at Greyhound were now expected to decline by 13 percent over the life of the new contract. Since labor costs were said to represent 62 percent of total costs of production for Greyhound, the full impact of the concession settlement should be to reduce operating costs by about 8 percent.

Strikers were never convinced that Greyhound needed the concessions to survive. Throughout the strike they and their union pointed to Greyhound's recent and current profits and to handsome salary increases for Greyhound executives. They suspected that the new management wanted to break the union. A source of resentment among them was that Greyhound, unlike other companies which claimed economic difficulties, never offered trade-offs for the concessions it demanded.

The strike left a bitter legacy for the workers. The ATU's chief negotiator promised that the union "will be prepared to restore balance to our relationship" with Greyhound. A local union president observed that the effect of Greyhound's hard line was to "solidify the union to an extent I would never have believed."[8] The outlook is for recurring conflict between ATU and Greyhound, barring some dramatic change, which is unlikely in the current institutional setting.

Conglomerate Multinational Employers

During 1953–68 a conglomerate merger wave affected American industry. The largest 200 U.S. manufacturing firms alone acquired some 3,900 companies worth more than $50 billion. Most of these combinations involved diversification rather than horizontal and vertical consolidation. International Telephone & Telegraph (ITT) typified the trend. In dozens of acquisitions, it was transformed from a telecommunications company to a conglomerate, with subsidiaries in baking, lodging, papermaking, auto rental, light bulb manufacturing, insurance, and many other lines of business. In the late 1970s, it was the nation's sixth largest industrial employer.

During this time, eight U.S.-based conglomerates together acquired 419 previously independent companies having assets of $13.2 billion. Just one of the eight had ranked among the nation's 250 largest industrial corporations in 1960, but by 1968 all of them were in the top 75.

The merger pace let up with the stock market decline of 1968 but resumed again in the early 1970s. This time cash-rich oil companies led the way. They bought vast coal reserves and metal ore deposits and acquired established firms outside the energy field, such as Mobil's buyout of Montgomery Ward and Exxon's takeover of Reliance Electric. In one week in 1981, oil companies put up more than $6 billion in attempts to acquire three large metal mining concerns. Later that year Mobile Oil, the nation's second largest energy company, tendered in excess of $10 billion to acquire controlling interest in Conoco, the nation's eighth largest, but was edged out by DuPont, which bid less but represented a more attrac-

---

[8]"If Anyone Won the Strike, Greyhound Did," *Business Week*, December 19, 1983, p. 39; "Greyhound Workers Accept Strike-Ending Settlement," *Daily Labor Report*, December 20, 1983, No. 245, p. 1.

tive parent company to Conoco management. The following year Marathon Oil was acquired by U.S. Steel after Mobil had attempted an unfriendly takeover.

The number of multinational corporations also increased greatly during this time as a result of acquisitions and capital transfers across national boundaries. By 1979 U.S.-based multinationals owned $193 billion in overseas assets, up 15 percent from the preceding year. Foreign-based multinationals increased their asset holdings in this country by 23 percent, for a total of $52.3 billion.

The largest five U.S.-based multinational investors in 1979 were four oil companies and Ford Motor; together they reported $237 billion in annual revenues and $8.2 billion in profits. Each had more than half its industrial assets and made more than half its profits overseas. The five largest foreign-based investors in this country included two oil companies, a South African conglomerate, and the West German retail grocer, Tengelman, which later acquired a controlling interest in A&P. Other familiar brand-name companies owned by foreign multinationals included Libby, Miles (Alka-Seltzer), Howard Johnson, Keebler, and Timex.

Impact on Labor Relations. Conglomerate organization theoretically gives management a tactical bargaining advantage over the unions. The conglomerate employer is, by definition, a multiindustry enterprise. This results in greater employer operating mobility than that of a union whose bargaining structure and representation rights rarely cross industry lines, greater financial leverage than that of a union whose members depend on a single business operation for their livelihood, and greater administrative range than a union whose decision-making options are limited to a single plant or industry. These administrative, financial, and mobility advantages enable the conglomerate to frustrate the collective bargaining process and impair the bargaining strength of the unions.[9]

Multinational organization of a firm compounds the problem for unions. Parallel production that spans national boundaries gives an employer domestic bargaining power because it represents alternative production sources in the event of a work stoppage. Unions also are less likely to learn about employer plans and decisions affecting their members and to confront company decisionmakers in collective bargaining when top management resides in another country.

---

[9]Kenneth V. Alexander, "Conglomerate Mergers and Collective Bargaining," *Industrial and Labor Relations Review* (April 1971), pp. 354–74.

In order to determine whether conglomerate multinational organizations can in fact undermine union power it is necessary to examine the labor relations experiences of one such firm.

Litton Industries

Founded in 1953 as a small electronics producer, Litton Industries was one of the first large conglomerate corporations. By 1969, it had acquired more than 100 independent companies. In 1980, it was the nation's 88th largest industrial corporation with annual sales exceeding $4 billion; it was the 41st largest employer with 75,400 employees. Litton's scores of subsidiary companies located here and abroad are distributed among the four product groups shown in Chart 1. Each group consists of several operating divisions and each division includes a number of goods and services specific to that group. Individual product lines range from navy destroyers to microwave ovens and services range from seismic explorations to medical research.

When profits and sales stagnated for Litton in the 1970s, the company divested itself of some traditional lines but continued to emphasize others, including military supplies, industrial equipment, electrical products, and office equipment and services. It meanwhile expanded operations in the high-growth areas of military equipment, oil industry services and equipment, and communications and data processing.

In most instances where Litton subsidiaries negotiate with unions, it is because the union already had representation rights when Litton acquired the firm. Unions have had great difficulty organizing the unorganized Litton facilities. Workers at its Triad-Utrad electrical products plant in Indiana tried unsuccessfully several times to unionize. The company resisted vigorously each time and numerous unfair labor charges were filed by unions against local management. On at least two occasions Triad-Utrad agreed to NLRB settlements in which workers it had fired during union campaigns were offered reinstatement with back pay.

Unions argue that such firings are effective and even profitable employer tactics to combat organization. Other workers are intimidated from getting involved and the organizing drive loses momentum; subsequent legal proceedings may continue until the union accepts a remedial settlement that protects disciplined workers but also closes out the organizing drive. In addition, the back wages and other costs incurred by the employer in violating the law may be

Chart 1. Litton Industries, Organizational Structure of Product Groups, and Selected Operating Divisions, 1963–81

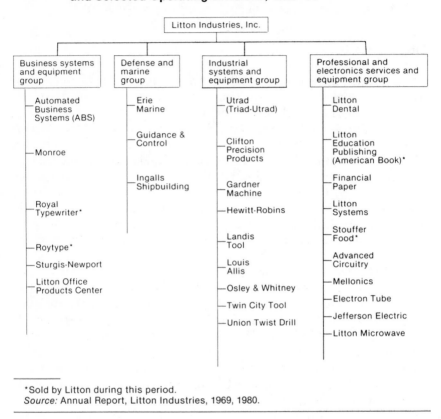

*Sold by Litton during this period.
Source: Annual Report, Litton Industries, 1969, 1980.

outweighed by the longrun gains from not having to bargain with a union.

During 1963–81 unions charged 29 Litton subsidiaries with unfair labor practices and the NLRB issued complaints in the 42 cases listed in Table 15. In 20 of them, the Board found labor law violations and the findings either were not appealed to federal courts or were upheld by the courts; in three other cases the Board found violations but was reversed upon appeal. In 13 cases the Board supervised voluntary settlements (once over union objections) in which subsidiary managers agreed to certain remedial actions, such as reinstatement with back pay for workers fired during union organizing drives, or one time where the union simply withdrew its charge without an apparent finding of employer violation of the law.

Table 15. Cases Involving Unfair Labor Practices Charges Brought By Unions Against Litton Industries' Subsidiaries and NLRB Complaints Issued, 1963–1981

Subsidiary (location)	Charging union	Case citations	Charges	Board finding or settlement
Advanced Circuitry (Springfield, MA)	Teamsters (IBT)	71-CA-7282 (1977)	Interference, discrimination	Violation (case closed upon compliance)
American Book (Florence, KY)	Papermakers	207 NLRB 154 (1973) 214 NLRB 413 (1974)	Interference Discrimination	No Violation Violation
Automated Business Systems (Clifton, NJ)	Electrical (IUE)	205 NLRB 532 (1973)	Interference, refusal to bargain	Violation
Automated Business Systems (Athens, OH)	Graphic Arts (GAIU)	9-CA-7745 (1974)	Interference	Settlement (posted notice)
Clifton Precision Products (Clifton Heights, PA)	Electrical (IUE)	156 NLRB 59 (1966)	Coercion, interference	Violation
Electron Tube (San Carlos, CA)	Engineers (OEIU)	20-CA-15163 and -266 (1981)	Interference, discrimination, coercion	No Violation
Erie Marine (Erie, PA)	Boilermakers	192 NLRB 119 (1970)	Interference, company union	Violation
Iron Workers		6-CA-5291 (1971)	Discrimination	Settlement (reinstatement with backpay; posted notice)
Financial Printing (Santa Clara, CA)	Printers (IPGCU)	256 NLRB 559 (1981) 32-CA-3160 (1980)	Refusal to bargain Refusal to bargain	Violation Violation
Gardner Machine (South Beloit, IL)	Auto Workers (UAW)	38-CA-1815 (1974)	Interference	Unilateral NLRB settlement (posted notice)

ULP Charges Against Litton Industries—contd.

Subsidiary (location)	Charging union	Case citations	Charges	Board finding or settlement
Guidance and Control (Woodland Hills, CA)	Machinists (IAM)	217 NLRB 34 (1975)	Interference, coercion, restraint	Violation (reversed in Second Appeals Court)
Hewitt-Robins (Columbia, SC)	Steelworkers	11–CA–4962 (1973)	Discrimination, interference	Settlement (backpay; posted notice)
Ingalls Shipyard (Pascagoula, MS)	Metal Trades Council AFL-CIO	143 NLRB 712 (1963)	Refusal to bargain	Violation
Jefferson Electric (Athens, AL)	Electricians (IBEW) Aluminum Workers	242 NLRB 417 (1979) 10–CA–15285 et al. (1979–80)	Discrimination, threats Various	Violation Violation
Landis Tool (Waynesboro, PA)	Aluminum Workers Teamsters (IBT)	251 NLRB 941 (1980) 190 NLRB 140 (1971)	Refusal to bargain Interference	Violation Violation
Litton Dental (Toledo, OH)	Teamsters (IBT) Teamsters (IBT) Independent	203 NLRB 143 (1973) 8–CA–7136 (1972) 8–CA–7146 (1973) 221 NLRB 98 (1976)	Refusal to bargain Interference Discrimination Interference	Violation Settlement (backpay) Settlement (election) Violation (reversed in Fourth Appeals Court)
Litton Microwave (Sioux Falls, SD)	Electrical (UE)	18–CA–7065 (1981)	Various	Violation
Litton Office Products Center (Statewide CT)	Clerks (UFCW)	1–CA–11659 (1976)	Discrimination	Settlement (charge withdrawn)
Litton Systems (Pleasanton, CA)	Teachers (AFT)	173 NLRB 153 (1968)	Discrimination	No Violation
Louis Allis (Evansville, IN)	Electrical (IUE) Electrical (IUE) Electrical (IUE)	182 NLRB 433 (1970) 190 NLRB 294 (1971) 193 NLRB 8 (1971)	Interference Refusal to bargain Interference	No Violation Violation No Violation

Mellonics (Woodland Hills, CA)	Independent	258 NLRB 623 (1981)	Interference	Violation
Monroe (Orange, NJ)	Electrical (IUE)	190 NLRB 516 (1971)	Interference	Violation (reversed in Fourth Appeals Court)
Osley & Whitney (Westfield, MA)	Electrical (IUE)	1-CA-7875 (1972)	Discrimination, refusal to pay	Settlement (reinstatement with backpay; posted notice)
Royal Typewriter (Hartford, CT)	Auto (UAW)	1-CA-7697 (1971)	Interference, assisting rival organization	Settlement (posted notice)
Royal Typewriter (Springfield, MO)	Allied Industrial Workers	209 NLRB 174 (1974)	Interference, refusal to bargain	Violation
Stouffer (New York, NY)	Teamsters	188 NLRB 79 (1969)	Refusal to bargain	Violation
Sturgis-Newport (Corinth, MS)	Machinists (IAM)	227 NLRB 1426 (1977)	Restraint, coercion	Violation
TRIAD-UTRAD (Blytheville, AR)	Auto (UAW)	217 NLRB 842 (1975)	Interference	Settlement (backpay)
TRIAD-UTRAD (Huntington, IN)	Auto (UAW)	25-CA-7618 et al. (1976)	Interference, coercion	Settlement (backpay; reinstatement)
	Sheet Metal Workers	25-CA-10439 et al. (1979)	Various	Settlement (backpay; reinstatement)
Twin City Tool (Grandview, MO)	Machinists (IAM)	17-CA-3645 (1968)	Discrimination	Settlement (backpay; posted notice)
	Auto (UAW)	17-CA-3493 (1968)	Discrimination	Settlement (backpay; posted notice)
UTRAD (Huntington, IN)	Electricians (IUE) and District 50	185 NLRB 49 (1970)	Interference, company union	Violation

Source: Published NLRB and Administrative Law Judge decisions.

This is a sizable number of cases, but more important are the repetitive character of subsidiary management practices that gave rise to the charges and the pattern of conflict labor relations that emerges at each stage of union-management relationships in Litton subsidiaries. This pattern reveals a history of aggressive and illegal behavior by subsidiaries in their responses to union activities.

Thirty-four of the 42 cases in Table 15, or 81 percent of them, involved events that occurred during union organizing campaigns or attempts to negotiate first contracts in 22 Litton subsidiaries. Subsidiary management response to union organization drives was similar in nearly a dozen separate Board decisions and voluntary settlements. A composite list of union charges in these cases would allege: (1) that managers interrogated and intimidated employees with predictions and threats of dire consequences should the union win, including loss of existing benefits and job conditions or eventual plant closing; (2) that they disciplined individual union sympathizers and activists; (3) that they made unilateral improvements in terms and conditions of employment and solicited employee grievances in order to persuade workers they did not need a union; and (4) that they created or supported internal labor organizations as an alternative to the outside union.

A case involving Litton's Landis Tool subsidiary is typical. The Board ordered a second representation election after management illegally questioned and observed employees, tried to get the workers to discuss grievances with supervisors when a Teamster organizing drive was underway, and created an impression that the plant would be closed if the union won the first election. The union lost by a wide margin but won the second election comfortably. Landis management challenged the union win on technical grounds and meanwhile refused to negotiate for a first contract. Nine months later the Board rejected the company's argument and ordered Landis to bargain. A contract eventually was signed.

The subsidiary was found not to have violated the law in resisting unionization and bargaining at the Louis Allis electric motors plant in Indiana, a facility Litton opened in the mid-1960s to parallel production of an older plant in Milwaukee, where a union was well-established. Twice the Board refused to find illegal interference with an electrical workers union's (IUE) subsequent efforts. Overturning a trial examiner's recommendation that a 1969 certification election lost by the IUE be set aside, a Board panel held that supervisors' references to other companies that, in their words, had "closed their doors permanently" after becoming organized, did not exceed the limits of permissible employer speech. The union continued its organizing efforts at the Evansville plant and was elected by a wide margin in 1970.

Louis Allis management refused to recognize the IUE after the union won the election at Evansville. The company raised procedural objections to the election and charged that the Board's regional director was biased. The Board rejected these allegations, refused to set aside the election, and ordered Litton to bargain with the union over a contract. After several months of unsuccessful talks, the IUE called a strike. Six weeks later, Louis Allis closed the Evansville plant with the walkout in progress. A year after the shutdown the Seventh Circuit Court affirmed the Board's ruling and ordered Litton to bargain with the IUE.

Litton closed plants or phased out particular operations in other locations either before scheduled representation elections were held or after unions had won elections. In each instance, Litton's size and range enabled it to obtain the discontinued production from alternative sources. A Mellonics computer software operation employing document analysts was shut down when workers began an organizing drive in 1980; a Sturgis-Newport business forms plant in Mississippi was closed after the Board scheduled a recognition election. A Financial Printing business forms plant in California was closed after the Board ordered Litton to bargain with a printers union that had won an election and been certified one-and-a-half years earlier. The company had refused to bargain while challenging the election results. The Aluminum Workers Union was certified at Jefferson Electric in February, 1980, filed refusal-to-bargain charges against the company in May, and obtained a Board order to bargain against Jefferson three months later. But it never did negotiate an agreement and was decertified by the workers in 1982.

Litton built a microwave oven manufacturing plant in South Dakota to parallel the production of a Minneapolis plant that had been built by Litton three years earlier and organized by the electrical workers' union (UE). Product lines then were phased out in Minneapolis and transferred to South Dakota. UE followed the subsidiary and won a certification election at the new plant. Subsidiary management refused to bargain on grounds that the election was invalid. Nearly four years after the election, Litton was found guilty of numerous violations of the law in its response to UE organizing and bargaining efforts.

Eight of the 42 cases arose in established bargaining units.

Most involved management actions that undermined unions as bargaining agents or threatened their representation status. In four instances, subsidiaries refused to bargain with incumbent unions, usually on grounds they no longer had majority support among the workers. This occurred at Clifton Precision Products, in both of Litton's domestic typewriter manufacturing plants, and at the New Jersey plant of Monroe. Each time the Board found illegal company behavior, but the Monroe decision was reversed in federal court. Apparently, all of these plants eventually closed. Another involved the Ingalls' shipbuilding subsidiary, where management refused to provide the union with bargaining information and made unilateral work rule changes; years later, Ingalls illegally eliminated an entire work shift after union stewards had filed too many grievances.

At Litton's Clifton Precision Products plant, subsidiary management tried to get an incumbent local of the IUE decertified. After a strike and subsequent negotiation of a one-year contract, the company urged and assisted workers either to withdraw from the union or revoke their dues checkoff authorizations. When the union sought to renegotiate the contract, Clifton instituted a unilateral wage increase and advised the IUE it was terminating the contract because it doubted the union's majority status. Prior to this management had improved benefits with a job posting system that promised participating employees "career advancement opportunities involving significant prospects of employee job security." Clifton then refused to bargain on grounds the IUE no longer had majority status among the workers. The Board rejected management's claim that it had a "good faith" doubt about worker support for the union.

An NLRB finding of illegal company interference with a decertification election at the Monroe division stemmed from an organizational change in which Litton divided a recent corporate acquisition into separate subsidiaries, Monroe Calculating Machines, and Automated Business Systems. The IUE, which had represented hourly workers at Monroe for some time, insisted that the workers be kept in the same bargaining unit and under the same contract despite the reorganization. Management objected and finally, in exchange for a small wage increase, the union agreed to separate the contracts.

When the parties began renegotiating the Monroe contract, however, a member of the bargaining unit filed a petition with the Board to decertify the union at Monroe. He also brought unfair labor charges against both the union and the company. This action prompted the parties to suspend negotiations and blocked the decertification election until the charges were resolved. When the Board rejected them, the individual filed an additional charge against the union, again blocking the election and stopping negotiations.

The second charge was also dismissed by the Board. Monroe management began holding personal interviews with each member of the bargaining unit to advise them of changes being made by management in the terms and conditions of employment. Included were a substantial wage increase—after years of minimal increases under collective bargaining—voluntary inclusion in Litton's nonnegotiated, contributory benefit programs, and a merit system to determine future wage increases. Then, two weeks before the scheduled decertification election, Monroe sent a letter to each hourly worker saying that the "increased wages, better fringe benefits and pension plans . . . will be possible if we have no union."

The Board found illegal interference by subsidiary management in the unilateral changes in benefits and conditions and the letter linking the improvements to decertification of the union. The results of the decertification election, in which the union was defeated, were thus set aside and a rerun election ordered. But the Fourth Circuit Court of Appeals reversed the Board and denied enforcement. The Court ruled that because Monroe management repeatedly acknowledged the company's low wage structure in comparison with those of area employers its conduct "was economically justified and was not instituted in order to influence the outcome of the decertification election."

Litton had closed several plants. Subsidiary managers sometimes threatened workers with plant closings if they voted in unions, struck, or failed to decertify established unions. This happened at the Automated Business Systems plant. Workers were told that if their union was not decertified in an upcoming election the plant might have to be closed. The gravity of this kind of warning during a tense election campaign prompted the Board to issue a bargaining order against the company. Until then, management had refused to bargain pending the outcome of the decertification election. In the words of the Board:

> It needs no extended discussion or lengthy list of authorities to demonstrate that threats of probable plant closings are among the most serious and most flagrant interferences with the right of employees to decide for themselves the question of union representation.[10]

---

[10]*Automated Business Systems* 205 NLRB 532, 84 LRRM 1042, 1048 (1973).

These cases raise the question whether Litton Industries, the parent corporation, has an overall antiunion strategy for individual subsidiaries. If it does, the NLRB could decide that it considers Litton and its dozens of subsidiaries to be a single employer. The Board then could order a Litton subsidiary to take special remedial steps, such as recognition and good faith bargaining with a union without the union's having won a recognition election, based not only on the behavior of that subsidiary but on the corporate-wide labor law record of Litton Industries. Such a turn of events would strengthen the hand of the unions, which so far have had little success against conglomerate multinational employers like Litton.

The Corporate Campaign Against Litton. During 1982–83, a coalition of international unions, including the three electrical workers' unions, conducted a nationwide campaign against Litton. One part of the effort involved the NLRB. Along with officials from the AFL-CIO's Industrial Union Department, which coordinates multiunion bargaining efforts with conglomerate companies, representatives from these unions met with staff lawyers from the Board to request that they treat Litton and its subsidiaries as a single employer when handling their unfair labor practices.

"We think we made the case that Litton has a corporate-wide antiunion strategy of manipulating and violating the labor laws," said a spokesman for UE. Litton's public relations director rejected the coalition's claim that the company had a pattern of repetitive labor law violations: "Over the past year, a dozen collective bargaining agreements have been renewed without any work stoppage, and 20 percent of all Litton employees are represented by a union, which is about the national average." With respect to the single employer issue, he denied Litton had a centralized labor relations policy. "Each division is a separate profit center and each is responsible for its own labor relations." According to Litton's director of labor relations, "I don't go anywhere unless I'm asked."[11]

That fall the original coalition members enlisted the support of others, including the Teamsters, various religious and community groups, and some elected political officials. The other part of the campaign included demonstrations outside Litton's Beverly Hills, California corporate headquarters, picketing at Litton's December, 1982 shareholders meeting, and introducing a resolution regarding the company's labor relations practices and frequent plant closings,

---

[11]Tamar Lewin, "Conglomerates: Test For Labor," *The New York Times*, January 11, 1983.

which was overwhelmingly defeated at the meeting but did gain the campaign considerable media attention. Additional demonstrations took place in San Francisco, Boston, and Washington, D.C.

The campaign focused on the stalemated contract talks and unfair labor practice charges at the South Dakota microwave oven plant. Both the company and the union devoted substantial time and money to the dispute. Asked by labor writer Henry Weinstein what the ultimate financial costs to the company might be, Litton's director of labor relations replied, "less than giving in to the union's demands."[12]

Appointment of a Labor-Management Committee. In October 1983 the union coalition announced it would be submitting a resolution to the upcoming Litton shareholders meeting calling on the company to obey the labor laws. Various church groups and officials vowed to support the resolution and indicated they would attend the meeting and speak out against what one of them called Litton's "socially immoral" and "socially destructive" labor relations activities.[13]

An event potentially more damaging to Litton than the attack on its public image occurred a few weeks later. NLRB General Counsel William A. Lubbers issued a policy directive to the Board's regional offices in which he instructed them to monitor Litton as a single company rather than a collection of unrelated holdings. This procedural change was the result of an internal Board review of all the Litton cases involving unfair labor practice charges. The General Counsel's office reported that while the evidence was insufficient to conclude that Litton is "virulently antiunion or a notorious labor-law violator," the 85 unfair practices filed against its subsidiaries since 1975 constituted "a substantial number" and that Litton had in fact centralized labor relations in some instances. These findings, said Lubbers, warranted the unusual review procedure.[14]

Litton representatives stated that the Board's action would not affect corporate behavior, but shortly afterward the company made a policy change. When the union coalition introduced its resolution at the December shareholder meeting, with sympathetic clergymen simultaneously addressing an anti-Litton rally underway outside,

---

[12]Henry Weinstein, "Litton: One Battle May Turn a War," *Los Angeles Times*, December 11, 1982, p. 20.

[13]Susan Dunlap, "Drive Pressed Against Litton Law-Breaking," *AFL-CIO News*, November 19, 1983, p. 1.

[14]"Labor Escalates Its Campaign Against Litton," *Business Week*, November 21, 1983, p. 48.

Litton chairman Fred W. O'Green announced a compromise. He proposed that shareholders approve appointment of a joint committee of company and union officials, to be chaired by a neutral outsider, to investigate the alleged labor law violations. "We now have to switch gears," he suggested, saying that the union campaign had been "counterproductive for both parties." Speaking on behalf of the 12 unions participating in the effort, AFL-CIO Industrial Union Department president Howard Samuels welcomed O'Green's proposal, which he claimed "puts us on the road toward a dialogue."[15]

In its first year report the committee said it had made significant gains in specific cases, identified the areas of "continuing friction," and suggested ongoing activities aimed at "diminishing the potential for future problems" between Litton subsidiaries and unions. Its "greatest success," according to the report, was assisting the parties to negotiate a contract at the Sioux Falls, South Dakota microwave plant. The settlement there came four months after an NLRB administrative law judge ruled that the company had failed to bargain with the union in good faith and ordered Litton to pay workers an estimated $1 million in back wages.[16]

Foreign-Based Multinational Employers

A variety of considerations have motivated foreign firms to locate production facilities in this country. Important factors are:

(1) access to American consumer markets, which are among the world's largest;

(2) the avoidance of possible protectionist measures against imported goods and services;

(3) the security afforded private capital in the United States compared to other parts of the world;

(4) the increased purchasing power of foreign currencies in the United States during most of the 1970s (though the trend was later reversed);

(5) the availability of Eurodollars in overseas banks for use in financing acquisitions of U.S. companies.

Domestic Manufacturing Plants of Foreign-Based MNCs. The labor relations policies of foreign-based firms operating in this

---

[15]Earl Gottschalk, Jr., "Litton Proposes Committee to Probe Its Labor Practices," *The Wall Street Journal*, December 12, 1983, p. 37.

[16]Henry Weinstein, "Group Resolves 2 of 3 Litton Labor Disputes," *Los Angeles Times*, November 22, 1984, pp. 1, 12.

country depend largely on their reason for locating here and their traditional attitude toward unions and collective bargaining. Volkswagen, for example, began assembling VW Rabbits in Pennsylvania in order to supply its large and growing share of the domestic small-car market, not to exploit labor. It did not resist UAW organization, although it asked for and received initial UAW concessions from the Big Three pattern.

Honda and Nissan (Datsun) have resisted U.S. unions and collective bargaining, which are unfamiliar labor institutions to them. Honda opposed the UAW's organizing drive at its Ohio assembly plant. Later the company was cited by the regional NLRB office for prohibiting workers from wearing UAW caps on the job. In another proceeding, the Board rejected Honda's plea for exemption from traditional Board standards because "the Japanese approach to labor relations is different." A year later, however, in what one of them described as "the beginning of a new era of cooperation," company representatives reversed the policy and said that Honda would no longer actively resist UAW organization efforts.[17]

Nissan was the object of labor violence at the construction site of its Tennessee truck plant after it had hired nonunion contractors. The company indicated it would resist unionization of the plant when it began full production. Nissan's chief executive officer of U.S. operations later told the first few hundred workers to be employed that the company would not welcome a union. "A lot of avenues of communication are just not open when you have a union shop," he was quoted as saying. "You can't build a quality product with an adversary relationship between unions and management."[18]

Michelin, a French-based multinational, located tire-making complexes in Canada and the United States in order to supply the North American market with radial tires which the domestic tire firms then were unable to compete against. It built plants in traditionally nonunion parts of both countries—Nova Scotia and the U.S. Southeast. None of them were organized by the United Rubber Workers union. The choice of location probably reflected the company's antiunion philosophy. The Michelin family, which continues to control the enterprise, says it does not recognize and bargain with unions anywhere in the world. "Those who exercise power but whose actions are not balanced by responsibilities are prone to excess," François Michelin said in explanation of his opposition to

---

[17]Clyde E. Farnsworth, "Honda Ends Opposition to Auto Union's Efforts," *The New York Times*, April 23, 1982, p. 39.

[18]"Building Trades Picket Nissan Plant Site," *Chicago Tribune*, February 4, 1981, p. 3.

unions. In 1980 the AFL-CIO Executive Council voted to put Michelin on the Federation's "unfair" list on the basis of union reports that the company had "unrelenting anti-union policies."[19]

The Swiss food conglomerate Nestlé also prefers doing business in North America. "The U.S. seems likely to continue along the path of economic freedom," Nestlé's managing director observed, "while Europe risks going in a more socialistic direction."[20] Labor relations at Nestlé's Fulton, New York, facility, its largest chocolate factory in this country, have been in conflict since the early 1970s. Strikes, one of them lasting five months, and frequent NLRB and arbitration proceedings have marred the relationship. At issue were management efforts, first, to replace separate craft classifications with a composite craft arrangement and, second, to resist coordinated bargaining attempts among domestic Nestlé unions.

Differing Union-Management Views. Opinion differs whether multinational corporate structure affects labor relations in the host country. Some observers argue that it does not, but they do so by limiting their definition of labor relations to exclude broader issues such as production location, technology, and processes. Under this definition, it is difficult to find a multinational impact, because day-to-day labor relations in host country plants normally are conducted by domestic professionals hired by parent firms for that purpose. Economic settlements customarily imitate domestic patterns and labor relations trends.

Others say that multinationals do have an effect. They expand the definition of labor relations to include traditional prerogatives of management, including investment and production choices. Their justification is that such decisions determine the environment within which bargaining occurs. Using this definition, they focus on the decision-making authority of company headquarters.

Compare the comments of a Ford Motor Company senior labor relations director with those of a representative of the international trade secretariat of unions of workers in the food industries of different nations. "Accepted by the unions or not," says the Ford official, "the prevailing and current management position is to consider basic investment and production development decisions as outside the scope of industrial relations matters appropriate for consultation or bargaining." The union representative rejected this view on grounds it would "avoid the issue and not talk about the

---

[19]"Michelin Goes American," *Business Week*, July 26, 1976, p. 59.
[20]Robert Ball, "Nestle Revs Up Its U.S. Campaign," *Fortune*, February 13, 1978, p. 80.

power relationships that exist between organized workers and employers."[21] The importance of multinational structures thus depends on which issues should be discussed at the bargaining table and the extent to which routine labor relations matters are determined by events beyond the immediate workplace.

Local Bargaining Case Study: Litton-Royal Typewriter

This case concerns negotiations prior to the shutdown of two Royal Typewriter plants by the parent company, Litton Industries. Domestic production was transferred to overseas typewriter subsidiaries.

Litton acquired Royal in 1965. Royal's headquarters and older manufacturing facilities were located in Hartford, Connecticut; a newer plant was in Springfield, Missouri. Within a few years, Litton acquired several more typewriter producers overseas, including the largest British and West German companies. Triumph-Adler of Germany boasted sophisticated research and development capability, far superior to that of Royal. It also had modern manufacturing plants and equipment. Soon after, perhaps as early as 1969, the parent corporation decided to phase down and close all its typewriter production units except in West Germany.

Shutdown of the U.S. operations began with the closing of the Springfield plant, where a local union of the Allied Industrial Workers represented about 1,000 hourly workers. The closing occurred in 1969 during an unfair labor practice strike. Both Litton and its subsidiary later were found in violation of the law for, among other things, refusing to bargain with the union initially over new contract terms and then over the decision to close the plant. Union negotiators were told, for example, that Litton headquarters would make the final decision whether to keep the plant open. Meanwhile, if the union had any proposals or suggestions on the decision, it should relate these directly to corporate management or through Litton's director of labor relations, who was heading Royal-Springfield's negotiating team. This approach to the matter made local bargaining meaningless. Union representatives could not make accountable the corporate managers who were making the final decision.

Management negotiators acknowledged as much. "We are

---

[21]Robert F. Banks and Jack Stieber, eds., *Multinationals, Unions, and Labor Relations in Industrialized Countries* (Ithaca, N.Y.: 1977), p. 45.

bringing this to you because we are required by law to do so," Litton's chief negotiator told the union at a crucial point in the talks.[22] He was referring to a recent case in which the Supreme Court ruled that employers had to bargain with unions over decisions affecting plant operations, including plant shutdowns, in addition to bargaining over the effects on workers of such decisions.

But the law does not say that either party has to agree to anything. This is especially significant in a plant shutdown situation where the strike threat is meaningless. Bargaining becomes pretense. When asked by the Springfield local whether a voluntary wage reduction would make labor costs competitive with those at alternative production locations, Litton's labor relations director conceded that wages are always an important consideration to employers in making such decisions. But in this instance, he added, the comparative wage advantages of the competing work forces available to the company made serious negotiations impossible. "I assume if your wages were down to an unrealistic level matching the Japanese or the Sicilians or some such thing, it might have a bearing," he explained, "but that is totally unrealistic, we all know."[23] Union negotiators declined to pursue the matter.

Production was transferred from Springfield mostly to Connecticut. Simultaneously, some production was being moved from Connecticut to overseas facilities, prior to the complete relocation of production in West Germany.

Negotiations at Hartford were frustrating for the UAW local which represented about 1,500 workers. Local officers suspected the plant might also be closed but they could not get local management to commit itself one way or the other.

The UAW did have a better tactical bargaining position than the AIW had in Springfield. It represented workers in both the main production plant and a nearby typewriter supplies manufacturing plant. Although Litton intended to close the production facility, and therefore could not be hurt by a strike there, it needed continued output from the supply plant, and therefore was more vulnerable to a stoppage than it had been in Springfield. Even though the Hartford plant also eventually closed, the union was able to negotiate a termination agreement with limited benefits for displaced workers. No final agreement was ever negotiated at

---

[22]Charles Craypo, "Collective Bargaining In the Conglomerate, Multinational Firm: Litton's Shutdown of Royal Typewriter," *Industrial and Labor Relations Review* (October 1975), p. 13.

[23]*Ibid.*, p. 18.

Springfield. In fact, more than a decade after the shutdown there, still being litigated by the parties were certain benefits that were owed the workers by Royal and a National Labor Relations Board order to negotiate job transfer rights of displaced workers.

The problems for the UAW at Hartford were its inability to get relevant data on the economic reasons behind the contemplated shutdown or to confront corporate decision makers regarding the shutdown. These were also major difficulties for the union in Springfield. Excerpts from a verbatim transcript of the talks demonstrate the UAW's experience.

Following an official announcement made at the bargaining table in September, 1971, that Litton-Royal was considering closing the plant, management asked the union, as it had in Springfield, to make suggestions and proposals for consideration in its deliberations.

> **Company:** We wish to take this opportunity to invite you to discuss ⟨the matter⟩ with us before we reach a decision. I want to assure you that no such decision has been made, and while we are considering these possibilities, we will take into consideration any thoughts, ideas or suggestions which you may wish to contribute to our decision-making.[24]

This statement was self-serving. It put the company on record as offering to bargain over union proposals regarding the shutdown in keeping with current labor law interpretations.

But in order to make realistic suggestions and proposals union bargainers needed more specific information than they were getting.

> **Union:** What are you looking for from the union, Jack ⟨the chief company negotiator⟩, in respect to the statement about soliciting ideas? Let's get specific. What do you mean by "ideas"? Are you talking about wage cuts? Extension of the contract? What are you talking about?
>
> **Company:** I am talking about anything that might contribute to being evaluated in an overall decision.
>
> **Union:** What would you—excuse me.
>
> **Company:** You ask what do I think? I do not think that is really a fair question. What I want to know is what you have that would influence our decision.

---

[24]This and subsequent quotations are taken from transcripts of negotiations between UAW Local 937 and Litton-Royal representatives in Hartford, Conn., during September 1971.

Union: What would it take to influence your decision, to reverse the trend?

Company: If I knew what you were giving me, I would be better able to answer.

Union: Well, we would like to know what you are thinking about in respect to the kinds of ideas we could come up with, if any. So I think it is incumbent upon you to suggest ways where you think the union can do certain things that might forestall—I did not say "guarantee," I said "might forestall"—any further moves. We would be perhaps in a better position to evaluate our position in respect to what ideas we might come up with.

I think if the company could give us some direct ideas, we could take these ideas under consideration.

Company: In essence, you are asking or soliciting from the company, ideas that you might propose to the company?

Union: No, that we might consider. That we might consider, not propose.

Company: Well, really, soliciting ideas from the company that the union might consider and . . .

Union: Evaluate and respond to.

Company: . . . evaluate and . . .

Union: . . . respond to, either affirmatively or negatively.

Company: I know what you are saying, but I would suggest this, that . . .

Union: Jack, let's lay the cards on the table. What are you beating around the bush for? When we find out what kinds of things you need, or what kinds of things you think you need that might change your company's position in respect to further moves, we certainly would be in a hell of a better position to respond. We are not going to just throw things out in the air and you will just keep saying, "That is not enough; that is not enough; that is not enough." We would like from you a clear expression from this corporation as to where they think the actions of the union might be conducive to changing the company plan. If there are none, so be it. . . .

Whatever you suggest might be impossible for this union to agree to, but I think we have to know, Jack, and let's lay the cards on the table. I do not think it surprises anybody, your announcement of today, because it has been rumored all around town, anyway. And it just seemed that it was coming at some time or another. When, is another thing.

The union requested that management provide it with specific information at the next scheduled bargaining session. "We cannot operate in a vacuum," its chief negotiator argued.

But at the next meeting, company negotiators had nothing new to offer. The union therefore made no proposals, arguing that "the burden of what is necessary to influence the company's decision rests upon this company."

> **Union:** You know obviously what it will take and what it will not take to alter a decision. We are asking you to be above-board and honest, stop fooling around, lay it on the table. What are you looking for? Are you looking for wage cuts, extensions, speedup, or any other things? Just say what you have in mind, and as I said before, unless it borders on the idiocy plane, certainly we will consider ⟨it⟩, as you said, in order to try to influence a decision which in my opinion has already been made.

This assertion sparked an exchange on employment in the plant's manufacturing department. The chief management negotiator responded to the UAW's complaint that it could not make proposals until the company provided substantive information. That is not so, he replied

> . . . your request to us to give you ideas, suggestions and so on so that you might determine whether this would be worthwhile to feed back to the company, should not relieve you of your own resourcefulness and responsibility to come up with your own ideas and suggestions or thoughts that you might have that might influence the company in its decision making.
>
> **Union:** Are you ready to make any determinations, as far as what you think is necessary to keep this facility here?
>
> **Company:** I have nothing to say concerning that at the present time. But I want to be sure that you understand that I cannot come up with things that you want to suggest; that is your job to do, not mine.

For the rest of that bargaining session the union negotiator pursued the matter without results. After nearly a month of further bargaining, the union, having despaired of getting the cooperation of local management, tried another approach. It asked that someone from corporate headquarters come to the table. This also failed.

> **Union:** How about ⟨our⟩ request that you bring somebody in to give us some information about what your problems are, the economic data, the production problems, what you expect to produce over there and what your problems are here? Bring somebody in that knows something. Bring him in to talk to us. Can we have somebody like that come in here?
>
> **Company:** We will completely dispose of that by saying no, we won't bring anybody else in.

Finally, the local union tried to communicate directly with Litton management. It sent a letter to Roy Ash, the president, asking him to clarify contradictory public statements by division and corporate officials concerning the Hartford plant. Litton executives earlier had assured a gathering of security analysts that Hartford production would be continued, but division managers had been telling union negotiators and the local press that the plant might be closed. Instead of explaining the contradiction, Ash referred the UAW letter to the Royal Typewriter division president who in turn passed it on to Royal's chief negotiator at Hartford, the same person who was refusing to elaborate on the situation at the bargaining table. He now sent union bargainers a letter inviting their "thoughts, ideas, or suggestions."

A few months later Royal management confirmed the Hartford plant would be closed permanently. Five weeks later the parties concluded a termination agreement. Each employee received a 5.5 percent wage increase until they were laid off. The 5.5 percent figure had nothing to do with conventional economic bargaining standards but instead was the negotiated rate then allowable under Phase II of the Nixon Administration's wage control program. This increase was the best the local union could do under plant closing circumstances. Union negotiators did not get severance pay benefits for displaced workers, as they had hoped to do. The union was powerless and Litton felt obligated neither to the workers nor the community for economic compensation for closing the plant.

Part of Hartford's production went to Litton's British typewriter plants at Hull and Leicester, a low-wage part of England. In January 1975, Litton gave five weeks' notice that both British plants would be closed and the work transferred to its West German operations. Litton had been locating Royal typewriter production in Britain since 1966, but partial data on comparative productivity suggest that in 1974, Litton was by far the most inefficient of four multinational typewriter manufacturers in the United Kingdom. Workers reacted against the shutdown announcement by occupying both plants in anticipation of government assistance to establish a worker cooperative to produce either a new typewriter or alternative products. Because of the heavy financial subsidies required and the slim survival chances a cooperative venture would have against global business equipment manufacturers, government help was withheld and the sit-in was ended six months later.

In 1979 Litton sold a controlling interest in its worldwide typewriter operations to Volkswagen of West Germany.

Summary

The conflict level is rising in established labor relations settings. Forces behind this change include managerial (and perhaps worker and public) hostility toward unions and collective bargaining; the rise of large diversified, global corporations; new production methods; government deregulation; the large number of unemployed workers who have no union allegiance and will take the jobs of striking union workers. New corporate structures reduce employer need to bargain and reach agreement with unions in particular locations. Production mobility and financial capacity enable employers to escape or overpower organized labor. Administrative centralization and operative secrecy allow them to initiate unilateral actions without effective union responses. The long-term consequences of this trend are uncertain, as are eventual union responses and the extent of future conflict bargaining.

Labor relations in the intercity bus industry involve fundamental differences in bargaining structures between two dominant firms. At Greyhound, the Amalgamated Transit Union succeeded in establishing a national bargaining structure and, as a result, the highest wages and benefits in the industry. It had the ability to stop Greyhound operations nationwide in the event of strikes. At Trailways, two dominant unions shared representation rights among separate operating units and several other units remained nonunion. This fragmented bargaining structure inhibited union effectiveness and resulted in much lower standards and negotiated settlements than at Greyhound. Integrated ownership and control of interconnecting bus lines enabled Trailways to cross-subsidize specific units in strike situations.

Unions tried unsuccessfully to strengthen themselves at Trailways by setting aside their rivalry long enough to petition the NLRB for a consolidation of the diverse bargaining units. Although the Board rejected their proposal as being inappropriate, the ATU eventually did organize the nonunion units of Trailways. The bargaining structure continued to be fragmented until the parties negotiated a concession settlement in 1982 which was applicable to all units.

The effect of weak union power at Trailways was to discourage Greyhound from accepting ATU demands that would further widen negotiated labor costs between the two. Impasses and strikes at Greyhound during the 1970s nevertheless usually ended with the ATU winning its objective.

Greyhound management was less concerned about a lengthy confrontation with ATU after the company diversified to become less dependent financially on the bus operations. So when the climate turned against organized labor in 1983 and government deregulation produced competitive conditions among alternative forms of transportation, Greyhound demanded substantial economic givebacks and language changes from ATU. A lengthy, bitter strike resulted in which the company hired strikebreakers and appeared intent on destroying the union. Eventually the strikers ratified a negotiated concession package because they feared the permanent loss of their jobs. Greyhound's union and workers vowed to be better prepared for battle in the next round of negotiations.

Conglomerate multinational corporate structures present a formidable threat to union power. They give employers operating mobility, financial reserves, and a system of managerial centralization that deprives unions of traditional strike power. The Litton Industries case details how difficult it is for unions to organize and bargain within this structural environment when the employer is determined to resist. A pattern emerges of bargaining impasses often followed by union decertification, plant closings and phasedowns, extended labor law litigation and numerous Board and federal court findings of illegal actions by Litton subsidiaries.

Foreign-based multinational employers have mixed effects on domestic labor relations, depending on their motives for locating in this country. They make initial and ongoing investment in plant and equipment which can make existing jobs more secure and productive and perhaps increase total employment. They also remove crucial economic decision making to organizations and individuals who are far removed from and unaccountable to domestic workers and unions. Conflict over unionization of workers occurred between the UAW and Japanese auto and truck manufacturers and between the building trades and Nissan in Tennessee. Michelin has domestic plants that have not yet been organized despite their potential importance to industry standards. The upstate New York plant of Nestlé experienced ongoing long-term labor relations conflict.

A detailed analysis of local negotiations over the shutdown of both Litton-Royal typewriter plants in this country shows that unions bargain under tactical disadvantages when they confront large, diversified multinational employers. Bargaining transcripts show that two unions were unable to obtain sufficient data and decision-making criteria for them to negotiate intelligently and effectively, were unable to face company policy makers at the bargaining table, and were unable to anticipate structural changes made by the employer.

Key Words and Phrases

pattern bargaining
consolidated bargaining
  structure
ratio of labor costs to total
  costs

conglomerate merger wave
unfriendly takeover
financial leverage
cross-subsidization

Review and Discussion Questions

1. What was the main reason for the historical wage and benefit differentials between Trailways and Greyhound?
2. What is the effect of conglomerate corporate structures on relative collective bargaining power of unions and corporations?
3. What has motivated foreign firms to locate production facilities in this country in recent years?
4. How do typical views of management officials of multinational corporations differ from those of their union counterparts?

Chapter Resources and Suggested Further Reading

The discussion on bargaining at Trailways is taken from Charles Craypo, "Bargaining Units and Corporate Merger: NLRB Policy in the Intercity Bus Industry," *Industrial Relations Law Journal* (Summer 1976); "Holiday Inns to Sell Bus Division," *Wall Street Journal*, August 20, 1979; and these federal court and Board cases: *UTU Local 1699 v. NLRB*, 546 F.2d 1038, 94 LRRM 2028 (CA DC, 1976); *Safeway Trails, Inc.*, 233 NLRB 1075, 96 LRRM 1128 (1977).

Information on the Greyhound strike comes from a variety of articles in the press and BNA publications. In addition to those identified in footnotes, major sources are: "Deregulation Will Take Bus Lines on a Rough Ride," *Business Week*, July 11, 1983; Steven Greenhouse, "The Reshaping of Greyhound," *The New York Times*, November 5, 1983; BNA, "Greyhound, Transit Union Hold First Talks Since Strike Began," *White Collar Report*, November 16, 1983; Henry Weinstein, "Strikers Clash With Police As Buses Move Out," *Los Angeles Times*, November 18, 1983; Damon Stetson, "Bus Line Strikers Vote Down Pact," *The New York*

Times, November 29, 1983; BNA, "ATU Workers Voting On Proposal From Greyhound; Approval Recommended," *White Collar Report*, December 7, 1983; BNA, "Transit Union Members Approve New Pact, End Walkout Against Greyhound Lines," *White Collar Report*, January 4, 1984. Greyhound's version of the economic issue is found in full-page advertisements in newspapers across the country on November 7 and November 30, 1983; the ATU's version is contained in an undated strike bulletin from union headquarters, "Fact Sheet: ATU Strike Against Greyhound."

Litton sources are: Securities and Exchange Commission, Form 10-K, Annual Report for the Fiscal Year Ended 1978, "Litton Industries;" "The Largest 500 Industrials," *Fortune*, May 4, 1981; Thomas O'Hanlon, "A Rejuvenated Litton Is Once Again Off to the Races," *Fortune*, October 8, 1979; Nick Galluccio, "The Housecleaning Is Over," *Forbes*, November 24, 1980; Michael L. Millenson, "Litton: An Industry Made For a Reagan Presidency," *Chicago Tribune*, April 13, 1981.

Sources for the references to Nestle's labor problems in New York are: Award of Arbitrator Irving Shapiro, In the Matter of Arbitration Between The Nestle Company, Inc., and United Food and Commercial Workers Union, Local 1974, RWDSU AFL-CIO, January 9, 1976; *Nestle Company*, 238 NLRB 92, 99 LRRM 1241 (1978); *The Nestle Company, Inc.*, 251 NLRB 1023, 105 LRRM 1382 (1980).

Sources used in the introduction to the section on conglomerate multinational employers are: "New Targets and Familiar Faces: The 100 Largest Foreign Investments in the U.S.," *Forbes*, July 7, 1980; Kenneth V. Alexander, "Conglomerate Mergers and Collective Bargaining," *Industrial and Labor Relations Review* (April 1971).

For a discussion of Litton's shutdown of its two typewriter plants in England, see Gerald Newbould and Peter Buckley, "Collective Bargaining in the Conglomerate Multinational Firm: Litton's Shutdown of Imperial Typewriter," *Labor Studies Journal* (Fall 1979).

9

Economic Bargaining Power

This chapter analyzes the dynamics of change in union and employer bargaining power in the private sector. It reviews the sources of union power and the standards used in economic bargaining that are described in the cases found in the preceding chapters. Relative power between unions and employers is defined and explained on the basis of the power relationships illustrated in these cases. The theme that emerges from this analysis is that relative bargaining power shifts over time with changes in industrial structures, production technologies, public policies, and worker attitudes and public opinion toward unions and collective bargaining.

The dynamics of comparative bargaining power are explained by the influence of either labor or industry over structure, technology, and policy. Changes in social opinion and mood are beyond the control of either party, but nevertheless greatly influence relative bargaining power. Institutional control over the sources of power are identified, explained, and even anticipated through detailed examination of individual cases. Study of a sufficient number of cases reveals the general trends and directions that are occurring in economic bargaining.

The Sources of Bargaining Power

The sources of union bargaining power are the industry's ability to pay higher labor costs and organized labor's ability to make the industry pay. Employers have the greatest ability to pay when they are efficient producers, are expanding output, and have pricing power in product markets. Control over prices results from one or more favorable conditions: consolidated industry structure and administered pricing to achieve target profits; government regula-

225

tion that prevents competition from new firms and allows existing ones to set prices; spatial limitations that protect the markets of firms covered by negotiated union contracts; and productivity gains that enable employers to offset higher labor costs.

Union ability to make an industry pay higher labor costs depends essentially on two factors—the extent of worker organization and the ability to stop production. The latter occurs when unions establish appropriate bargaining structures and maintain exclusive representation by one union or effective coordination by two or more of them. Apart from these institutional characteristics, equally important but less tangible determinants of union power are the quality of union leadership and the extent of rank-and-file militancy. The specific ingredients of union power are complete unionization of the relevant work force, which includes those workers who make goods and services that sell in competition; elimination of directly competitive unionism, where two or more unions represent different groups of workers and do not coordinate their efforts but instead work against one another when they negotiate economic settlements; consolidation of bargaining structures so that union work stoppages shut down all or most of management's production activities and union negotiators are able to confront employer decision makers directly at the bargaining table.

Early unions seldom were successful against monopolized or oligopolized industries. In late nineteenth century American transportation, communications, and steelmaking, large employers readily disposed of threats from craft and industrial organizations alike. Established unions and spontaneous worker movements were crushed by unassailable corporate power. Despite temporary gains around the turn of this century and again during World War I, organized labor was virtually eliminated from basic industry. Craft unionism survived, however, in construction, printing, rails, and other segments of the private economy. But the result was a highly segmented and decentralized union movement that had no political or industrial base of power and was therefore vulnerable to employer initiatives because of its narrow, special interest character.

The situation changed in the 1930s. Employers imposed job speedups, harsh working conditions, and substantial wage cuts. It became increasingly difficult for them to contain worker resentment in this environment. General strikes and worker sitdowns plagued industrial communities and basic manufacturers until the CIO unions finally won bargaining rights in most industrial sectors. There was also a resurgence of craft unionism in places where AFL organizations had lost ground during the 1920s. Craft unions accepted the industrial union structure where that was necessary for them to protect their traditional work jurisdictions or to expand into new ones.

Economic Bargaining Standards

The standards used in economic bargaining reflect prevailing industry and economic conditions. Unions view profits and productivity as evidence of employer ability to pay. Profits may be a signal that product market conditions will permit employers to pass on higher labor costs in the form of higher prices. Productivity gains warrant higher earnings, but often at the expense of those workers who are displaced or deskilled by new machines and processes that improve efficiency.

Two other bargaining standards—cost-of-living and comparability—originate outside the industry environment. Cost-of-living becomes an important factor whenever inflation erodes workers' real earnings. Union negotiators act under rank-and-file pressure to establish or strengthen contract escalator clauses. Their ability to do so is an important index of union bargaining power. Comparability is a standard the unions use to extend their bargaining power with one firm or group of firms to other locations where they may not be as strong. Such momentum can also carry from one industry to another.

Comparability became a sign of union power following the post-World War II rise of national bargaining by CIO unions in concentrated industries. Workers in one industry compared their earnings and job conditions to those in similar industries and refused to accept anything less. Key settlements in basic industry spread to fabricator and supplier firms and sometimes even into unrelated sectors of the economy. Comparability was a powerful political force inside unions, and at times would override economic differences among firms and industries to produce similar economic settlements in dissimilar economic environments.

Recently, however, comparability has been a management issue. Givebacks and concessions have been demanded of unions on the basis of differences in labor costs among competitive enterprises. In some instances, concessions were made even where economic conditions differed among the firms that got them, apparently because concession bargaining was already widespread in that industry or geographic location.

Variations in Bargaining Power

Bargaining settlements differ considerably among industries. The differences are attributed to variations in industry organization, technology, profit and productivity levels, growth rates, extent of unionization, bargaining structures, and settlement patterns among industries. Individual case studies explain such deviations.

Of the craft bargaining cases discussed in Chapters Four and Five, labor registered impressive long-term gains in three: construction, printing, and airlines. In each instance, specialized crafts organized their relevant work forces sufficiently to capitalize on generally favorable economic conditions. Employers in these industries are structurally fragmented and dependent on individual crafts for continued production, so strikes and strike threats become powerful bargaining weapons during prosperity.

Craft unions historically decentralized their bargaining structures. This enabled them to choose strategic strike targets, reach agreements, and then use those settlements as comparability standards for other employers. Pattern-plus bargaining became common. Strong individual crafts set the pace—typographers in printing, machinists in airlines, and the mechanical trades in construction. In each industry union leverage was enhanced by the natural perishability of the product or service—a daily newspaper, an airline ticket, a fixed-time building contract. Institutional sources of union power complemented favorable environments of spatial limitations in printing and construction and government regulation in airlines.

Industrial unions, by contrast, had their greatest successes against concentrated basic manufacturing industries. Conditions in autos and steel, for example, were ideal for union strength. Secure domestic oligopolies practiced administered pricing to achieve target profit rates. Unionization of workers was industrywide, rank-and-file members typically were militant and supportive of union leadership and objectives, and national master agreements were reflected in strong pattern bargaining. Similar environments characterized other oligopolized industries.

But not all industrial unions were successful against oligopolized industries. Islands of nonunion or independent operations persisted in oil refining, where technology permitted continued production during strikes and bargaining structures were too fragmented for effective job actions. Industry technology and bargaining units were similar in chemicals, where no union was able to organize enough of the relevant work force to establish its economic position.

In men's clothing and other nonconcentrated manufacturing industries, industrial unionism and bargaining were not as beneficial to workers as in the oligopolized sectors. The difference can be attributed to large numbers of small and dispersed employers, easy entry of nonunion firms into the industry, product price competition at home and import competition from low-wage producers abroad, and erratic profits and low productivity gains that restrict employer ability to pay. No matter how successful unions are in organizing their relevant work forces or establishing appropriate negotiating structures in these industries, their bargaining potential is necessarily restricted. Now, with the return of sweatshops and homework to domestic garment manufacturing, unions are in jeopardy of being further weakened.

Conflict bargaining erupted throughout the private sector in the late 1970s and early 1980s. It broke out in industries with previously stable labor relations and in those where collective bargaining was new. It occurred in manufacturing as well as in construction, transportation, and services; it involved salaried and professional as well as blue-collar workers. The yearly number of union decertification elections increased almost fourfold (from 230 to 902 cases) between 1960 and 1980, and unions lost roughly three of every four of them. Employers adopted increasingly tough and aggressive bargaining stances and in many instances replaced striking workers with union and nonunion strikebreakers.

The new conglomerate and multinational corporate structures weaken union power. At the organizational level, they give large employers such flexibility in plant location and production choices that existing bargaining arrangements become structurally inappropriate and therefore ineffective for unions. At the administrative level, they consolidate managerial authority among diverse and isolated production units. This centralization insulates top management decision makers from unions in the separate plants and divisions where labor contracts are negotiated. It also shields the corporation and its operating subsidiaries behind consolidated financial statements and unclear, inaccessible lines of internal authority, thus making it impossible for unions in fragmented units to negotiate intelligibly or forcefully over management policy, performance, and intention.

New corporate structures and increasing global competition for markets that were once dominated by U.S. manufacturers have completely altered post-World War II economic bargaining relationships between industrial unions and basic industries. Faced with intensive price and quality competition from foreign-made products, domestic oligopolies have terminated operations, transferred production elsewhere to get cheaper labor, and bought time to refurbish and reorganize their production plants and revamp and redesign their product lines. The labor relations stability that characterized these industries disappeared in the growing controversies over employer concession demands, job transfers and displacements, and labor-management frictions on the shop floor.

Controlling the Sources of Union Bargaining Power. The case studies described here suggest a relationship between relative bargaining power and control over the environment within which negotiations occur. The sources of union bargaining power at a particular time reflect institutional conditions such as the extent of unionization or the degree of employer dependence on skilled labor. But new organizational structures, technologies, and public policies, as well as shifts in worker and public attitudes toward unions, give rise to changes in the sources of bargaining strength. Whichever party influences these processes is able to shape long-term relative economic power.

Labor is at an institutional disadvantage in this regard. It controls neither the structure of business enterprise nor the introduction of production technology. In market economies, this authority rests with managers. Unions have the legal right to bargain over the effects of such changes on the terms and conditions of employment, but not over the decisions themselves. Whether to expand or relocate production, for example, is not a mandatory bargaining item, nor are decisions to diversify operations through corporate acquisitions, to introduce robots or computers into the workplace, or to start up a nonunion subsidiary in competition with the unionized shop.

Except in the rare instance where management has previously negotiated away the right to make such decisions unilaterally, labor cannot automatically challenge them at the bargaining table. Labor tries instead to offset the effects by adopting union and bargaining structures and by devising new strategies both at the bargaining table and beyond that traditional arena. But for unions to respond effectively as a movement requires a degree of unity, mobility, and flexibility that is institutionally impractical among traditionally independent, fragmented, and market-oriented labor organizations and which never characterized American labor in the past. The task presently appears to be doubly difficult because of labor's public disfavor and limited political effectiveness.

There is an ironic twist in this link between environmental change and bargaining power. Unions typically achieve bargaining leverage when they organize workers and negotiate contracts that reflect existing employer structures and production methods. They begin to lose that power when the old structures and methods change but their organizational and bargaining structures do not. Institutions effective in the past now are inappropriate because they are frozen in time. Master contracts no longer cover the industry's relevant work force whenever firms relocate their production or imports capture domestic markets. Local craft agreements no longer protect skilled workers when area employers find alternative methods and sources of production through new technologies and nonunion workers.

The implication is clear: established union power fades with time when it rests on transient market conditions. Time alters industry environments in ways that subvert organized labor. Of course, employers also must cope with change, but they have greater resources with which to do so, particularly if they are large. Unions, by contrast, do not have direct access to the institutional sources of change. Unable to determine the course of events—to create situations or shape public policies—unions become reactive rather than active. They are forced to devise strategies and structures suitable to unfamiliar, hostile environments. They did not bring about the new environments, and indeed probably resisted them, but now they must be institutional vehicles through which workers accommodate themselves to structures, processes, and practices that are essentially antiworker in their consequences.

Organized labor has not had much recent success as a political movement or a shaper of public policy. Pro-collective bargaining sentiment in this country peaked with the Wagner Act of 1935. Subsequent modifications of the National Labor Relations Act in 1947 and 1959 retreated from the social principle of collective bargaining as the preferred method of dispute resolution. The revisions narrowed the scope of bargaining and made it more difficult for unions to organize workers in unfriendly settings. In addition, administrative labor law recently has turned against unions and collective bargaining: the National Labor Relations Board has taken a restrictive position on matters involving union and collective worker rights under the law. In 1978, union-supported NLRA amendments that would have given union organizing drives more protection against hostile managers and management consulting firms failed to pass in Congress.

Other policy changes have gone against labor. In trucking, airlines, and telecommunications, government deregulation has hurt existing union power. In the health care field, federal government efforts to curtail rising medical costs have put pressure on hospital and nursing home managers to resist labor cost increases at the bargaining table. In state and local government, removal of federal funding results in service cutbacks, job reductions, and diminished bargaining power for public employee unions.

All in all, labor has fared badly in recent years in either controlling or influencing its collective bargaining environment. In a concluding section of this chapter, a look will be taken at factors that have been more favorable to labor.

The Dynamics of Bargaining Power

Industrial organization. Corporate organization is an important determinant of bargaining strength. Experiences in two industries, telegraphy and basic steel, demonstrate how corporate consolidation of product markets and production processes made it impossible for workers to organize effective unions. Consolidation of Western Union after the Civil War destroyed the natural bargaining power of skilled Morse telegraphers and defeated their efforts to establish collective bargaining or bring about any of the other solutions they thought might resolve the emerging labor-employer conflict in telegraph offices: increased competition within the industry, government regulation or ownership of telegraphy, or direct employee control of major telegraph companies.

Formation of the U.S. Steel Corporation in 1901 virtually monopolized the domestic iron and steel industry. It also enabled owners to reverse the earlier gains of the Amalgamated Association, a craft union that had successfully organized most of the mills in the mid-Atlantic and Great Lakes states and had the power to block production by the largest firms. But the creation of U.S. Steel automatically nullified the Amalgamated's grip on the industry by structurally integrating union and nonunion facilities. Since the purpose of industrial monopoly is to restrict product supply and raise prices, the company simply closed many of the mills where the union was strongest and withheld recognition from it in nonunion locations. In a desperate move, the Amalgamated called a companywide strike against U.S. Steel for companywide recognition and negotiations. It was decisively defeated. The union never recovered from its loss and eventually was driven from the steel industry. Steel and telegraphy remained unorganized until the 1930s, when protective legislation, worker militancy, and better coordinated and financed unions finally succeeded where earlier efforts had failed.

Once the concentrated industries were unionized, their strong financial and growth performances contributed to union bargaining power. The institutional linkage that developed between industry concentration and industrial union success is essential to an understanding of economic bargaining in recent decades. It explains why CIO unions were able to negotiate wage and benefit improvements that lifted their members into middle-level standards of living and provided them and their families with considerable economic security. Favorable market environments encouraged basic manufacturers to negotiate hefty gains with minimal resistance and labor strife.

The structural connection also explains why American unions opposed the practices of industrial oligopolies until they had organized them and established centralized bargaining structures, at which time they dropped their opposition in exchange for a negotiated share of the gains and a cooperative, mutually beneficial economic relationship. It was in the short-run interest of the workers that their unions should capitalize on the market power of these firms when bargaining wage and benefit improvements. Rapid, unilateral changes in the industrial setting soured the relationship, however. For instance, the organizational diversification of integrated steel companies and the widespread phasedown of operations illustrate the problems that could befall workers and unions that depended on traditional corporate structures for their continued institutional power.

Furthermore, as the Litton case study discussed in Chapter 8 shows, global and conglomerate corporate structures present unions with still more challenges. And recent events in the intercity bus industry demonstrate the adverse impact on unions of diversified holding company structures. Larger social trends also affect union capability. The outcome of the Greyhound strike was influenced by the force of a nationwide union concession trend, high levels of sustained unemployment, and public indifference or antagonism toward unions.

Established union power in the crafts also is being affected. As Chapters 4 and 5 show, common ownership of union and nonunion construction operations undermines craft organization in that industry; conglomerate ownership of commercial print shops and consequent mobility of operations and locations erases the tactical edge previously held by print crafts in the traditional job centers; the rise of chain newspaper holding companies strengthens employer ability to withstand union job actions against individual papers; deregulation of airlines permits the entry of new or subsidiary carriers that operate as nonunion entities and capture shares of the market from established carriers with which airline unions bargained from a position of strength.

Industrial Restructuring and Plant Closing. The major changes in industrial organization that concern unions are the wholesale deterioration of American manufacturing and the widespread plant closings that have accompanied this decline. Over the past two decades, manufacturing corporations have disinvested in their traditional operations and gone into other businesses, many of them speculative, nonproductive enterprises. In the alternative they have relocated production from one part of the country to another and from domestic to overseas sites. Industrial restructuring eliminates union power where it occurs and also has a debilitating effect on labor elsewhere. Seymour Melman, an industrial engineering professor, attributes these dislocations to changes in industrial management, specifically to fundamental shifts in managerial values, training and advancement, and reward systems.

> By the 1960s the ideal type, as portrayed in management journals, had become the financier-strategist, the shrewd, nimble operator who combined disparate firms into conglomerates that maximized the short-term profit-making opportunities afforded by tax laws, securities transfers, the milking of production assets and other financial legerdemain. This is a world of money-making, one that can prosper even as production is neglected or transferred to distant lands. In this world, the optimum condition is profit without any production.[1]

Melman's thesis is that this reorientation from production to finance carried with it an inevitable decline in America's productive capacity. Domestic capital was exported to other countries either to build overseas production facilities or to make speculative investments in foreign businesses; the numbers of managerial and supervisory personnel grew relative to those of professional, technical, and production workers because management wanted greater control over organization and production processes; money was put where it would make the highest rate of return in the short run,

---

[1]Seymour Melman, *Profits Without Production* (New York: Alfred Knopf, 1983), p. xiii.

rather than where it would produce the greatest amount of goods and services or the largest number of jobs. In addition, according to Melman, a soaring U.S. military budget compounded the problem. Huge government purchases made without regard to price eventually transformed America's historically cost-efficient machine tool industry, which lies at the core of every mass production industry, from a competitive, technologically competent supplier to a regressive sector addicted to cost-plus-profit government contracts. In 1978, the United States imported more tools than it exported for the first time in its industrial history; by 1980, domestic factories supplied fewer than three out of four machine tools used in this country and the prices of those they made for the military were rising 20 percent annually.[2]

Growing production inefficiencies in the basic manufacturing industries, together with steadily rising negotiated labor costs, prompted large, financially mobile manufacturers to diversify into other lines of business and shut down or relocate existing production. These actions disarmed unions at the bargaining table. There were threats of job displacements if unions did not agree to contract concessions. The workers were losing their militancy and employers had considerable excess production capacity. Job actions at the point of production had little force once the production sites themselves were irrelevant to profits and therefore useless to industry.

Plant closings and phasedowns became crucial variables in bargaining outcomes throughout the industrial northeast quadrant of the nation. The experiences of one such factory town doubtlessly reflect those of others. A study of economic dislocation in South Bend, Indiana during 1954–83 reveals 27 separate plant closings and numerous phasedowns during the 30-year period.[3] Between 1961 and mid-1983, the South Bend area lost more than 4,000 manufacturing jobs and gained nearly 32,000 nonmanufacturing jobs, mainly in the service and trade sectors. The ratio of manufacturing to total employment dropped during this time from 42 to 26 percent. Between 1953 and 1983, more than 35,000 jobs disappeared in the area's eight largest manufacturers, including the 1963 shutdown of Studebaker, a second-tier auto producer that in 1953 had employed more than 20,000.

---

[2]Ibid., p. 40.

[3]Charles Craypo, "The Deindustrialization of a Factory Town: Plant Closings and Phasedowns in South Bend Indiana, 1954–1983," in Donald Kennedy, editor, Labor Studies Series, vol. II, *Labor and Deindustrialization: Workers and Corporate Change* (University Park, Penn.: Pennsylvania State University, Labor Studies Department, 1984).

Of the 27 plant closings during 1954–83, 23 were made by absentee owners, 18 of them by large diversified corporations that had no further operating or administrative need for their South Bend facilities. A total of 11 shutdowns involved established manufacturing operations in which production either was terminated altogether or relocated in southern plants owned by the parent companies. Another 12 closings involved manufacturing plants and one financial institution that had been acquired by outside firms and later were closed when the parent companies relocated production operations in their mainly southern plants. Only four of the closed facilities were locally owned and operated; one of these closings occurred after the local company diversified itself and built a southern manufacturing plant but kept its administrative headquarters in South Bend. Another closing by a locally-owned firm concerned a large building contractor that had diversified into construction development and contract management operations and liquidated its original construction business.

The largest number of manufacturing jobs disappeared as a result of five terminations of large-scale operations that were located in South Bend but controlled by absentee corporations. In each instance, the South Bend products were not competitive in domestic sales markets, usually because of the entrenched market positions of large established firms. Because of their size and diversity of operations, the absentee companies survived these shutdowns better than displaced local workers did. Studebaker, for example, had acquired at least 11 unrelated businesses during the four years before terminating its domestic auto production in 1963. A few years later, it was reorganized as the conglomerate Studebaker-Worthington.

High labor costs and union contracts often were cited by corporations as reasons for local plant shutdowns, especially after 1975. Labor costs probably were motivating factors in some of the earlier shutdowns as well, but by the mid-1970s it had become commonplace to blame economic dislocation on high labor costs. A survey of labor relations experiences in these shutdowns shows, however, that with few exceptions the South Bend unions had agreed to economic concessions when employers demanded them prior to the closings. On other occasions, labor tried unsuccessfully to negotiate givebacks that might reverse plant closing decisions. But local managers said it was useless to try to make the plants cost-competitive through labor concessions. Direct labor costs realistically could not be reduced enough to be competitive in the South and overseas.

Furthermore, most of the plants had become rundown and inefficient in the absence of capital investment and proper maintenance
for long periods of time.[4]

Technology

Technology is crucial to relative union-industry bargaining
strength because it determines the quantity and quality of labor that
is needed in the production process. Thus it creates or destroys
union power. In one instance, it might make employers dependent
on certain job skills; in another, it can make previously crucial skills
obsolete. Much of the final impact on workers depends on how craft
and industrial unions respond. The dominant institutions in market
capitalism favor technological change that is unrestricted by labor's
self-interest. Therefore, when individual unions try to stop new
technology, they usually are simply brushed aside. Crafts that have
accommodated themselves to new methods, however, usually suffer
initial membership declines but manage to survive. Industrial
unions seldom attempt to prevent new production methods; instead
they try to negotiate income security provisions for displaced workers and meanwhile to qualify their members for the new jobs.

New technologies produce mixed results for workers and
unions. Some jobs, either skilled or unskilled, are downgraded or
eliminated as a result of new machines and processes. Others are
upgraded and expanded. Regardless of the net effect, however,
unions must deal with the dislocations that inevitably accompany
new technology. Innovation affects the relevant work force, the ap-
propriateness of traditional bargaining structures, and the application of legal regulations and remedies regarding labor relations. Because continued union power usually depends on the preservation of
established methods and practices, technology almost by definition
is a destroyer of labor's economic leverage. The challenge to unions
therefore is to make timely adaptations to technological change.

---

[4]The most important determinant in whether a plant closes is whether the owner invests
in building and equipment. In a survey of 171 plant shutdowns made by the nation's largest
500 corporations during the 1970s, inefficient, outdated facilities and machinery was the
most frequent reason given by managers for the closings. High labor costs and militant
unions were mentioned as reasons less than half as often. The author concluded that "the
clear culprit in closings of both new and old facilities is inefficient production technology. In
nearly half of all closings the factory slipped—or perhaps we should say was allowed to slip—
into poor technological and management practices." Roger Schmenner, "Every Factory Has
A Life Cycle," *Harvard Business Review* (March/April 1983).

The responses of the Graphic Arts Union to rapid and fundamental changes in print technology, described in Chapter 4, demonstrate a generally effective union policy in the face of immediate job threats.

Paradoxically, just as some workers suffer from the advent of technology, others suffer when their employers do not adopt modern plant and equipment. Failure of the domestic steel industry to build new mills and to install capable, efficient machinery contributed heavily to the recent disinvestment and massive job losses in steel. For years, American workers have had to make steel in ill-designed buildings with outdated equipment.

Microelectronics. The leading edge of technological change in today's workplace is microelectronics. The potential for electronic-based changes in design, organization, and production pervades both office and factory. Microelectronic technologies center around the computer. Computers essentially store and process information. When linked to the instruments of production, they transform office typewriters into word processors and electro-mechanical tool-making machines into programmed, numerically controlled instruments. They record and calculate credit card charges and then bill the customer; they guide the movements of robots that spray-paint manufactured parts, weld joints, and assemble electronic components. They locate and move warehouse inventory and sort out commercial fish catches for canning.

Microelectronic technology substitutes electronic impulses for printed words and numbers. In the process, it displaces workers who type, file, copy, and deliver office paper and replaces them with those who operate and monitor the machines that memorize, calculate, and circulate the information.

In addition to the job displacement effect, electronic devices also monitor and record individual work performance. Office workers increasingly come under surveillance by the very machines they operate. Computers connected to video-display terminals used by telephone operators keep track of work performance at each station; central office switching systems can record the frequency and duration of phone calls made by everyone in the office; insurance claims handlers are monitored by the data processing machines they operate.

Systemwide electronic switching exchanges link office data and communications equipment: computers, word processors, copiers, and telephones. The result is not yet a "paperless office," which is still just an office manager's dream, but it is an important step in that direction. Recent advances make it possible for small and medium-sized offices to adopt data storage and processing practices that previously were practicable only in large workplaces. Electronic machines thus can be designed and installed to reinforce the customary hierarchical workplace. They centralize and regiment production by enhancing supervisory control while diminishing the autonomy and operating discretion of individual workers and work groups.

Like the "paperless office," the "automated factory" is still not a practical reality. Electronic technology approaches that ideal, however. Computers are used in manufacturing mainly for numerically controlled machine tooling, assisted design and production, industrial robots, and computer-controlled systems of material refining and processing. They lower production cost by replacing hourly wage earners with computerized machines that are programmed to simulate the human motions of skilled and unskilled workers.

Numerical control is a process that applies computer technology to industrial machining. The resulting process requires less-skilled operators and automatically controls machine feed and speed rather than leaving it to worker discretion. Unless experienced operators are trained to program the computers, they become deskilled and possibly displaced by this kind of technology.

Machine programming itself, however, is being automated through electronic technology. Computer-assisted manufacturing prepares the programs that operate numerical control machines and supervise production processes. Computer-assisted manufacturing and computer-assisted design can be combined in a way that merges electronics and engineering in order to store and process vast amounts of technical data. In theory this combination ultimately creates the "automated factory" in which plant design is computer-determined, tool machining is computer-programmed and controlled, and production operations are roboticized.

Robots presently are not dominant in American industry but their potential is enormous and they are being introduced at a rapid pace. Advances in electronic technology steadily lower the production costs of robotic control units and make industrial robots more cost-competitive with production labor. By the 1980s, robots capable of performing unsophisticated assembly operations cost the equivalent of about three years of average production worker earnings, meaning that a robot working double shifts for 18 months would pay for itself in saved labor costs. Meanwhile, robots are becoming increasingly capable of performing work tasks that require human sight and touch, which makes them employable in many more job classifications and product lines.

The closest approximation now to the automated factory is the self-regulating continuous flow operation of an oil refinery, chemical plant, paper mill or any other workplace where raw materials are processed. Computers measure and report flow rates and pressures and through automatic sensors determine necessary adjustments and changes; they either signal human monitors of needed changes or perform the tasks themselves. The most sophisticated of these systems also analyzes product quality and self-adjusts plant operations. As this level of capability spreads to other industries, additional workers and occupations will be made obsolete.

Electronic technology is an explosive technology that can suddenly and unexpectedly change entire industries and clusters of related industries. Employers and industries that make use of it will improve their competitive position at home and abroad. But technologies are not neutral. Some kinds make firms more competitive by enhancing worker skills, hence making them more productive and therefore more justified in raising workers' economic living standards. Others make firms competitive by deskilling workers and driving down their bargaining power despite productivity increases. Which type of technology will actually be introduced depends on employer choices. How workers are affected will depend on how well unions represent them in the process of change. In any event, the impact is almost certain to be dramatic and uneven.[5]

Public Policy

The third category of change is the policy-setting within which unions organize and bargain with employers. This includes labor relations law and the micro- and macroeconomic policy decisions that affect bargaining environments.

---

[5]On the other hand, rapid technological change in a nonunion industry can cause such instability and uncertainty that workers are attracted to collective bargaining as a self-defense mechanism. Evidence suggests that when business offices and banks introduce electronic technologies, working conditions deteriorate and labor relations become impersonal and arbitrary. Employees begin to look at unionization more sympathetically than they might have in the past. In its clerical organizing campaign at Columbia University, for example, the UAW indicated it would negotiate a "technology bill of rights" for employees if selected as the bargaining agent. Unilateral introduction of VDTs was a key issue in the organization of Equitable Life Assurance office workers in Syracuse, N.Y., and prompted a strike by Blue Cross/Blue Shield employees in San Francisco. "Personnel Administrators Discuss 'Hot Issues' In Banking Industry," BNA, *White Collar Report*, vol. 56, No. 12, September 26, 1984, pp. 370–71.

Labor Law. Policy objectives generally change over time with changes in the economic and social philosophies of those who have political power. Like technology, public policy is seldom neutral in application, even with sincere efforts to adopt a balanced approach. Enactment and enforcement of labor law necessarily favors one side or the other. Adoption of one economic policy over another normally creates economic situations that are favorable to the bargaining position of one party. America experienced about 70 years of rapid industrial growth after the Civil War, during which there were no federal statutes to settle labor disputes and to moderate industrial conflict. This laissez-faire tradition ended abruptly in the 1930s with passage of the Norris-La Guardia Act, which curbed the use of court injunctions to prohibit union activities, and the National Labor Relations Act (NLRA), a decidedly pro-collective bargaining law. Collective bargaining is still the favored policy solution to industrial conflict in both the private and public sectors despite erosion of the NLRA by the Taft-Hartley (1947) and Landrum-Griffin (1959) amendments.

Administration of the NLRA by the National Labor Relations Board (NLRB) is an important aspect of public policy and affects relative bargaining power. Early Board policy favored union organization and broad bargaining rights for labor, but in recent years the Board has been unsympathetic to complaints and legal interpretations initiated by unions. This change is notable in the gray areas of legislative enforcement where policy precedents are not yet clearly established. But it is also evident in the recent reversal of established Board doctrines such as those requiring employers to bargain over plant and production relocations, protecting workers who refuse to perform assigned job tasks on health and safety grounds, and prohibiting employer interrogation of workers during union organizing drives.[6] The overall result has been to make it more difficult for unions to organize new workers, expand the scope of bargaining, and defend themselves against rising antiunion activities of management. If the trend continues, it is likely that unions will not resort to legal remedies as exclusively as they have in the past and to that extent the resolution of industrial disputes will occur outside the scope of federal administrative law.

Aside from the shift in Board sentiments, unions are put at a disadvantage in the current labor relations climate because of the

---

[6]*Illinois Coil Spring Co., Milwaukee Spring Div.*, 265 NLRB 206, 111 LRRM 1486 (1982); *Myers Industries, Inc.*, 268 NLRB No. 73, 115 LRRM 1025 (1984); *Rossmore House*, 269 NLRB No. 198, 116 LRRM 1025 (1984).

Act's underlying premise regarding appropriate sanctions against violators. Federal labor law, unlike criminal law, is remedial rather than punitive. Employers and unions normally are not punished for repetitive labor law violations except in notorious instances of illegal behavior, such as the highly publicized case of J. P. Stevens' opposition to unionization of its southern textile mills. Remedial labor law seeks to remedy the effects of illegal behavior rather than to punish the offender. It tries to restore the relationship between labor and management to what it was before the offense occurred.

The Litton Industries case in Chapter 8 illustrates the remedial approach in practice. Before 1984 the pattern was for the Board and the courts to examine independently each complaint and judgment involving Litton subsidiaries rather than to consider them in relation to one another for evidence of companywide labor policies that would merit punitive sanctions. Partly as a result of the law's remedial principle, Litton was able to respond aggressively and often illegally to union organizing and negotiating activities at numerous locations before the NLRB General Counsel's office began to consider Litton's overall record before the Board. Unions were thus weakened and thwarted by unpunished illegal actions throughout the company for a long period of time. The cost to the company in terms of the remedial sanctions issued by the Board would not have equaled the benefits it gained by not having to recognize and bargain with unions during that time.

Government labor relations policy affects relative bargaining power in still other ways. The Davis-Bacon Act requires that construction workers on federally-funded projects be paid wages equivalent to the average wage standard in that labor market area. Administrative practice in the matter has been to equate the negotiated wages between local building trades and employer associations with area wage standards. Davis-Bacon therefore encourages contractors to use union labor and pay union scale on projects that are federally financed or supported. This interpretation enhances the bargaining power of construction unions because it increases the amount of "union" work in particular labor markets. Legislative attempts in the 1980s to repeal Davis-Bacon and the state laws that have been patterned after it were defeated by construction union lobbying efforts. Then, however, the Reagan Administration used its executive powers to restrict the use of negotiated wages as a standard for determining Davis-Bacon prevailing wage levels.

Economic Policy. Public policy decisions in economic matters occur at the industry (micro) or national (macro) level. Microeconomic policy choices affect labor in specific industries, such as government deregulation and foreign trade. Macroeconomic policies influence overall levels of economic activity, including employment, inflation, and growth rates. Macroeconomic decisions have a less direct effect on relative bargaining power in specific industries, but they can seriously disrupt short-term power relationships in industries that are especially sensitive to business cycles.

Microeconomic deregulation of the transportation and communications industries damaged union power by exposing high-wage employers to competition from firms operating outside master labor agreements and customary settlement patterns. This cause-and-effect relationship is described in the discussion of airline bargaining in Chapter 5. Reduced union effectiveness is also evident in the wake of federal deregulation of telecommunications and interstate trucking. Entry of nonunion competitors and breakup of the Bell System threaten national contracts in telecommunications. The unions now negotiate with the fragmented corporate components of the former AT&T holding company. These regional companies themselves are branching into new fields and organizing integrated operating subsidiaries. AT&T kept its long-distance telecommunications network intact, but competitors like MCI and Sprint, both nonunion companies, are eroding that market. Its telecommunications equipment manufacturer, Western Electric, also is under competitive pressure from a host of overseas and domestic suppliers. The long-run effect is likely to be the displacement of unionized jobs under national economic contracts and the expansion of nonunion employment in the industry.

In interstate trucking, the entry of thousands of mostly small nonunion carriers following industry deregulation undermined the integrity of the national master freight agreement between the Teamsters and the major trucking associations. The nonunion share of the industry rose sharply and many of the unionized carriers asked Teamster locals to exempt them from the economic terms of the national contract. In 1984, Teamster national leaders negotiated a rider to the existing interstate trucking contract which would have allowed a two-tiered wage system for new hires. The settlement was overwhelmingly rejected by the members.

Policy decisions regarding foreign trade directly affect industry ability to pay in economic bargaining. The discussion in Chapter 7 describes the overriding importance of trade policy in recent contract bargaining in the steel industry.

The same is true in autos. The principal policy objective of the

UAW has been its proposed domestic auto content legislation. This approach would require that cars sold in the United States contain a designated ratio of domestically-manufactured parts and components that is proportionate to the manufacturer's total sales volume in this country. Such a law would strengthen the union's position at the bargaining table by regulating capital investments in the industry for both foreign and domestic producers. It would guarantee that manufacturing operations be located in this country and therefore be accessible to UAW organizing efforts and possible inclusion within the union's national settlement pattern. Big Three demands for union concessions under threats that they will relocate plants or subcontract parts production or that they will close domestic plants due to imports would lose force under auto content legislation. U.S. auto firms do not support the union on this issue, presumably because domestic production requirements would hinder their own global mobility.

National labor market policies influence union bargaining power, to the extent that they determine the availability of nonunion workers as a source of labor for employers in strike situations or with regard to production relocations. Government policies that reduce financial assistance to unemployed workers and persons not in the labor force have a negative impact on union workers. They create a pool of indigent workers who are potential strikebreakers and they raise the cost to employed workers of resisting employer demands at the bargaining table and then being dislocated by subsequent plant closings and phasedowns. The ease with which Greyhound recruited strikebreakers during the 1983 strike dramatizes the significance of recent changes in federal labor market policy.

A survey of these changes shows that the cost of being unemployed has risen sharply. Unemployment insurance payments have been taxed, and extended unemployment benefits eliminated or reduced. Trade adjustment assistance for workers who have been displaced because of foreign imports has been virtually abolished. Public service employment, such as that provided for in the Comprehensive Employment and Training Act (CETA), has been done away with as a part of national employment policy. Welfare recipients have been taken off the eligibility rosters or had their benefits reduced. Finally, federal aid to students in higher education has been slashed.

The economic reasoning behind these policies is that assistance programs subsidize long-term idleness. Benefit payments to persons who are capable of working interfere with normal market pressures on them to search for and accept jobs that may not be to their liking. Financial assistance therefore should be limited to job search, relocation, and worker training activities. Regardless of whether one accepts this argument, its adverse effects on the bargaining power of organized labor are unmistakable.

Macroeconomic Policy. Government policy regarding overall levels of unemployment and inflation is not neutral in its impact on relative negotiating power. A policy decision to combat inflation with tight monetary measures and the resultant economic recession are sure to weaken labor at the bargaining table. During recessions, the negotiating agendas of industrial unions emphasize income and job security issues rather than new economic gains. Members of unions in industries that are hit hard by high interest rates, such as the building trades, experience both high levels of and prolonged unemployment and a loss of bargaining power.

It is important then that macroeconomic policy in the United States has been to tolerate relatively high levels of unemployment and to use economic recession and unemployment as policy weapons in the fight against inflation. It is evident from comparisons of unemployment and inflation rates in the United States and other industrialized countries that American policy makers have preferred high joblessness to high prices in the economy. Table 16 lists average yearly indexes of consumer prices and unemployment rates

Table 16. Average Rates of Unemployment and Inflation in Ten Industrial Nations, 1974–82

Nation	Average unemployment rate	Average consumer price index (1967 = 100)
Canada	7.7	212
U.S.	7.2	206
Great Britain	6.9	336
Netherlands	6.3	214
France	5.6	249
Australia	5.5	251
Italy	3.7	320
W. Germany	3.5	163
Sweden	2.1	229
Japan	2.0	250
Average 1974–82	5.1	243

Sources: U.S. Department of Labor, Bureau of Labor Statistics, *Handbook of Labor Statistics,* Bulletin 2175 (Washington: December 1983), pp. 440–441; Joyanna Moy, "Recent Labor Market Developments in the U.S. and Nine Other Countries," *Monthly Labor Review* (January 1984), p. 45.

for the United States and nine other industrial economies during 1974-82.

Aside from Canada, the United States had the highest average annual unemployment rate of the industrial countries included in the table. Aside from West Germany, it had the lowest rate of inflation during this time. Compared to Sweden, the U.S. economy averaged 5 percentage points more unemployment and 23 index points less inflation annually. While the U.S. average annual unemployment rate exceeded the average for all ten countries by 2.2 percentage points, the Swedes nevertheless managed to achieved the next to lowest unemployment level and a level of inflation that was below the overall average.

Indeed, the relative experiences of the high and low-unemployment economies in Table 16 cast doubt on the belief that unemployment is a necessary trade-off for price stability. The four nations with the lowest levels of unemployment—Japan, Sweden, Germany, and Italy—experienced an average index of consumer prices of 240, compared to an average figure of 242 among the four nations that had the highest unemployment levels—Canada, the United States, Great Britain, and The Netherlands.

The Decline of Union Bargaining Power

A "social contract" between U.S. labor and industry emerged in the years following World War II. It was a tacit agreement: industry accepted unions and collective bargaining, but with the understanding that organized labor would not try to infringe upon management's decision-making authority in the planning, production, and marketing of goods and services. Instead, unions would limit themselves to negotiating the terms and conditions of work. In theory, this understanding confined labor's role to participating with employers in the determination of immediate issues. In practice, it resulted in formal collective bargaining and written contracts that specified workplace standards and procedures, "bread and butter" matters including wages, hours, fringe benefits, seniority systems in layoff and promotion, union security, and grievance and arbitration processes.

Labor contract language also imposed constraints on management involving things such as arbitrary work assignment, but it seldom directly challenged the hierarchical structure of work or undermined the traditional decision-making prerogatives of management. Unions negotiated earnings and conditions, content to let employers run the business while labor bargained on the basis of bottom-line performance: profits, productivity, and comparability with other industries and enterprises.

Implicit in this relationship was the assumption that things would continue as they were. Unions expected institutional and industrial reliability. They took for granted the continuation of their mature collective bargaining relationships with employers and the durability of industrial production. Business cycles might shift relative bargaining power temporarily from one side of the table to the other, but the fundamental negotiating principle of economic give-and-take with ultimate accommodation and compromise would prevail. So, too, would economic expansion continue along with rising living standards for workers.

But the social contract is being ignored, or at least greatly compromised. What was assumed to be permanent has proven transient. Employers no longer accept unions and bargaining as part of the inevitable routine. In the past they believed that the alternative to formalized bargaining relationships was industrial anarchy, where militantly irresponsible elements would prevail over discipline and stability in the workplace. Unions and bargaining were the lesser of two evils. Now, however, they have reason to believe that there is an alternative to union labor relations. Unions and bargaining are now the less desirable of two options—the union shop or the open shop, and "responsible" unions or no unions. The nonunion setting is not only preferable to them, but for the first time in 50 years it is also possible. This does not mean that all or most employers will try to oust incumbent unions, but it does suggest that they might seize the opportunity to weaken union influence considerably.

Organizational and economic environments have changed. Widespread terminations and relocations of production activities remove the industrial base upon which the social contract once rested. As described above, overall economic performance has not matched that of the decades in which the social contract was evolving.

Unions are responding to these adverse conditions in both traditional and innovative ways. At the bargaining table, they try to negotiate job security protections for the most vulnerable members and income maintenance provisions for those already displaced. In the field, they seek to organize workers at new production locations and, in order to offset membership losses in traditional jurisdictions, also to organize those who work in the industries that have not yet been effectively unionized and in sectors that are replacing the declining industries.

The union efforts so far have produced limited gains. Job and income security clauses are difficult to negotiate under conditions of economic duress; often they are granted only as trade-offs for long-term job and production guarantees and on the condition that the union recognize management's right to displace additional workers if future business conditions require it. Union organizing drives often lose momentum and fail when they are confronted with determined employer resistance or worker indifference. Even so, steady organizing and contract advances have been made in certain non-manufacturing sectors.[7]

Innovative union responses employ strategies and weapons that are appropriate to situations where conventional practices are inappropriate. These include, among others, corporate campaigns, coordinated union organizing drives, and control over worker pension fund investments.

Corporate campaigns, like the one involving Litton Industries described in Chapter 8, have had varying degrees of success against that company, J. P. Stevens, and Beverly Enterprises, a nursing home chain. What distinguishes these corporate campaigns from traditional union offensives is that they exploit the financial and administrative aspects of business enterprise rather than depend on job actions to stop production in situations where that is impractical. They bring pressure on the target company's directors, shareholders, and financial sources as a way of forcing management to change its labor policies.

Unions have begun coordinating their membership organizing campaigns more than in the past. A number of concentrated drives in targeted locations have been undertaken in which one or more departments of the AFL-CIO coordinate the activities of several affiliated unions. The object is to create an organizing momentum that will affect a wide range of area industries and trades, resulting in successful certification elections and ultimately in the formation of a viable labor movement in that region. The tangible gains made from these efforts have been limited, but even by undertaking them,

---

[7]Health care is one example. Contrary to the trend against labor generally, unions have been winning elections steadily in that industry. One union won three of every four of its NLRB certification elections during the first half of 1984. Some four million U.S. health care employees are eligible for unionization.

labor unions acquire organizing experiences and skills that are prerequisite to future advances.

Multiunion organizing efforts also focus on specific industrial sectors. Usually these are coordinated by specific AFL-CIO departments, such as the Industrial Union Department, the Food and Allied Service Trades Department, and the Building Trades Department. Preliminary joint union activities in the health care industry have been initiated by the Federation's Department for Professional Employees. In addition, several unions have increased their organizing budgets and field staffs, among them the Food and Commercial Workers and the Service Employees International Union and, outside the AFL-CIO, Teamsters and Mine Workers.

Union control over pension investments is a potentially powerful tool in shaping economic structures and relationships. In 1983 the assets of all private and public sector pension funds in this country totaled $1.15 *trillion*, one-third of which is in union negotiated pension funds. This represents a huge source of investment capital that could be used strategically by unions to determine future directions in job creation and location. Union-controlled pensions, which are common in the old AFL trades, can be invested directly by unions subject only to legal regulations regarding the fiduciary responsibility of trustees; industrial union pension funds, however, are administered mainly by employers as a result of labor law provisions and industrial relations custom. Apart from some building trades unions that have made direct pension investments into unionized construction work and a few public employee associations that participate in pension investment decisions, most unions have not begun to use this potentially powerful instrument of control.

The future of union economic bargaining power in this country is uncertain. It is presently in decline. If this condition is due mainly to economic recession and short-term industrial dislocation, organized labor should be able to regain its previous strength at the bargaining table without having to make significant organizational and behavioral changes. But if it is more deep-seated than that, as the analysis and case studies in this book suggest, unions will have to reexamine the present usefulness of structures and approaches that were successful in the past. In that event, pure-and-simple economic bargaining cannot continue to occupy the central position that it has held during most of American labor relations history. Instead, it will be supplemented or challenged by alternative methods of industrial dispute resolution that are now emerging.

Chapter Resources and Suggested Further Reading

Industrial restructuring and its impact on union bargaining power are discussed in Barry Bluestone and Bennett Harrison, *The Deindustrialization of America: Plant-Closings, Community Abandonment, and the Dismantling of Basic Industry* (1982); Seymour Melman, *Profits Without Production* (1983); Donald Kennedy, ed., *Labor and Deindustrialization: Workers and Corporate Change*, vol. II, Labor Studies Series (1984); Robert Kuttner, *The Economic Illusion: False Choices Between Prosperity and Social Justice* (1984). On the causes of global decline of American industry, see Robert H. Hayes and William J. Abernathy, "Managing Our Way to Economic Decline," *Harvard Business Review* (July/August 1980).

The impact of technology on labor is an issue that has generated a considerable body of literature. The current debate started with Harry Braverman, *Labor and Monopoly Capital: The Degradation of Work in the Twentieth Century* (1974), which argues that in market economies new technology is introduced mainly to enhance employer control over workers. An in-depth case study of the U.S. machine tool industry follows this line of argument but broadens the Braverman argument to include larger social issues: David F. Noble, *Forces of Production: A Social History of Industrial Automation* (1984). Also see David F. Noble, *America By Design: Science, Technology, and The Rise of Corporate Capitalism* (1977) for a social history of U.S. business and technology. Two other works in the Braverman tradition are Andrew Zimbalist, ed., *Case Studies in the Labor Process* (1979), and Mike Cooley, *Architect Or Bee?: The Human/Technology Relationship* (1980), which examines the effect on industrial engineers and designers of computer-aided design and production systems. Another case study that considers technology in terms of relative labor-management control is Keith Dix, *Work Relations in the Coal Industry: The Hand-Loading Era, 1880–1930* (1977). This theme is also evident in Ian Reinecke, *Electronic Illusions: A Skeptic's View of Our High-Tech Future* (1984).

Two additional works also focus on relative labor-management control, but critique the Braverman analysis: Charles F. Sabel, *Work and Politics: The Division of Labor in Industry* (1982), and, from Great Britain, Stephen Wood, ed., *The Degradation of Work?: Skill, Deskilling and the Labour Process* (1982).

The origins and evolution of American labor law are described in Karl E. Klare, "Judicial Deradicalization of the Wagner Act and the Origins of Modern Legal Consciousness, 1937–1941," *Minnesota Law Review*, vol. 62 (1978); and James B. Atleson, *Values and Assumptions in American Labor Law* (1983).

A recommended survey of micro- and macroeconomic policies as they affect labor is Howard M. Wachtel, *Labor and the Economy* (1984). Dual labor market and segmented labor market theories are described and analyzed in Peter B. Doeringer and Michael J. Piore, *Internal Labor Markets and Manpower Analysis* (1971) and David M. Gordon, Richard Edwards, and Michael Reich, *Segmented Work, Divided Workers: The Historical Transformation of Labor in the United States* (1982). For a critical analysis of federal labor market policies, see Sam Rosenberg, "Reagan Social Policy and Labour Force Restructuring," *Cambridge Journal of Economics* (1983), pp. 179–96. A more general discussion is Sar Levitan and Clifford M. Johnson, *Reviving the Promise of Opportunity in America* (1984).

Topical Index

About the Author

Charles Craypo is Professor and Chair, Economics Department, University of Notre Dame. He also has been a faculty member and labor educator at Michigan State University, where he received a doctorate in economics, Pennsylvania State University, and Cornell University. His major publications are in *Industrial and Labor Relations Review, Journal of Industrial Relations Law*, and *Labor Studies Journal*, and in edited books on labor and employment issues. He is currently co-directing a national research project on employee-owned companies and economic redevelopment programs.